ROBERT HAMILTON MOORE

GEORGE WASHINGTON UNIVERSITY

HANDBOOK OF
Effective Writing

HOLT, RINEHART AND WINSTON
New York · Chicago · San Francisco · Toronto · London

July, 1966

Copyright © 1965, 1966 by Holt, Rinehart and Winston, Inc.
Copyright © 1955, 1959 by Robert Hamilton Moore
All rights reserved
Library of Congress Catalog Card Number 66-12616
25811-0716
Printed in the United States of America

PREFACE

As students and courses change and textbooks proliferate, there would seem to be a place for a relatively full, yet not exhaustive handbook to be used with a rhetoric, a rhetoric-reader, or a collection of readings, either as a supplementary textbook or, in courses whose students no longer need class discussion of mechanics, as a desk reference during the writing and revising of themes.

Since the handbook section of my *Effective Writing* has recently been thoroughly revised, its publication as a separate handbook seems timely. It is purely a handbook; I have made no attempt to add capsule discussions of matters properly handled by a rhetoric, because rhetorics in plenty are available for those who desire them. It is accordingly concerned solely with grammar, punctuation, and other conventional mechanics. With the addition from the fuller text of abbreviated chapters on the conventions of outlining and of research papers, it provides what I regard as the essential guidance on mechanical problems.

Since the rhetorical effect will be equally unfortunate if a locution strikes the reader as either stilted or careless, the *Handbook* attempts to take into account both the results of linguistic study and the convictions of many readers about what good usage ought to be. I have not hesitated to recommend particular usages where recommendations seem desirable, but I have also tried to make the student aware of the need for choice and to provide realistic grounds for choosing.

Throughout the discussions of grammar, syntax, and punctuation, I have made use of varying systems of analysis, usually approaching the same point from various directions, since some students find one approach helpful, whereas some best use another one. I have, however, retained traditional terminology wherever possible, because, despite its weaknesses, it remains the only terminology that all students and all teachers find familiar, regardless of what other terminology they may also have met.

Robert Hamilton Moore

Washington, D.C.
November 1965

CONTENTS

Grading Chart	*Front cover*
Correction Symbols	*Back cover*
Preface	v

1. THE MOST COMMON ERRORS — 1

Detailed Table of Contents	1
Fragmentary Sentences	4
Comma Splices	5
Run-on, Run-together, or Fused Sentences	6
Excessive Coordination	8
Faulty Subordination	11
Dangling Modifiers	12
Misplaced Modifiers	13
Reference of Pronouns	16
Agreement of Pronouns	19
Agreement of Verbs	22
Sentence Construction (shifts)	26
Faulty Parallelism	29
Awkwardness	31

2. GRAMMAR — 35

Detailed Table of Contents	35
The Importance of Grammar	38
The Functions of Sentence Elements	41
The Basic Sentence Patterns	51
Parts of Speech and Functions	53
Formal Groups (phrases and clauses)	87

3. PUNCTUATION — 100

Detailed Table of Contents	100
The Importance of Punctuation	104

vii

Two Fundamental Principles — 105
The Comma — 107
Other Marks of Punctuation — 135

4. SPELLING — 153

Detailed Table of Contents — 153
Historical Background — 154
The Importance of Spelling — 157
Improving Spelling Deficiencies — 157
    Personal Spelling List — 158
    Diagnosing the Trouble — 158
    Using the Dictionary — 160
    Visual Spelling — 162
    Finger Spelling — 163
    Memory Aids — 163
    Regular Patterns — 165
    Spelling Rules — 167
    Spelling Lists — 170

5. MANUSCRIPT CONVENTIONS — 178

Detailed Table of Contents — 178
Legibility — 180
The Page — 181
Paging — 182
Endorsement — 182
Final Revision — 182
Titles — 184
Capitalization and Lower Case — 184
Italics — 187
Hyphens and Syllabication — 188
Abbreviations — 192
Representation of Numbers — 192

6. OUTLINING — 195

Detailed Table of Contents — 195
The Informal Outline — 195
The Formal Outline — 196

The Sentence Outline	199
The Topic Outline	202

7. THE RESEARCH PAPER   207

Detailed Table of Contents	207
The Use of the Library	208
Research Paper Procedure	217
The Preliminary Bibliography	217
Taking Notes	227
Plagiarism through Ignorance	229
The Final Outline	231
The Final Paper	231
Sample Short Research Paper	240

8. GLOSSARY OF TROUBLESOME PHRASES   249

Index   271

1

The Most Common Errors

Frag	* 1.	Fragmentary sentences, 4
		a. No complete main clause, 4
		b. Afterthought modifiers, 5
		c. No finite verb, 5
		d. Fragments in dialogue, 5
Cs	* 2.	Comma splices, 5
		a. Rule, 6
		b. Comma splices in dialogue, 6
Run-on	* 3.	Run-on, run-together, or fused sentences, 6
		a. Rule, 6
		b. No connective and no punctuation, 7
Co-ord	* 4.	Excessive coordination, 8
		a. "Stringy sentences," 8
		b. "Choppy sentences," 8
Sub	* 5.	Faulty subordination, 11
		a. Illogical subordination ("Upside down subordination"), 11
		b. Overlapping subordination, 11

* There are exercises for items marked with an asterisk.

Dng * 6. Dangling modifiers, 12
　　　　　　a. Dangling participles, 12
　　　　　　b. Dangling infinitives, 13
　　　　　　c. Dangling elliptical clauses, 13
　　　　　　d. Confused thought, 13

Mm　 * 7. Misplaced modifiers, 13
　　　　　　a. Carelessness, 14
　　　　　　b. *Only*, etc., 14
　　　　　　c. "Squinting modifiers," 15

Ref　 * 8. Reference of pronouns, 16
　　　　　　a. Implied antecedents, 16
　　　　　　b. Ambiguous antecedents, 17
　　　　　　c. Antecedents in subordinate constructions, 18
　　　　　　d. Demonstratives with implied antecedents, 18

PAgr　 * 9. Agreement of pronouns, 19
　　　　　　a. Person, 19
　　　　　　b. Gender, 19
　　　　　　c. Number, 20
　　　　　　　　1) Antecedents with *and*, 20
　　　　　　　　2) Antecedents with *or* or *nor*, 20
　　　　　　　　3) Affirmative and negative antecedents, 20
　　　　　　　　4) *Either*, etc., 21
　　　　　　　　5) *Each*, etc., plus a plural modifier, 21
　　　　　　　　6) *None*, 21
　　　　　　　　7) Collective antecedents, 21

VAgr　 *10. Agreement of verbs, 22
　　　　　　a. Person of nouns, 22
　　　　　　b. Singular subjects plus plural modifiers, 22
　　　　　　c. Singular subjects with *as well as*, etc., 22
　　　　　　d. Subjects with *and*, 22
　　　　　　e. Subjects with *or* or *nor*, 22
　　　　　　f. Affirmative and negative subjects, 23
　　　　　　g. Subjects and subjective complements, 23
　　　　　　h. Subjects after the verb, 23
　　　　　　i. Indefinite pronouns, 23
　　　　　　j. *None*, 24
　　　　　　k. Collective nouns, 24

THE MOST COMMON ERRORS

        l. Relative pronouns, 24
        m. Quantities, 24

Cst   *11. Sentence construction (shifts), 26
        a. Point of view, 26
          1) Shift in tense, 26
          2) Shift in mood, voice, and person, 26
        b. Sentence patterns, 27
        c. Faulty predication, 27
          1) Illogical use of "to be" (False equation), 28
          2) Faulty appositives, 28
          3) Incomplete or illogical comparisons, 28

//Cst   *12. Faulty parallelism, 29
        a. Similar ideas, 30
        b. Dissimilar ideas, 31

K   *13. Awkwardness, 31

    The purpose of this chapter is to bring together in one place the most common errors in grammar, syntax, and punctuation. (The most common error of all, misspelling, is treated in a chapter of its own, Chapter 4.) We shall consider these common errors briefly and illustrate their nature and the methods of correcting them. Working with this chapter as you revise your themes should result in your learning to avoid the errors altogether. Some, though not all, of the errors discussed here are considered in more detail in other chapters, often from a slightly different point of view. You should consequently follow up all cross-references to other parts of the book, to be sure you thoroughly understand the errors you are making in your themes before you attempt to correct them. If you find terms that are unfamiliar to you, consult the index or your dictionary. If the explanations in the text are still not clear, consult your instructor.

    The first three errors we need to consider—fragments, comma splices, and run-ons—result primarily from carelessness in punctua-

Frag ──────────────── THE MOST COMMON ERRORS

tion or from inability to recognize grammatically complete ideas. If they persist in your themes despite your efforts to eliminate them, it will suggest that you are unable to identify the fundamental constituents of the sentence. You may need to study the chapters on effective sentences and on grammar carefully.

1. FRAGMENTARY SENTENCES—Frag

A sentence, in the context in which it appears, conveys a complete idea. Sometimes, especially in dialogue representing conversational speech or in informal writing representing the free flow of easy thought, complete ideas are readily conveyed by grammatically incomplete sentences which, being appropriate, are very effective. But normally, especially in serious exposition and argument, your reader will expect a subject and a finite verb in a grammatically independent predication.

Faulty fragmentary sentences (and we are concerned here exclusively with faulty ones) are usually of two kinds: They may be long strings of modifying phrases and clauses, but with no complete independent clause to carry the burden—imposing, but actually saying very little; or they may be afterthought modifiers that really belong to, and should have been connected with, a preceding main clause. Fragments of the first type need a main clause. Fragments of the second type need to be repunctuated to tie them onto the main clause they are modifying. (See also P12e.) A few students write faulty fragments of a third type: fragments that contain only a verbal instead of a finite verb.

Often, if you read aloud what you have written, the tones and pauses of your own voice will warn you that your punctuation is misleading or that you have forgotten to complete your thought. But to use this test on your own writing, you must read the signals your punctuation and phrasing actually give. If you read what you *meant* to say, instead, the test will not help you.

a. No Complete Predication

I think the idea expressed by Jacques Barzun of offering lectures or general courses for nonscience majors, which would give a general understanding of scientific principles and methods and yet not force a student who will never be a chemist to wade through a lab manual and still come out with no clear idea of science.

COMMA SPLICES ─────────────────────────── **Cs**

Do not, as this student has done, allow mere length to confuse you. Such a fragment often accompanies the use of too long and too complicated sentences.

b. Afterthought Modifiers or Appositives

He was here Wednesday afternoon. Immediately after he arrived from New York. (*A comma instead of a period, or no punctuation at all, would make such a passage more effective.*)

I do not believe the argument that Professor Barzun presented. Because a laboratory course at least introduces a student to scientific techniques, without which no real understanding of methods or even principles can exist. (*Comma. The second word-group is merely a modifier.*)

A student cannot merely be told, for example, that measurements must be precise, but must have experience. For instance, the dismay of missing an "unknown" because of a few too many drops of a reagent. (*Perhaps a dash. Dismay is in apposition to experience.*)

c. No Finite Verb in a Main Clause

The doctor whom I consulted recommending no strenuous exercise. (***Such a fragment may result from the careless omission of a linking verb, or perhaps from inability to distinguish between finite verbs and verbals.***)

Our language governs the way we think, but at the same time the way we think, governing as it does the kind of language we can use. (*The first clause is complete, but not the rest of the sentence.*)

d. Fragments in Dialogue (see also P5e)

In normal speech, of course, incomplete sentences are common, and dialogue often uses them. But in punctuating dialogue and accompanying orientation phrases, be careful not to create unintentional fragments which would not convey complete ideas in normal speech.

FAULTY: "I am quite sure," he insisted. "That you are wrong."
CORRECTED: "I am quite sure," he insisted, "that you are wrong."

2. COMMA SPLICES (OR COMMA FAULTS, OR COMMA BLUNDERS)—Cs

A comma splice results when two independent clauses are run together with insufficient punctuation. (See also P1.) Your instructor will regard repeated comma splices as serious errors because repeated comma splices, like repeated faulty fragments, suggest that

Cs/Run-on   THE MOST COMMON ERRORS

you are unable to recognize complete ideas. The "rules" are simple. Learn first to follow them implicitly, and later you may learn how to modify them to suggest subtle sentence relations.

a. Rule: Independent clauses not connected by *and, but, or, nor,* **or** *for* **are separated by a semicolon or made into two sentences.**
(But see also Excessive Coordination, pages 8–9, and P1.)

A comma splice results when a comma is used instead of the semicolon.

> Certain bacteria, such as *Escherichia coli* and many soil bacteria, bring about the reduction of nitrates to nitrites, nitrogen as nitrates is essential to plant growth. (*A semicolon after* nitrites, *or a period, would prevent confusion. The comma splice results because the comma is insufficiently heavy to identify the main break in the sentence.*)
>
> Soil bacteria of all types are useful, however, they do not all function to the same end. (*Conjunctive adverbs, like* however, *are not simple conjunctions.*)

Many writers use commas, however, when the clauses are short and the connection is so close that no confusion will result.

b. Comma Splices in Dialogue (see also P5e)

In punctuating dialogue and accompanying orientation phrases, be careful not to create unjustifiable comma splices.

> COMMA SPLICE: "I will not go," he said, "you may be sure of that."
> CORRECTED: "I will not go," he said. "You may be sure of that."

3. RUN-ON, RUN-TOGETHER, OR FUSED SENTENCES—Run-on

Even worse than the comma splice, which confuses the reader by tying together two independent clauses with a comma when a semicolon is needed, is the run-on sentence, which jams together two independent clauses with no punctuation at all.

a. Independent clauses connected by *and, but, or, nor,* **or** *for* **are generally separated by a comma, unless the clauses are short and the connection is very close.** Failure to use such a comma may result in a confusing run-on sentence.

> I intend to go with your brother and you may do as you please.

RUN-TOGETHER, OR FUSED SENTENCES ———— **Run-on**

b. **Most confusing of all are two independent ideas without any sort of connective and without any punctuation.**

> Students should be careful of punctuation trouble will result if they are careless. (See Cs2a.)

NEVER "correct" a comma splice by removing the comma, leaving no punctuation at all. The resulting run-on sentence will be worse than the original error.

EXERCISE

In the following passage, identify and correct all fragmentary sentences, comma splices, and run-on sentences.

> A common college phenomenon which worries students and their parents more than it should, the mood of cynical disillusionment which overtakes almost all intelligent students sooner or later. It comes most often to sophomores. Which is one reason sophomores are so hard to tolerate. Sometimes it does not come until the junior year rarely does it come as early as the freshman year or as late as the senior year. But come it nearly always does and for very good reasons. For one thing, the hitherto unquestioned certainties which the student brings to college with him in his mental baggage without really knowing why he believes them are not only laid open to question, but are sometimes dismissed as not being even worthy of consideration. Then, the study of the way we think and of the logical fallacies which trip the unwary, the study of the nature of evidence and of the dangers of gullibility, the confusing difference between fact and opinion—all of these suggest that a case could be made for almost any idea or any side of any argument. And instructors who are equally intelligent and equally admirable maintain sharply opposed opinions, class discussions develop convincing arguments for adopting contradictory conclusions. Truth seems undiscoverable and even reasonable probability seems all but unattainable. Disillusionment, skepticism, and cynicism—doubting everything but doubt itself—offer an uncomfortable but fairly dependable protective armor and the more sensitive the student, the more eagerly he dons it. To wear it defiantly until increasing knowledge and growing wisdom enable him once again—this time through his own thinking—to say with some confidence, "This I believe."

7

Co-ord   THE MOST COMMON ERRORS

4. EXCESSIVE COORDINATION—Co-ord

Frequent comma splices or run-on sentences (see above) are usually a sign that the writer uses too many compound sentences, consisting of equal (coordinate) independent clauses. A compound sentence, remember, says to the reader, "Here are two independent ideas, neither modifying the other—equally important, yet together expressing a single, unified idea." Such a logical relation is fairly rare in mature thought. Far more often one of the ideas is in some degree and in some manner really subordinate to the other, and the sentence pattern expressing them should reflect the true relation of the ideas.

a. "Stringy Sentences"

Avoid the excessive coordination of "stringy sentences," long chains of primer sentences tied together with *and*'s or *but*'s or *so*'s.

> I came early on registration day, and I knew exactly what I wanted to take, but I had to wait in long lines everywhere I went, and my adviser insisted that I take chemistry, and several of the classes I wanted were full, and the cashier said my papers were filled out wrong, and nothing worked right for me, so I spent all day, and even then I ended up with a terrible schedule.

These clauses are roughly parallel, but because the ideas are not logically equal, the parallelism is faulty. To reflect the thought accurately, the sentence should be broken up, and some of the independent clauses should be reduced to subordinate clauses or modifying phrases.

> Although I came early on registration day and knew exactly what I wanted to take, I ran into long lines, closed classes, an adviser who insisted on adding chemistry to my program, and a cashier who sent me back to correct my papers. It took me all day to register, and even then I ended up with a terrible schedule.

b. "Choppy Sentences"

Avoid "choppy sentences," incoherent passages lacking the transitional words or phrases that would indicate the relation between the ideas.

EXCESSIVE COORDINATION — Co-ord

> Flying is an excellent way to travel. There are long stretches of boredom. The passengers sitting by the windows can see very little. Passengers in the aisle seats can see nothing at all. One can pass the time by reading and eating. The air lines provide up-to-date magazines and excellent food. The fares are high, but roughly equivalent to those of Pullman travel. Accidents are usually fatal, but are very rare, considering the passenger-miles traveled. Flying is comfortable and is the fastest form of transportation. To get from one place to another, flying is best.

That paragraph is bumpy and confusing, but all it lacks is adequate transitions.

> Flying is an excellent way to travel. In spite of the long stretches of boredom resulting from the inability of the passengers by the window to see very much and of those in the aisle seats to see anything at all, one can pass the time by reading the up-to-date magazines and eating the excellent food provided by the air lines. The fares, it is true, are high, but they are roughly equivalent to those of Pullman travel. It is also true that accidents are usually fatal, but they are very rare, considering the passenger-miles traveled. Most important of all, flying is comfortable and is the fastest form of transportation. For those who wish primarily to get from one place to another, flying is best.

In developing the ability to write flexible sentences and paragraphs, and incidentally in developing your own ability to think clearly, take great care in subordinating lesser ideas to greater. According to the relative importance of the ideas, use single-word modifiers, phrases rather than clauses, compound subjects and compound verbs, subordinate clauses rather than main clauses. Save your main clauses for your most important details. Shift the position of the main clauses in your sentences, and shift the position of the lesser modifiers, so that emphasis will fall where you want it. Attempt consciously to use all the elements of the English sentence that you know, varying your sentence patterns to reflect your thought as exactly as possible. Avoid, of course, confusingly involved sentences, and avoid sentences chopped up by too many parenthetical elements. Keep your reader and the effect you want to make always in mind. If you do all of that, sentence variety will automatically follow.

Co-ord _____ THE MOST COMMON ERRORS

EXERCISE

Rewrite the following passages so that they will clearly reflect the writers' thought, without choppiness and without confusing complexity. Reorganize if necessary.

1. There are only two times a day in which a man can get himself into trouble. One is daytime. The other is nighttime.

2. Big-city intellectuals dislike Suburbia. They say suburbanites must conform. The suburbs are dull. No intellectual challenge is provided. None is tolerated. The houses are all alike. Status symbols are all-important. The size of one's car or power mower determines position. Whether one lives in the middle of the "project" or on the edge is important. The PTA is the center of life. Children take up all their parents' time. Men commute. It is a woman's world.

3. Shopping centers are replacing the downtown stores as the source of the family's needs and the result is that the middle of most cities is blighted and so more people move away or stay away and so more deterioration follows and city businessmen and city planners are worried, but no very satisfactory solutions have yet been found.

4. A modern drugstore is likely to be a member of a chain. They are all alike. The doors are marked "In" and "Out." Near the doors are cash registers. They are inside a fence with turnstiles. Only the tobacco counter is outside the fence. The fountain lunch counter may be too. It will be along one side. Behind the fence are aisles of shelves full of goods. Above the shelves are signs saying "Cosmetics," "School Supplies," "Cameras." It is hard to know where to look for what you want. At the back are the drugs. The store is clean, but it is all impersonal and I miss the old drugstore.

5. I turned restlessly in my bed this last morning of camp, aware only of the sound of my own thrashing movement and of the whimper of a nearby screech owl, trying to forget the litter we had made in packing up to leave, trying to forget the work which had yet to be done before we could get away. But incautiously glancing at the filthy floor, with duffel bags and suitcases standing open amid the still unpacked spoils of camping, eagerly awaiting the yet-to-be-stored miscellany of toothbrushes, wash

FAULTY SUBORDINATION ——————————— **Sub**

cloths, soap, towels, forgotten whistles, trophies, leather work, the shorts and socks and shoes and blouses which could not be put away until just before our departure made me suddenly conscious of the many tasks remaining to be done before our departure and exhausted me in the very prospect; so, pulling the rather soiled top sheet up over my head, I made a final effort to go back to sleep.

5. FAULTY SUBORDINATION—Sub

a. Illogical Subordination ("Upside down subordination")

Avoid illogically subordinating major ideas to minor ones.

When the attempt was made to hold up the First National Bank, I was just walking down Main Street, paying no particular attention to anything. (*Surely, the attempted holdup is more important even to an egocentric writer than the fact that he was walking inattentively down the street. Putting that idea in the main clause would give it more emphasis.*)

As I was walking down Main Street, paying no particular attention to anything, the attempt was made to hold up the First National Bank.

Usually, the context makes clear what should be important and what is minor.

b. Overlapping Subordination

Avoid overlapping subordination, the awkward repetition of identical forms of pronouns, of subordinating conjunctions, or of prepositions.

This is a job which I will do with a zest which cannot be exceeded.
She said that she would take that one and that I should take this one.
He failed because he couldn't answer the exam questions because he hadn't slept the night before.
I will go with you with pleasure.

If modifiers or other elements are parallel in importance, however, the repetition of connectives clarifies the relationship. Do not vary connectives merely for the sake of change.

EXERCISE

Rewrite the following passage to correct any faulty subordination.

Dng ———————————— THE MOST COMMON ERRORS

The pattern of your sentences should reflect your thought, because you should choose and arrange sentence elements carefully. Main clauses imply important ideas. Subordinate clauses should express ideas that are secondary but which are still of major importance. Though lesser ideas may go into phrases or single words (a strong single word may be more emphatic than a flabby phrase). The beginning and the end of a sentence are usually more emphatic than the middle. An inverted sentence pattern is more emphatic than a normal one, and a modifier out of its normal position—if the relationships are clear—is more emphatic than one standing where it would be expected to stand. By varying these elements by changes in structure and position, and by carefully introducing concepts in the order in which you want them considered, you may control your reader's responses to your thought by suggesting the importance of each point by the weight you give it.

6. DANGLING MODIFIERS (See also pages 88–97.)—Dng

As you practice using different kinds of sentences, developing your ability to write mature and flexible sentences that will reflect the turns of your thinking, you may find yourself sometimes writing dangling modifiers. Do not allow the recurrence of the symbol **Dng** to discourage you from further experiments; you cannot learn to handle new tools skillfully without practice. Instead of being discouraged, learn how to avoid dangling modifiers and how to recognize and correct such dangling modifiers as may have slipped in during the heat of composition. When you have done that, you will have mastered a new sentence pattern that will be very valuable to you.

Dangling modifiers are verbal clusters or elliptical adverbial clauses with nothing to modify.

a. Dangling Participles

DANGLING: *Seated one day at the organ,* a new chord shaped itself under my fingers. (*Who was seated?*)

CORRECTED: *Seated one day at the organ,* I played a strange new chord. (*Main clause revised to contain a modifiable word.*)

CORRECTED: *As I was seated one day at the organ,* a strange new chord shaped itself under my fingers. (*Participial phrase changed to adverbial clause. Notice that this sentence, though structurally satisfactory, is stylistically weak because of the shift in voice.*)

MISPLACED MODIFIERS — Dng/Mm

b. Dangling Infinitives

DANGLING: *To learn to handle new tools,* repeated practice is necessary. (*Who is to learn?*)
STILL DANGLING: Repeated practice is necessary *to learn to handle new tools.*
CORRECTED: *To learn to handle new tools,* you must practice repeatedly. (*Main clause revised to contain a modifiable word.*)
CORRECTED: *Before you can learn to handle new tools,* repeated practice is necessary. (*Infinitive phrase changed to adverbial clause.*)

c. Dangling Elliptical Clauses

DANGLING: *When planning to move,* damage to some of your furniture should be accepted as inevitable. (*Who is planning?*)
CORRECTED: *When planning to move,* you should accept damage to some of your furniture as inevitable. (*Main clause revised to contain a modifiable word.*)
CORRECTED: *When you are planning to move,* damage to some of your furniture should be accepted as inevitable. (*Elliptical clause expanded to full clause. This revision may be stylistically awkward. A "correction" may still produce a weak sentence.*)

d. Confused Thought

The hardest kind of dangling modifier to discover and correct in revision results from a basic confusion of thought. It can take many forms.

On my first day in high school, too unnerved to eat breakfast, I left the house twenty minutes early—much to my mother's dissatisfaction. (*The dissatisfaction must refer to the failure to eat, not to the early departure. The sentence will have to be completely rewritten to make it clear.*)

Many modifiers which are technically dangling do not cause any confusion at all; you can find examples in all but the most formal writing. You need to be aware of the problem, nevertheless, for a dangling modifier of which you are unaware may raise a laugh over a point you meant very seriously.

7. MISPLACED MODIFIERS—Mm

Misplaced modifiers are modifiers which are all right in themselves, and do have something in the sentence to modify, but which are put in the wrong place, so that they seem to modify an element you did not mean to qualify. The essential difference between dangling modifiers and misplaced modifiers is that the former cannot fit logically anywhere in the sentence; the latter merely do not belong where you put them.

Remember that *modifiers go as near as possible to the elements they modify.* An adjective (word, phrase, or clause) will consequently try to attach itself to the nearest noun; an adverb will try to attach itself to the nearest verb, adjective, other adverb, or the whole clause in which it appears. Whether modifiers precede or follow the element they modify, and whether their position is fixed or is relatively free is a complicated matter of structure and idiom. If you are uncertain about that, see Chapter 2. If a modifier is placed near an eligible element which it was not intended to affect, the modifier has been misplaced and confusion will certainly follow, sometimes with unintentionally amusing results.

Correcting a misplaced modifier is easy: Move it from the confusing position and put it where it will be clear. Sometimes, as in the first example below, you may need to rephrase the whole sentence.

a. Carelessness

MISPLACED: Look at that odd boy with the checked trousers about a block behind.

MISPLACED: Friday I started for the ocean in a jeep which was about two hundred miles away.

MISPLACED: I have been looking forward to taking English for a long time.

MISPLACED: Professor Snodgrass objects to students who sleep while he is lecturing shamelessly.

b. *Only,* etc.

One special problem causes particular trouble: *Only* and *almost* and *nearly* and *completely* are words that in informal English may move around in a sentence rather freely. There is no real confusion when we say,

> This bus driver only drives as far as Clarksburg.
> The fullback only smokes after the football season.

But many readers have been taught to object to such floating adverbs, and sometimes there might possibly be a question as to what

MISPLACED MODIFIERS _____ **Mm**

we really mean. And sometimes the misplacing of such adverbs can be a serious functional error, making it impossible for the reader to be sure what you mean.

> He almost solved the problem in his head. (What does that mean? Was the problem ever solved?)

To be sure that your writing is clear and to avoid distracting your reader unnecessarily, it is best to put such adverbs as near as possible to the elements in the sentence they are intended to modify.

> This bus driver drives only as far as Clarksburg.
> The fullback smokes only after the football season.
> He solved the problem, but he finally had to use pencil and paper.

c. "Squinting Modifiers"

Another special problem arises with a modifier which stands between two elements it might modify, so that the reader cannot tell which it was intended to affect. (It is called a "squinting modifier" because it looks both ways. Perhaps "cockeyed modifier" would be a more accurate name.)

> CONFUSING: The man who is honest usually is happy.
> IMPROVED: The man who is honest is usually happy.

Such modifiers are perfectly clear when they are spoken, because the pitch and juncture given them makes confusion unlikely. But no such aid to understanding is present in the written sentences.

The problem often accompanies comma splices or run-on sentences.

> CONFUSING: I will not go, until you have apologized, I will not even stir from this chair.
> IMPROVED: I will not go. Until you have apologized, I will not even stir from this chair.

EXERCISE

In the following sentences, distinguish between dangling modifiers and misplaced modifiers. Rephrase all faulty sentences to correct the errors.

> 1. Having always enjoyed reading, standard grammar and idiom have never been any trouble to me.

15

Ref _____ THE MOST COMMON ERRORS

2. To absorb English idioms from reading, your reading rate must not be extremely fast.

3. Seven miles below me I could see the pattern of the river system very clearly.

4. To find an unoccupied parking place, a fireplug should be found.

5. When parked by a fireplug, a ticket is not unexpected.

6. Thoroughly boiled, she served the cabbage and announced dinner.

7. Studying calculus, the neighbor's children are distracting.

8. Do not cross yellow line when on your side.

9. She talked to the professor with knowledge and understanding.

10. To avoid parking problems, the bus is best.

11. Our dog is as old as my sister, who is fourteen but still in good health.

12. Although very well constructed, Mary lives in an old and odd-looking house.

13. His lectures are confusing, and I fear sometimes intentionally confusing.

14. After spending two weeks fishing in the mountains, the office seemed very confining.

15. Howling through the treetops, I could hear the wind.

8. REFERENCE OF PRONOUNS—Ref

Third person pronouns substitute for nouns already explicitly expressed in the sentence or passage. Rarely, demonstrative or relative pronouns refer to and summarize a concept clearly implied by a whole preceding predication. (See pages 42, 56.) Until you are sure of the clarity of your writing, be certain that there is an expressed substantive near enough to the pronoun for the reference to be unmistakable, and be certain that there is only one eligible antecedent to which the pronoun might refer.

a. Implied Antecedents

Avoid using a pronoun to refer to an antecedent which has been merely implied by the preceding phrasing.

REFERENCE OF PRONOUNS _____ **Ref**

> I have always envied the teacher's life, and I have decided to become one. (*Teacher's is an adjective in function, not a noun. The noun teacher, to which the pronoun is intended to refer, does not appear in the sentence at all.*)
> I accept the Universe! which, on the whole, is just as well. (*Such a pronoun really refers to the idea of* acceptance, *implied by the verb. The construction is well established, and if no confusion results, no one will notice it. It is not used, however, in strictly formal writing, and you might well avoid it in college work.*)

b. Ambiguous Antecedents

Do not use a pronoun to refer ambiguously to one of two or more eligible antecedents.

> John handed Elmer *his* book.

Ambiguity also occurs when forms of the same pronoun are used to refer to different antecedents.

> When a driver is waiting for a parking space and another driver edges in ahead of *him, he* may try to cut *him* off. (*The reader may be able to solve the puzzle, but the writer's job is to set no puzzles in the first place. It is never adequate to say, "Oh, you know what I mean." The reader is concerned with what you have said.*)
> If the skin receives too much sugar, *it* stores *it* up, and *it* interferes with the normal functioning of the oil glands.

Be particularly careful of using *it* as a pronoun and *it* as an expletive in the same sentence. If there is any possibility of ambiguity or awkwardness, avoid the construction.

> *It* is a stubborn condition, and *it* is hard to correct *it*.

Ambiguity can also occur through the position of eligible antecedents in the sentence.

> The Buick skidded on the wet pavement and crashed into a shed. *It* was totally demolished. (*Pronouns tend to refer both to the nearest eligible antecedent and to an eligible antecedent functioning in the same way as the pronoun. Here, it could refer either to* Buick *or* shed, *since both are third-person singular,* Buick *and* it *are both subjects, and* shed *and* it *stand side by side.*)

Avoid the awkwardness of parenthetical explanation of ambiguous pronouns. It is better to be clear in the first place.

Ref ─────────────────────── THE MOST COMMON ERRORS

> WEAK: John said that *he* (John) would do *his* (Jim's) work for a slight fee.
>
> BETTER: John promised to do Jim's work for a slight fee.

c. Antecedents in Subordinate Conjunctions

Avoid using a pronoun to refer to an antecedent functioning in a subordinate construction.

> I envy the life of a teacher, and I plan to become *one*. (Teacher, *the intended antecedent, is merely the complement in a modifying phrase, and consequently the reference is obscured.* One *tends to refer instead to* life, *the nearest major eligible noun*.)

d. Demonstratives with Implied Antecedents

If you use the demonstratives to refer to an implied antecedent (see page 16), be sure the reader would have no trouble supplying the omitted substantive.

> ACCEPTABLE: Many teachers will object to demonstratives lacking a clear antecedent. *This* [objection] should be considered before you employ the construction.
>
> CONFUSING: The first step in planting a lawn is preparation of the soil. *This* must be turned over to a depth of six inches. In former days, *this* was accomplished by using a spade and a strong back. Now one can rent a small tractor and do the work faster and more efficiently. *This* also breaks up the soil into a fine texture in the same operation.

EXERCISE

Clarify all confusing pronoun reference in the following sentences.

1. As the fan oscillated on the rickety table, it squeaked.
2. Because I thought they were very good, I gave the books to my nephews.
3. An emotion does not explain its meaning. It has none; it must be provided for it.
4. Before heads of state are driven through the streets of Washington, they are decorated with flags and hosed down if they need it.
5. Jane looked despairingly at the battered copy of the outside reading list. It was barely legible, and it was so long it would take forever to read every book in it.

AGREEMENT OF PRONOUNS — **PAgr**

6. I had always supposed that college courses would be easy for me, but it assumes a preparation I have not had.
7. It said in the paper that it will snow, and if it does, it will tie up the holiday traffic.
8. With her figure, she should never have bought that dress. It bulges in all the wrong places.
9. John told Jim that he would do his English lesson.
10. The archaeologists are contradictory in this report on the evidence concerning Cretan writing, which is confusing.

9. AGREEMENT OF PRONOUNS—PAgr

Pronouns agree with their antecedents in person, gender, and number. "To agree" means to correspond in form. If the antecedent is third person, masculine, and singular, for example, the pronoun will be third person, masculine, and singular. The antecedent of first and second person pronouns is determined by context. All nouns, including clauses and phrases, are treated as third person.

a. Person

Pronouns agree with their antecedents in person. There is only one point that needs to be mentioned. The indefinite pronouns (*one, each, everyone, everybody,* and so on) are third person in origin, but *you,* used informally as an indefinite pronoun, is second person. *You* may be used only when all readers might reasonably accept it as personal in reference.

Avoid, for example, sentences beginning: "Have you ever looked at yourself in your new dress and thought . . . ?" Half of the human race would have to say, bristling, "No, of course not!"

b. Gender

Pronouns agree with their antecedents in gender.

In English, gender is determined by sex and consequently causes little grammatical trouble. If the antecedent names a female, the pronoun is feminine; if the antecedent names a male, the pronoun is masculine; otherwise the pronoun is neuter. The few exceptions (ships, for example, are feminine) cause no trouble.

In sentences containing both masculine and feminine antecedents, a masculine pronoun alone is sufficient.

> RIGHT: Every man and woman votes according to his own best judgment.

19

UNNECESSARILY ELABORATE: Every man and woman votes according to his or her own best judgment.

c. Number

Pronouns agree with their antecedents in number.

The men went their way.
The man went his way.

The following complications need to be examined.

1) ANTECEDENTS WITH *and*

Two or more antecedents connected by *and* take a plural pronoun, regardless of the number or position of the individual nouns.

Bill and Elizabeth went to New England for their vacation.
The foreman and the men did their work efficiently.
The men and the foreman did their work efficiently.
BUT: Every bolt and cog in the machine does its share of the work.

2) ANTECEDENTS WITH *or* OR *nor*

Two or more singular antecedents connected by *or* or *nor* take a singular pronoun.

John or Joe will get his way.
Neither John nor Joe will get his way.

If the antecedents differ in number, the pronoun agrees according to the logic of the idea.

Neither the captain nor the men knew what initiated their action.
Neither the captain nor the men knew what initiated his action.

3) AFFIRMATIVE AND NEGATIVE ANTECEDENTS

If one of two antecedents is affirmative and the other negative, the pronoun agrees with the affirmative antecedent.

The men, but not the superintendent, will be paid extra for their overtime work.
Not the superintendent, but the men, will be paid extra for their overtime work.

AGREEMENT OF PRONOUNS **PAgr**

4) *Either,* AND SO ON

Either, neither, everyone, nobody, and so on, are treated as singular in formal writing and take singular pronouns. Informally, they often take plural pronouns. Be sure that the form you use is consistent with the tone of your paper.

> FORMAL (usually preferred in college writing): Everybody in the class conscientiously did his own work.
> INFORMAL AND COLLOQUIAL: Everybody did the best they could.

The reason for the difference is that formal English tends to follow the form of the words; informal and colloquial English tend to follow the meaning. If in a formal context you find you have written a sentence which demands that the second pronoun be plural, recast the sentence to avoid the indefinite pronoun.

> After the completion of the ceremony, everyone entered their automobiles and formed a procession.
> After the completion of the ceremony, the participants and the spectators entered their automobiles and formed a procession.

5) *Each,* AND SO ON, PLUS A PLURAL MODIFIER

Each, either, neither, everyone, and so on, followed by a modifying phrase containing a plural noun, are still singular (but see point 4, above) and take a singular pronoun.

> Each of the students did his best.
> Neither of them was present when his name was called.
> Every one of them misunderstood the problem and consequently got his answer wrong.

6) *None*

None may be either singular or plural.

> None of them deserves credit for his work.
> None of them were there when they were called.

7) COLLECTIVE ANTECEDENTS

Collective nouns (naming groups of things) are either singular or plural, depending on whether the writer means to refer to the group as a unit or to the individual members of the group. A

PAgr/VAgr — THE MOST COMMON ERRORS

pronoun agrees with the intended number of the collective antecedent.

> RIGHT: The board of directors announced its decision.
> RIGHT: The board of directors voted to pay themselves extra fees.

10. AGREEMENT OF VERBS—VAgr

A verb agrees with its subject in person and number, whatever the subject is and wherever in the sentence it is located.

The following complications need to be examined.

a. Person of Nouns

All nouns are third person. The point is more important than it may sound. No one in college ever writes "He don't," but many college students write sentences with singular nouns as subjects and a *don't* somewhere along the line as a verb.

b. Singular Subjects plus Plural Modifiers

A *singular* subject followed by a phrase containing a plural noun is still singular and takes a singular verb.

> The silhouette of the mountains looms against the evening sky.

c. Singular Subjects with *as well as,* and so on

A *singular* subject followed by a parenthetical phrase introduced by *as well as, in addition to,* and so on, takes a singular verb.

> Monday, as well as the remaining days of the week, begins very early in the morning.
> The happy laughter of the children, in addition to the banging of the garbage cans they are playing with, distracts me badly.

d. Subjects with *and*

Two or more subjects connected by *and* require a plural verb.

> Marjorie and Lois were glad to see each other again.
> Men and women are accorded equal voting rights.

e. Subjects with *or* or *nor*

If two or more subjects of differing number are connected by *or* or *nor,* the verb agrees with the nearest subject.

AGREEMENT OF VERBS VAgr

> The teacher or the students are wrong.
> The students or the teacher is due for a surprise. (*If such sentences seem awkward or illogical, they may always be rephrased.*)
> The students are due for a surprise, or the teacher is.

f. Affirmative and Negative Subjects

If one of two subjects is affirmative and the other negative, the verb agrees with the affirmative subject, regardless of which is nearer the verb.

> Not the general, but the privates, were unhappy at the thought of a night march.
> The privates, but not the general, were unhappy at the thought of a night march.

g. Subjects and Subjective Complements

The verb agrees with the subject, not the subjective complement.

> The only drawback to the apartment is the neighbors' noisy children.

h. Subjects after the Verb

The verb agrees with the subject even when the subject follows the verb, as it does in questions and after the expletive *there*.

> Is Lois sitting in that uncomfortable chair from choice?
> Are there any reasons for your decision?
> There are three reasons for my decision.

(The expletive *it* also throws the logical subject after the verb, but with *it* the verb is always singular, even though the logical subject may be plural.)

> It has been seven weeks since we have seen her.

i. Indefinite Pronouns

The indefinite pronouns (*each, everyone, everybody,* and so on) are singular and require a singular verb.

> Everybody has done his work promptly.
> Each of the students has done his own work.
> Every man and woman has contributed greatly.

23

j. *None*

None may be either singular or plural.

None of them deserves credit.
None but the brave deserve the fair.

k. Collective Nouns

Collective nouns may be either singular or plural, depending on whether the writer is thinking of the group as a unit or of the individual members of the group. The verb agrees with the intended number of the collective subject.

SINGULAR: The board of directors decides all policies.
PLURAL: The board of directors vote themselves extra fees for every bit of extra work they do.

l. Relative Pronouns

If the subject is a relative pronoun, the verb agrees, for all practical purposes, with the antecedent of the pronoun.

There are many men who are always too tired to work.
He is one of those men who are always too tired to work. (*The logical relation of the ideas can be seen more readily if the sentence is rearranged: Of those men who are always too tired to work, he is one.*)

There are old and honorable literary precedents for *one of those men who is* (Addison, Swift, Johnson, Jefferson, Macaulay, *et al.*), but many readers still strongly object to it.

He is the only one of those men who is not always tired. (*In this sentence, the adjective clause modifies the singular* one: *Of those men, he is the only one who is not always tired.*)

m. Quantities, and so on

Quantities considered as units, fractions modified by a phrase containing a singular noun, and some nouns plural in form but singular in meaning—all express singular ideas and take singular verbs.

Two weeks is the normal vacation period in business.
Two-thirds of the crop is ruined.
Mathematics is a confusing subject.

AGREEMENT OF VERBS _____ PAgr/VAgr

Two-thirds of the apples are spoiled.
The news is good tonight.

EXERCISE

Choose the correct form from the pairs in parentheses in the following sentences.

1. On the library steps there (has, have) gathered the usual group of students, men and women, to smoke and relax.
2. Relaxing on the library steps is one of the numerous ways which students (has, have) to avoid studying.
3. Every one of the few students who (is, are) too far behind in (his, their, his or her) work to relax (wishes, wish) (he, they, he or she) had studied earlier.
4. Either you or she (is, are) going to give tomorrow's speech.
5. Glenn is the only one of all of the students on this campus who (was, were) voted Most Likely to Succeed in high school who (shows, show) that (his, their) success may be academic.
6. Either of the candidates (is, are) well qualified because of (his, their) past experience.
7. The student body anxiously (awaits, await) the Registrar's reports of (its, their) grades.
8. Intelligence and application—(this, these) (constitutes, constitute) the secret of success in college.
9. (Is, are) any of the proposed solutions to the problem of poverty likely to work in all circumstances?
10. Either the instructor in the classroom or the deans of the various colleges and divisions (handles, handle) disciplinary problems.
11. The recognition of negative characteristics, as well as awareness of similarity, (is, are) essential to making satisfactory classifications.
12. Nine-tenths of what one learns in class (is, are) probably going to be forgotten before long.
13. The one-tenth that (remains, remain) (is, are) your general education.

14. Even in your professional specialty, three-fifths of your knowledge (is, are) all that you are likely to retain for instant use, of the five-fifths you originally learned.

15. Everybody (has, have) to hope that (he, they) will not need part of the dormant two-fifths of (his, their) information in an emergency.

11. SENTENCE CONSTRUCTION (SHIFTS)—Cst

a. Point of View

In your English classes you may have heard "point of view" used in a rhetorical sense to refer to the position or attitude from which events are seen or ideas are considered—the "Speaker" behind a piece of writing. Here, we use it in a grammatical sense, related but more tightly restricted, to refer to consistency in grammatical forms—to tenses and sequence of tenses, to mood, to voice, to person, and to number; or it may refer to a structural or a logical consistency from one end of a sentence to the other.

The fundamental principle is clear: The writer must keep in mind his relationship—in time, mood, number, and so on—to what he is saying. Changes within a single theme or even a single sentence are not only possible, but are sometimes mandatory. What is important is that *shifts in point of view should not be illogical.*

1) SHIFT IN TENSE (THE TIME RELATION OF VERBS AND VERBALS)

The bull still had lots of life in him when the picadors entered the ring. These men teased the bull until he charges them. They then gouge the bull's back with their long lances. The ground was becoming stained with blood wherever the bull stands. (*Shift from past to present to past to present.*)

Taxing up to the hangar, the pilot went in to make his report. (*The action named by the particple occurred before that of the main verb; a perfect participle,* having taxied, *would express that time relation.*)

2) SHIFT IN MOOD, VOICE, AND PERSON

The process of carving figures from soap begins with the collection of materials. The would-be sculptor needs an idea, a bar of soap, and a small-bladed knife. First, carve out the rough outlines.... (*Shift from indicative mood, third person to imperative mood, second person.*)

SENTENCE CONSTRUCTION — Cst

He browns the meat and the onions. Then the sauce is poured over the meat . . . . (*Shift from active voice to passive voice.*)

If one is to get from college all that college can give, you must put into college all that you can give to it. (*Shift from third person* one *to second person* you.)

b. Sentence Patterns

In addition to the shifts in point of view just illustrated, another kind of shift is very common. In the heat of composition, students often begin a sentence according to one pattern and then forget where they were going and shift in mid-sentence to a different pattern altogether. Or revision of one part may throw another part off.

In its simplest form, this kind of shift may merely repeat an element already included.

I knew that, if I left the job to her, that she would do it in the least efficient way.

Or some vital element may be omitted from the sentence, such as parts of a verb phrase or prepositions demanded by an idiom.

This problem has and will be carefully studied. (*Omitted:* been, *to complete the verb phrase* has been.)

I am as good or better than you. (*Omitted:* as, *leaving the idiomatic comparison* as good as *unfinished. Perhaps the best phrasing for that idea:* "I am as good as you, if not better.")

Or if the writer jumps across a gap in the thought in mid-sentence, the two ends of the sentence may seem to have little or no structural or even logical connection with each other.

Watching us intently, nevertheless the sun went down immediately behind the deer, which made them a difficult target for all our care to prevent discovery.

To have been able to judge exactly what the scope of registration would be this year would have been hard to predict.

c. Faulty Predication

A predication is a statement of an idea, but a faulty predication is literal nonsense. Usually, it burbles out in the haste of composing and is not caught in revision because the writer reads what he meant to say instead of what he put down on the page.

Cst   THE MOST COMMON ERRORS

1) ILLOGICAL USE OF *to be* (FALSE EQUATION)

    The most comfortable method of traveling is an automobile.
    The copper wheel process is one of the best types of ornamentation.
    Many automobile accidents are youth and the desire to show off. (*Perhaps that nonsense results from the omission of* caused by, *but as it stands, the predication is faulty.*)
    To her grandchildren, a grandmother is a doctor, teacher, part-time parent, playmate, and many other occupations.
    I intend to illustrate my thesis by examples which are the chief reasons for the development that took place. (*In this sentence, the choice of a more exact verb than* are *would have solved the problem. Presumably the student avoided* illustrate *and* exemplify *to prevent repetition. It would have been better to change the infinitive.*)

A few constructions which logically result in false *to be* equations are increasingly common, but many readers object to them and are distracted.

    Doing well in college is when you make the Dean's List.
    A construction to watch out for is where .... (*A thing is never a* when *or a* where. *Suspect any* is when *or* is where *sentences.*)
    The reason I won't go is because .... (*This phrasing is becoming increasingly common, but it is still wordy, if not ungrammatical. Avoid* reason is because. *Say "I won't go because ..." or "The reason ... is that ...."*)

2) FAULTY APPOSITIVES

    The play irritated my father, an unmitigated piece of trash. (*The appositive belongs to* play, *not to* father. *Yet it stands by* father.)
    Mary flirted openly with Kenny, a sure sign that she was quarreling with Bill. (*What substantive does* sign *repeat?*)
    Skill with any musical instrument requires diligent practice, a category into which I certainly do not fit. (*Nothing in the main clause names a category.*)

3) INCOMPLETE OR ILLOGICAL COMPARISONS

    My study habits are better than John. (*Omitted:* than John's are. *This is both incomplete and illogical.*)
    I am so tired tonight. (*We can stress* so *in speaking, but in writing it suggests* so tired that ... *and seems incomplete.*)

FAULTY PARALLELISM   Cst/ //Cst

Swimming is one of the most relaxing and beneficial exercises of any other sport. (*The* other *makes nonsense of the sentence.*)

Alert students are sometimes troubled by the distinction between figures of speech (such as metaphor, metonymy, and synecdoche) and faulty predications. The difference is that the good figure of speech is appropriate and intentional; the faulty predication results in inappropriate nonsense. Furthermore, the faulty predication is not the same as a faulty figure of speech. The first results from lazy carelessness in the choice of diction (usually *to be* instead of a more exact verb) or from failure to recognize other pairings of unlike ideas. The second results from a misguided effort to gain clarity by an inappropriate figure. The writer of a faulty predication plods indifferently into a logical quagmire; the writer of a poor figure of speech leaps without looking and lands with an intellectual pratfall.

Sometimes—in the heat of composition—two or three ideas overlap and get scrambled. This sort of shift (and any of the others) can happen to the best of us. But it is a sad freshman who does not recognize and correct such shifts when he revises his themes, as the writer of the following sentence, faced with an extra semester of instruction and practice, should have realized.

> When I consider the above-mentioned mistakes plus some others, it will all boil down to the fact that it is the cause of disinterest or just trying to get by, because yet today there remains the fact that the taking of this course is still a means toward an end and still not caring whether I make a *D* or *A* but only whether I pass or flunk is the only interest I have for this course because my true interest is numbers and their association to each other and not with the association of words and ideas of words which would make my other courses easier, if I had a control over my English or rather rhetoric.[1]

FAULTY PARALLELISM—//Cst

Putting similar ideas into similar constructions is an important device for securing effective sentences, for obvious reasons. The human mind likes to run in grooves, and a reader is pleased by skillfully repeated patterns. Parallelism, the deliberate use of similar

---

[1] From "Rhet as Writ," *The Green Caldron: A Magazine of Freshman Writing*, published at the University of Illinois. Reprinted by permission.

//Cst _____ THE MOST COMMON ERRORS

constructions for similar ideas, is very common as a result. It is so common, in fact, that your reader will be irritated and confused if you fail to use parallel patterns where he expects them or do use them with dissimilar ideas where he does not expect them.

a. Similar Ideas

Use similar constructions to express similar ideas.

FAULTY: I enjoy swimming, hiking, and to fish.
PARALLEL: I enjoy swimming, hiking, and fishing. (*Three gerunds are parallel; two gerunds and an infinitive are not.*)
FAULTY: He was an old man of ninety-seven and tired.
PARALLEL: He was an old man of ninety-seven, and he was tired. (*Two clauses are parallel; a clause and an adjective are not.*)
PARALLEL: He was an old, tired man of ninety-seven. (*Two adjectives are parallel.*)
FAULTY: This is an important job and which must be done carefully.
PARALLEL: This is a job which is important and which must be done carefully.
PARALLEL: This is an important job, and one which must be done carefully. (*Two nouns, job and one, are parallel; a noun and an adjective clause are not.*)
NOT PARALLEL, BUT CORRECT: This is an important job which must be done carefully.

Notice that all the examples of faulty parallelism so far considered result from misuse of the coordinating conjunction *and*. *And* connects only equal elements.

A similar error results from misuse of the correlative conjunctions, such as *either–or, neither–nor, not (only)–but (also)*, which always work in pairs to connect equal elements.

FAULTY: Either John will do this job or let it slide.
PARALLEL: John will either do this job or let it slide.
FAULTY: Not only will John do this job, but ask Frances to help him.
PARALLEL: John not only will do this job, but will ask Frances to help him.

When you use correlative conjunctions, be sure each member of the pair is followed by grammatically similar elements.

Other kinds of faulty parallelism are more complex, sometimes involving a lack of logical comparability even though grammatical

AWKWARDNESS //Cst/K

parallelism is maintained, or otherwise failing to balance ideas which ought to be treated alike.

> Here is the typical regular Navy officer of today: an average of seven years in the service, high school graduate, has a good technical education through a service school, is usually quite competent, and well satisfied with his career.
> No one really cares what you do, but only can you keep it secret.
> By using the French idioms in each lesson, the student is able to enlarge his vocabulary, also making him able to express himself more accurately. (*This one is the kind that poses problems for the instructor. It might be marked* //Cst, *or* Cst, *or even* K.)

b. Dissimilar Ideas

Do not use similar constructions to express dissimilar ideas.

The principal trouble here arises with constructions that look like A, B, and C series, but do not deal with logically similar elements.

> FAULTY: I put on a surgical gown, a skull-type cap, and tied a mask around my face.
> CORRECTED: I put on a surgical gown and a skull-type cap, and tied a mask around my face. (*The first* and *now connects two nouns,* gown *and* cap; *the second connects two verbs,* put on *and* tied. *The comma separates the dissimilar elements.*)

In revising your themes, be alert for all such shifts in construction. Remember that although you may know what you mean, your reader must depend on what you actually say.

13. AWKWARDNESS—K

A final problem which remains to be mentioned is that of awkwardness. It is a complex problem which may take many forms and may be related at one and the same time to weakness in grammar, to shifts in construction, to the uncertainty in diction and idiom which plagues those who have never done much reading, and to haste in writing and slackness in revising. It is very hard for an instructor to put a finger on, because it results in writing which is not exactly ungrammatical but is certainly not fluent.

The following passages, for example, offer nothing which a student should be proud of having written. They could be analyzed in detail, and their weaknesses could be specifically indicated. Yet

31

few instructors have the time for such detailed analysis as would be required, and the margins of themes leave too little room. Most instructors, consequently, would mark them as awkward and hope that the student, when he revised his theme, would ask himself, "Now, what did I really mean to say here? What would be the easiest way to say it?"

> Had not the people of the ages been able to record their history and do so well, we would be lost in knowing about the past.
>
> There was no grammar as such, because everybody would not have been in that class if he or she did not know it.
>
> I could get little satisfaction from having helped to any extent mentally subnormal children if I were one in a grade-series of teachers. With a limit to the time or level of development, the teacher cannot fully practice a good program with a follow-up and check to keep the children from backsliding or becoming fixed at one level when there is more capacity than has been developed.

And finally:

> In speaking to friends and fellow students and also from my own personal experience, I have found it rather difficult to advance in position in the business world without a college education. I have always worked with one idea in mind, that is, the hope of advancement. In this hope I am at this time deeply disappointed. I have failed to reach the step of the ladder that I feel I am capable of standing on. Why? Well, my superiors have told me that I have not sufficient education. I pointed out to them that I did have the experience and intelligence to handle the job. In this they agreed, but they wanted the piece of paper to show that I had had the education. At this stage, I could not produce the evidence. So the only outlook I had was to enter college.

How would you mark a passage like that to show the student his weaknesses? Every line has something wrong with it, and yet very few of the errors are so clear cut that reference to the handbook would do very much good. In despair, the instructor contented himself with the general comment: "A good deal of awkward phrasing, in which you don't say quite what you mean. See me in conference."

There is no quick cure for a bad case of awkwardness, but practice in writing, reading aloud what you have written, attentive-

AWKWARDNESS   **Cst/ //Cst/K**

ness to the rhythms and idioms of Standard English as you read what others have written, care in knowing before you write what you want to say, and critical revision of what you have written—all these will help.

EXERCISE

Rewrite the following passages to make them clear and effective. Identify the kind of error involved.

1. As the plane droned on, some talked, watched movies, read, and others were asleep.
2. As soon as they are corrected, these inadequacies in the curriculum will improve the college greatly.
3. To appoint Ira to a committee is to be sure that, though it may take time, that the job will be well done.
4. The grill work is well-designed, unobtrusive, and stainless steel.
5. One should work carefully and do the best that you can do, within the limits of the importance of the task.
6. We were playing football in the side yard and having a lot of fun until Uncle Will comes out and starts coaching.
7. I have a great deal of interest and respect for your opinion.
8. Among the numerous skills developed by a good course in English composition are a knowledge of the basic structure of the language and confidence in your ability to express yourself fluently.
9. My grandmother is acquisitive and retentive—anything and everything from old dresses and letters and knickknacks to long since abandoned old rocking chairs in the attic.
10. My ability to play basketball was not great, but it was at least better than the average boy.
11. Sawmills, mining wastes, atomic energy plants, and chemical refuse are responsible for the pollution of salmon streams.
12. The biggest change from high school to college was the differences in teaching.

13. The average American traveling in Europe does not know the languages of the country he is in nor anything about the customs. They are Ugly Americans.

14. Wherever one goes in this country, you find people having different ideas on that which it is necessary to be done, but all of them Americans and wanting what is best for everybody, which makes education important and a free press.

15. Abolishing poverty, not only in Appalachia but in the blighted hearts of city slums, is a vital problem for all of us, and which will take time to solve.

16. Roses are perhaps the most popular flower, but they are hard to care for, being more susceptible to insects and disease.

17. The town's present real-estate assessment is $25,643,159.00, which under the statutory law of 18 percent pertaining to debt limit of real estate, is $4,615,768.62.

18. Love may be based on common interests, or on loneliness and propinquity, or for many other reasons.

19. The easiest way to write faulty predications is out of your head.

20. Professor Snodgrass was maneuvered into resigning, the best thing President McClanahan has done since taking office.

2

Grammar

Gr   Grammar

The importance of grammar, 38
The functions of sentence elements, 41
    1. The sentence itself, 41
    2. The elements of the sentence, 42
* 3. The functions, 43
       a. Subject, 43
       b. Verb, 44
       c. Complement, 44
          1) Subjective, 45
          2) Predicate adjectives, 45
          3) Objects of verbs, 46
              Direct object, 46
              Indirect object, 46
              Objective complement, 46
          4) Objects of prepositions or of verbals, 46

* There are exercises for items marked with an asterisk.

   d. Modifier, 48
   e. Connective, 48
   f. Absolute, 49

The basic sentence patterns, 51

Parts of speech and functions, 53
 * 4. Nouns, 54
   a. Definition, 54
   b. Classes, 54
 * 5. Pronouns, 56
   a. Definition, 56
   b. Classes, 56
   c. Troublesome relatives, 57
   d. *Who, which, that*, 57
  *e. Case, 58
    1) Subjective complements, 59
    2) Words in pairs, 59
    3) After *than* or *as*, 60
    4) Modifying gerunds, 60
    5) Subject of infinitive, 60
    6) With the infinitive *to be*, 60
   f. *Who* and *whom*, 61
    1) Subject in a clause, 61
    2) Object of a verb or verbal, 62
    3) Object of a preposition, 62
   g. *Whose*, 62
   h. Person, number, gender, 62
  6. Verbs, 63
   a. Definition, 63
  *b. Kinds, 65
    1) Transitive, 65
    2) Intransitive, 65
    3) Linking, 65
  *c. Number, 67
  *d. Tense, 68
    1) The six basic tenses, 68
    2) Other tense forms, 69
   e. Tense Problems, 70

             1) Past for past participle, 70
             2) *Of* for *have,* 70
             3) *Shall* and *will,* 71
             4) Overuse of *would,* 71
             5) Special uses of the present, 71
                    Habitual action, 72
                    Universal truth, 72
                    Historical present, 72
             6) Sequence of tenses, 73
       * f. Mood, 73
         g. Voice, 74
  * 7. Verbals, 75
       a. Gerunds, 75
       b. Participles, 76
             1) Present, 76
             2) Past, 77
       c. Infinitives, 77
       d. Split infinitives, 78
       e. Verbals in fragments, 78
       f. Tense sequence with verbals, 79
    8. Modifiers, 80
       * a. Adjectives, 80
       * b. Adverbs, 81
         c. Verb-adverb phrases, 83
         d. Confusion of adjectives and adverbs, 83
    9. Connectives, 84
       a. Prepositions, 84
       b. Conjunctions, 84
             1) Coordinating and correlative, 85
             2) Subordinating, 86
       c. Conjunctive adverbs, 86
   10. Interjections, 86

Formal groups, 87
   * 11. Phrases, 87
       a. Verb phrases, 87
       b. Prepositional phrases, 87
       c. Verbal phrases, 88

Gr ──────────────────────── GRAMMAR

       1) Gerund phrases, 89
       2) Participial phrases, 89
       3) Absolute phrases, 89
       4) Infinitive phrases, 90
 12. Clauses, 91
    a. Independent clauses, 92
    b. Dependent clauses, 92
       *1) Noun clauses, 92
       *2) Adjective clauses, 94
       *3) Adverb clauses, 96

THE IMPORTANCE OF GRAMMAR—Gr

For those who cannot trust their own language habits, some knowledge of "grammar" offers the easiest way of correcting habits that are not in accord with general educated usage, of learning to recognize and avoid "mistakes"—whether those mistakes are functional, actually getting in the way of the reader's comprehension, or merely conventional, violating an established usage although not preventing understanding.

You already know most of the grammar of spoken English, though you probably do not know how to explain it in words and very likely have never thought of most of it as grammar at all. But you do speak English. You know the basic forms of English words (*morphology*), the basic ways to arrange them (*word order*), and the use of words that mean little in themselves (*function words*) but indicate the relationships of more meaningful words. Most remarkable of all, you know how to pitch your voice, high or low or gliding from one pitch to another, to give variations of meaning to an utterance. You know how to give greater or less vocal emphasis to parts of an utterance. You know how to vary the pauses between parts of an utterance to join or separate what would otherwise be a meaningless series of sounds. In other words, you know how to use the very important devices of *pitch, stress,* and *juncture*. In spoken English all of these are fundamental parts of the grammar. And the spoken language is the vital, living language.

GRAMMAR _____ **Gr**

Written English is a complicated set of symbols that represents spoken English, but in some ways does it awkwardly. The difficulties you may have with written English are our primary concern. Many of them arise because written English lacks the pitch, stress, and juncture signals of spoken English, except as typography and punctuation can suggest them. Others arise because morphological changes in the forms of words (showing tense, case, number, and so on), which once were of major importance, are now incomplete remnants of a dead system and consequently are sometimes hard to remember. Still others arise because written English must be fuller, clearer, and more precise than spoken English; you cannot merely write down what you might say. And still others arise because you have never seen much sense in learning a subject that did not seem to have much use outside an English class; consequently, though you have met "grammar" often, you may never have learned how to make use of what you know.

But now, having entered college, you are preparing yourself for admission to the educated minority, and you need to know the minority dialect used by educated people. Again, you already do know most of it, but wherever your habits differ, you need to learn the constructions that educated speakers and writers use—particularly educated writers.

For it is the usage of those who are presumed to know the language best that makes the "rules" of the educated dialect, not logic nor lawgivers nor the practice in other dialects, though all of those to some extent influence educated usage. And to learn to adjust your habits to educated usage, you must know something of the basic structure of the language. Grammar, of whatever kind (and there are several kinds), is an attempt to classify the elements of a language in order to describe how its works. Just as algebra is generalized arithmetic, English grammar is, or should be, generalized English, by which one can make or understand meaningful statements about the language instead of having to treat every new sentence as a new and unique phenomenon. Language is less exact than numbers, and grammar is less fixed and less complete than algebra. Scholars still strongly disagree about what approaches, what systems of classification, and what terminology provide the

39

best description of Modern American English. (It has been wisely said that all grammars leak.) But for all the disagreements, it is possible to generalize about what usually occurs. We shall use familiar terminology wherever possible, borrow from varied approaches to grammar when it is convenient to do so, and try to describe the national, current, and reputable usage that makes up the language of the educated man.

But it is not enough to say of a disputed locution that it is nationally and currently used by most reputable writers. There is a time lag in grammatical understanding, as there is in many things. The primary purpose of all worthwhile writing is to convey the writer's idea as effectively as possible to the reader he wants to reach. Those readers may not be as sophisticated linguistically as the writer is; they may respond unfavorably to a construction that he knows is quite well established, and the possibility of such an unfavorable response must be considered. Suppose, for example, that the writer ends a sentence with what looks like a preposition. He may know it is not a preposition, but is an adverb, and that English has long made use of verb-adverb combinations to produce new verb-ideas. (For example, in the phrase *to put on shoes, put* and *on* combine to express the idea of the formal *don,* itself an old and now forgotten verb-adverb phrase, *to do on. Shoes* is the object of the verb-adverb combination, not of *on* alone. Because this adverb *on* looks like the prepositional *on,* however, the student would perhaps do well to avoid it at the end of a sentence. It will seldom be noticed anywhere else.) If the reader is startled by any construction and loses track of what the writer is trying to say because he thinks instead of the way the idea is phrased, there is a flaw in the writing which reduces the effectiveness of the paper. So we shall sometimes say, "This is not wrong. Don't worry about it when others use it. But avoid it yourself, because many readers will be distressed and distracted by it." Alexander Pope is now somewhat out of fashion, but his advice is still good.

> Be not the first by whom the new is tried,
> Nor yet the last to lay the old aside.

We shall try to find a middle ground and to recommend constructions which are clear, modern, and effective.

THE SENTENCE ITSELF ———————————————— **Gr 1**

THE FUNCTIONS OF SENTENCE ELEMENTS

1. THE SENTENCE ITSELF—Gr 1

Grammar is chiefly concerned with the sentence. Although consistency in grammatical point of view does relate one sentence to another in such matters as tense and person and number, most grammar consists of analyzing the elements of one individual sentence at a time. We shall be working with sentences throughout most of this chapter.

But what is a sentence? Basic though the concept is, and familiar as the word is, "a sentence" is so hard to define that we can best fall back on combining many definitions, each clarifying some one aspect of the sentence and all together suggesting the meaning. The word *sentence* is related to the word *sense,* and in very general terms, a sentence is an utterance that makes sense in itself, in the context in which it appears. The old grade school definition is inadequate: "A sentence is a group of words having a subject and a verb and expressing a complete thought." But not all sentences have a subject and a verb, though most of them do. And what is a complete thought? It is a structure that makes sense in itself, in its context. Someone asks a question, and you answer, "Yes." In its context, *yes* makes sense, and in speech or writing dialogue it is certainly a sentence. "Where—?" "The drugstore." "Ouch!" "George?" These could all be sentences—minor sentences, though not full sentences.

But in written English, especially outside of dialogue or stream-of-consciousness prose, sentences usually are also grammatically complete with subject and verb and a complete idea. For grammatical completeness alone, another definition has been phrased: A sentence is "a structure not included by any formal device in any larger structure"—by such elements, that is, as subordinating conjunctions, like *until* or *if.* "George is here" is a sentence, but "If George is here" is not; it is made dependent on some kind of larger structure by that *if.*

Still another definition looks to the spoken language for its clues, but written sentences can be read aloud and tested by the clues offered by the voice; so this definition can be useful too:

41

"A sentence is an utterance between two full stops of the breath, usually ending with a change of pitch." With practice, you can hear the signals of pitch, stress, and juncture (pauses). We will need them often.

Many other definitions have been phrased, but we can get along with a combination of these three: "A full sentence is a grammatically complete and independent utterance, spoken between full stops of breath and ending usually with a change of pitch; it makes sense in itself and in its context." It is a *predication*, an expression of a fully formulated thought. Much of the rest of this chapter will be concerned with examining details behind that definition.

2. THE ELEMENTS OF THE SENTENCE—Gr 2

English, as a spoken language, is made up of sounds and sound combinations, and anyone who pretends to anything like a thorough understanding of the language must know what they are and how to identify them. We do not need to be so thorough. It is interesting to know that there are different grammars and different approaches. Depending on our approach, we could learn to say that the elements of the sentence are phones, segmental phonemes, suprasegmental phonemes, or morphemes, or constituents, or clusters, or vowels and consonants, or words and phrases, or headwords, or kernels and strings, or transforms, or various other things. Those terms and many others are important to one or another of the currently active attempts to describe Modern English.

Unfortunately, none of these new grammars is complete or foolproof, and there is none with which all college students are already familiar. For our purposes, even though the traditional terminology of Latin-based grammar causes some trouble when it is applied to English, we can perhaps get along best with the terms most students already know, and merely modify, at need, the way we look at them. In those terms, the elements of the written sentence are letters and words representing sounds. The words are roots (or stems), and one or two to a word, and part-words like prefixes and suffixes (*ex-*, *-ible*, *-tion*). Some words are only roots, some are prefixes and roots, some are roots and suffixes, and some are all three. Sometimes each word functions as a unit (as in

THE FUNCTIONS _____ Gr 3/3a

Frank snores. Charlie catches fish. Some students are lazy), but they sometimes go together in word-groups with the whole word-group functioning as a unit (as in [*The old man*] [*in the corner*] [*has been sitting*] [*in my favorite chair*] [*since the day before yesterday*], [*when he first came in*]). Some of the word-groups are phrases, some are clauses, and some are just clusters of words attached to a major word, the "headword" in the group. Whether the functioning unit is a single word or a word-group makes very little difference in the way the unit functions.

3. THE FUNCTIONS[1]—Gr 3

Whether as single words or as word-groups, all elements of the sentence (with the single exception of the expletives *it* and *there*, in *It is* and *There is/are* sentences) function in one of six ways, as *subjects, verbs, complements, modifiers, connectives,* or *absolutes*. These functions must be understood, because we shall be using these terms constantly throughout the chapter.

a. *Subject:* **A word or word-group indicating the topic of the sentence, telling what the predication is about.** (*Test: Who* or *what* did or is or has done to it whatever the sentence asserts?)

  S
John teaches.

     S
The squirrel in the tree jabbered incessantly.

       S
Whoever left the door open should have shut it.

       S
To leave doors open in winter is foolish.

     S
Does *the draft* disturb you?

  S
It does.

[1] For this simplification of Otto Jesperson's analysis of functions, I am especially indebted to George A. Gullette and James M. McCrimmon, *Writing Effectively* (New York: Holt, Rinehart and Winston, 1941).

Gr 3a–c _____ GRAMMAR

The subject normally precedes the verb in statements and exclamations, and normally follows the verb or splits a verb phrase in questions.

b. *Verb:* A word or word-group that tells what the subject does or is, or what is done to it. (*Test:* What does the subject *do? Is* it something? *Is* something *done to* it?)

    S   V
John *teaches*.

  V S   V
Does John *teach?*

       S   V
The squirrel in the tree *jabbered*.

     S V
The noise *is* incessant.

S   V
It *becomes* worse by the minute.

             S   V
Much fruitless thought *has been expended* on the nature of the verb.

V
Sit down.

The verb normally follows the subject in statements, and precedes the subject or straddles it in questions. In requests or commands (imperatives) the subject normally does not appear at all.

c. *Complement:* A word or word-group that completes an otherwise incomplete idea initiated by a verb, a verbal, or a preposition.

Complements are restatements of the subject, or modifiers of the subject, or objects. (*Test:* The subject acts on *whom* or *what?* The subject is *what?* Something is IN, ON, UNDER *what?*)

      S   V   C
Dr. Reesing teaches *"The Age of Milton."*

THE FUNCTIONS _____ **Gr 3c**

      S   V   C
"The Age of Milton" is *a senior course.*

     S   V   C   C
The course is *a requirement* FOR *English majors.*

       C   V   C
In studying *Milton,* read *the text* carefully.
   (*Studying,* as a verbal, may itself require a complement.)

  S V   C
Muriel is IN *the library.*

  S   C V   C
Relaxing IN the *library* is *popular.*

    V   C   C   C
Please give *me your name and address.*

   S   V C   C
Dr. Reesing is *chairman* OF *the department.*

The complement normally follows the verb, verbal, or preposition.

1) COMPLEMENTS MAY RESTATE THE SUBJECT

Subjective complements follow forms of the verb *to be* and a few other "linking verbs," like *to become,* which assert conditions or states of being; subjective complements tell what the subject is.

    S   LV   C
Dr. Reesing is *chairman* of the department.

  S LV   C
Honesty is the best *policy.*

       S LV   C
The best policy is *honesty.*

2) COMPLEMENTS MAY MODIFY THE SUBJECT

Predicate adjectives also follow *to be* or other linking verbs.

Gr 3c   GRAMMAR

     S LV C(M)
Grass is *green*.

     S   LV   C(M)
Relaxing becomes *habitual*.

     S   LV C(M)
Relaxing is *pleasant*.

3) MOST COMPLEMENTS ARE OBJECTS

They follow verbs of action in the common actor-action-goal pattern of the sentence. There are three types of these.

                     V   C
DIRECT OBJECT: The storm destroyed the *village*.

            V   C
Dr. Reesing teaches *"The Age of Milton."*

              V C   C
INDIRECT OBJECT: Give *me* the *book*. (*Book* is the Direct Object. Such a sentence always has two objects; the Indirect Object precedes the Direct Object; the two complements name different things.)

         C   C
Tell the *dean* the *truth*.

                       S   C   C
OBJECTIVE COMPLEMENT: The fraternity elected *Richard president*. (*Richard* is the Direct Object. Such a sentence always has two objects; the Direct Object precedes the Objective Complement, and the two complements name the same thing.)

4) OBJECTS OF PREPOSITIONS OR OF VERBALS

Complements may be the headwords in prepositional phrases (see pages 87–88), or they may complete verbals instead of verbs (see pages 75–79). Both are *objects*.

      C
IN the *room* . . .

THE FUNCTIONS _____ Gr 3a–c

        C
TO the *barricades!*

        C
FLYING an *airplane* . . .

        C
TO TELL the *truth* . . .

        C   C
I want you TO TELL me the *truth*. (The phrase *you to tell me the truth* is direct object of *want*.)

Subjects, verbs, and **complements** are the most important elements of the sentence. Everything else is related to them in one way or another.

EXERCISE

In the spaces to the left, indicate the function of each italicized element. Use the symbols S for subject, V for verb, and C for complement.

_____ 1. Some women *should be struck* regularly, like gongs.

_____ 2. I never struck a *woman*, dear, for sport.

_____ 3. Sentences 1 and 2 are *quotations* which do not necessarily disagree.

_____ 4. Great minds often *flock* together.

_____ 5. *Flying an airplane* is more exciting than driving a slow car.

_____ 6. *Whoever attempts to fly an airplane,* however, should have had some experience.

_____ 7. In an emergency, inexperienced people *have* sometimes managed to fly.

_____ 8. As Icarus found, though, the novice is seldom *successful.*

_____ 9. Give *Icarus* credit for trying.

_____ 10. The credit given *him* might take the form of a commemorative wreath.

Gr 3d–e GRAMMAR

d. *Modifier:* A word or word-group that describes or limits, or qualifies, or identifies some other element, making it more specific.

Modifiers may affect subjects, verbs, complements, other modifiers, or even whole predications. (*Test:* Does an element serve to make some other element more specific?)

        M(C)

Andrea was *absent.* (Describes Andrea, and also completes the incomplete verb-idea.)

    M   M

The *absent* Andrea slept *late.* (*Absent* describes Andrea; *late* tells how she slept.)

  M M   M

The old man *in the corner* . . . . (Tell which man, describes and identifies.)

  M   M M

Jack's car was damaged *very badly.* (*Jack's* identifies the car; *badly* qualifies *was damaged,* and *very* qualifies *badly.*)

    M

If it does not rain soon, the crops will be ruined. (Qualifies the whole main predication.)

The positions of modifiers are sometimes fixed and sometimes flexible. We shall examine that problem as we consider types of modifiers later. Notice, at the moment, that they tend to stand as near as possible to the elements they modify.

e. *Connective:* A word or word-group whose chief function is to tie parts of the sentence together, indicating subordination or coordination between the parts, reducing a main element to a modifier, or doing something similar.

In addition to this grammatical information, they convey various ideas of relationship: *in* is not *under; and* is not *but; instead of* is not *in addition to.* They are very important in enabling us to express complicated ideas. (*Test:* Does the word or word-group work chiefly to show connections between major elements in the sentence?)

THE FUNCTIONS _____ Gr 3e–f

>   **Con**
> The old man *in* the corner . . . (Makes *corner* a modifier of *man*.)
>
>   **Con**
> *In spite of* his laziness, he accomplished a good deal. (Ties *laziness* to the main idea and sets up the conditions under which he worked.)
>
>   **Con**   **Con**   **Con**
> Writing *and* speaking have much *in* common, *but* are not identical.
>
>   **Con**   **Con**
> *Because* they are similar, one cannot always test the clarity *of* written
>
>   **Con**   **Con**   **Con**
> English *by* ear alone, *since* what is clear *when* it is spoken may not
>
>   **Con**
> be clear *when* it is read.

Connectives usually begin the word-groups to which they belong, and most of the time they stand between their word-groups and the sentence elements to which their word-groups are connected.

f. Absolute: A word or word-group included in the sentence but having no grammatical effect on it.

Terms of address, grunts and groans, digressive comments, and so on are all absolutes. (*Test:* Does the element in any way change the grammatical structure of the rest of the sentence?)

>   **A**
> *Dean Linton,* what should be done with a student who is absent all the time? (The absolute aims the sentence at its target, but has no grammatical effect.)
>
>   **A**
> The answer, *of course,* is that such a student should fail. (*Of course* comments on the obviousness of the idea, but it does nothing else.)
>
>   **A**
> An alert student—*but I do mean "alert"*—can learn enough grammar to correct his bad habits. (The digression comments on the main idea and emphasizes part of it, but does nothing else.)

49

Gr 3d–f GRAMMAR

A

There is, *alas,* not much hope for an inert student. (Just a groan.)

Absolutes may appear anywhere in the sentence. Notice that they are always set off from the rest of the sentence by commas.

In summary, except for the expletives *it* and *there,* all elements in an English sentence function in one (occasionally two) of these six ways: as Subjects, Verbs, Complements, Modifiers, Connectives, or Absolutes. So do the *separable* elements within word-groups. Once we realize that fact and learn to identify these six functions, the patterns of English become relatively easy to understand.

EXERCISES

A. In the following sentences, underline all single-word modifiers, connectives, and absolutes. Above each, identify the function by the symbols M, Con, or A.

1. These ashtrays do not always prevent cigarettes from rolling off and burning the table.

2. Regardless of how one feels in winter, in summer no one objects to an invasion of a polar-Canadian air mass.

3. Bright, clear, invigorating days, with low humidity and low temperatures, are Canada's gift to the United States.

4. When they come, muggy air from the Gulf of Mexico is pushed back toward the Gulf.

5. I hope, of course, that Canadians do not begrudge us the temporary use of their air.

6. Oh, let us rejoice in the existence of that long, undefended border between the two nations.

7. The liberal arts and the sciences have been called two separate cultures, because the specialists in one often know too little about the other.

THE FUNCTIONS _____ Gr 3a–f

8. In the twentieth century—the age of space and plastics—can anyone be considered liberally educated if he knows nothing about science?

9. Can any scientist be considered educated at all if he knows nothing of those liberal arts by which man has always developed his most human, or humane, potentialities?

10. If ever there really are two separate cultures, Lord Snow and Mr. Leavis, they both will be destroyed.

B. By means of the symbols S, V, C, M, Con, A, analyze the function performed by each word in the following sentences.

EXAMPLE:
        S   V M C Con M   C   Con V Con M   C
John hit the ball over the fence and ran to first base.

1. Swimming in the ocean is fun.

2. I dislike grammar.

3. The clock struck twelve.

4. Snodgrass is the treasurer of the club.

5. Oh, how I hate arising in the morning!

6. Shannon and I worked on the magazine.

THE BASIC SENTENCE PATTERNS

We have sketched the nature of sentence elements and the ways in which those elements can function. Now we need to look briefly at the basic patterns of English sentences. Subjects, verbs, and complements are relatively limited in the positions they may assume, because *word order* is one of the most important grammatical devices in modern written English. In Anglo-Saxon days, when form changes were elaborate, word order was less important, and English, rather like Latin, could indicate function by the forms

Gr ──────────────────────────────── GRAMMAR

of the major words. But now we have few form changes (just enough, in fact, to cause us trouble occasionally). We depend chiefly instead on word order and function words to mark grammatical function. Consequently, although variety of pattern is still possible, there are basic patterns we normally use. If you know them, they can often help you to identify subjects, verbs, and complements that are otherwise obscure.

All sentences do one of four things: make statements, ask questions, issue commands or requests, or utter exclamations. For the first two, there are eight common structural patterns, for the third there are six, and for the fourth there are three. Any of them may admit additional elements, such as modifiers, but the elements listed are essential to the pattern.

Statements—active

1. S V—Mortals die.
2. S LV M—Washington is beautiful.
3. S LV C$^{(SC)}$—Deans are administrators.
4. S V C$^{(DO)}$—Deans counsel students.
5. S V C$^{(ID)}$ C$^{(DO)}$—Addison gave Ann a kitten.
6. S V C$^{(DO)}$ C$^{(OC)}$—We made Eisenhower President.
7. It is M S(word-group)—It is unlikely *that he will appear.*
8. There LV S M—There are difficulties here.

Questions—active

Patterns 1 through 6: S V+? V S+? V S V+?

1. Mortals die?
2. Is Washington beautiful?
3. Are deans administrators?
4. Do deans counsel students?
5. Did Addison give Ann a kitten?
6. Did we make Eisenhower President?

Pattern 7: Is it M S?—Is it unlikely that he will appear?
Pattern 8: LV there S M?—Are there difficulties here?

Commands and requests

Patterns 1 through 6: The S disappears from the statement pattern. Only *second-person* statements with some form of future verbs can be transformed into requests.

PARTS OF SPEECH _____ **Gr**

    Statement: S V + __ You will report for induction.
    Command: V + __ Report for induction.
    Statement: S V + __ You will send me the free booklet.
    Request: V + __ Send me the free booklet.

Patterns 7 and 8 do not occur.

Exclamations

  1. *How* or *what* S V __ How it rains.
  2. *How* or *what* C S V __ What a joke it was.
  3. *How* M S V __ How green the grass is.
  (Stress and pitch signals may lend other patterns exclamatory force in spoken English. An exclamation point may do the same in writing.)

PARTS OF SPEECH AND FUNCTIONS

    The most familiar, but in some ways the least satisfactory method of classifying sentence elements is as "parts of speech." Because the established terms are familiar and convenient, everyone who discusses English grammar uses them in some degree; consequently it is essential to know them. But it is also important to realize that the system is not foolproof. First, it is not a system of logical classification in which one and only one set of criteria is applied throughout. (Of the customary eight parts of speech, some are classified by meaning, some by function, and some by position in the sentence.) Second, it is a system designed to describe Classical Latin and not Modern English, and although the two languages are related, the system does not fit English perfectly. Third, the same word in English may function in several different ways, so that a word may be a subject in one sentence, a verb in another, and a modifier in a third, or even belong to one class by form but another by function, like possessive pronouns. We shall try to solve these problems by classifying words according to their function in a given sentence. We shall try to define the parts of speech by their most common meanings, their forms, and their characteristic functions.

    We usually identify eight parts of speech: *nouns, pronouns, verbs, adjectives, adverbs, prepositions, conjunctions,* and *interjections.* In addition to these, there are the verbals, which it is convenient to consider separately.

4. NOUNS

a. Definition

Nouns are names, and often names are nouns. They name people, places, things, qualities, and concepts: *Jack, Kankakee, desk, warmth, honesty.* Here we classify by meaning.

Nouns have characteristic forms. They usually may be either singular or plural: *boy-boys, ox-oxen, witch-witches* (but *mush, news* have only one form). They may have a possessive form: *boy's, ox's, witch's-witches'.* They may be preceded by *a, an,* or *the.*

Nouns function as Subjects, as Complements, and sometimes as Modifiers.

    S   C
The *snow* drifted across the *roads.*

    M   S
The *mountain passes* were choked.

   C   S
In *time,* all *traffic* stopped.

    M   S
The *weatherman's prediction* was fulfilled.

Or nouns may be appositives to Subjects or Complements, renaming the idea more specifically and functioning the same way.

   S   S
His *sister, Mary,* was here. (*Mary* is an appositive, in apposition to *sister.*)

As Subjects or Complements, the position of nouns is determined by the basic sentence patterns. As Modifiers, they precede the words they modify, usually other nouns.

b. Classes

From different points of view, nouns may be classified in several ways. There are *common nouns* and *proper nouns:* the first name groups of things; the second name individuals. There are *abstract nouns* and *concrete nouns;* the first name intangible concepts; the second name tangible things. There are *general nouns*

NOUNS   Gr 4a–b

and *specific nouns:* the first name classes; the second, units within those classes—and a noun may be general in respect to some other noun and specific in respect to a third noun. Notice that these three classifications overlap. Every noun may be classified in all three ways. *Harry,* for example, is at once a proper noun, a concrete noun, and a specific noun. *Virtue* is common, abstract, and general.

COMMON NOUNS: desk, virtue, boy, copper
PROPER NOUNS: Tom, Dick, Harry, the White House
ABSTRACT NOUNS: virtue, truth, beauty
CONCRETE NOUNS: desk, boy, Harry, the White House
GENERAL NOUNS: vegetable, plant, organism (*Each of those is more general, dealing with a larger class, than the one before it.*)
SPECIFIC NOUNS: tree, oak tree, the Treaty Oak (*Each of those is more specific, dealing more nearly with a unit, than the one before it.* Tree *is specific in relation to the general noun* plant, *above.*)

Nouns offer very little trouble, except for the difficulty of realizing that an intangible abstraction, like *truth,* is a thing, and that its name consequently is a noun. When a word functions as a noun, that is, as Subject or Complement, you may call it a noun (or a substantive). Even words which normally function in other ways may be called nouns (or substantives) when they function as Subjects or Complements; or they may be classified by form according to their normal use. Either way, you may get into an argument.

Many are called; *few* are chosen.

You may say that *many* and *few* are Subjects and so are nouns; or you may say that what is meant is *many men, few men,* that the true subjects are "understood," and that *many* and *few* are adjectives and Modifiers. In either event, you should be prepared to defend your decision against disagreement.

EXERCISE

Underline the nouns in the following sentences and identify the function of each as Subject or Complement.

1. Many freshmen are confused by terms they hear during the first semester in college.
2. A few definitions of common words might be useful.

Gr 4/5a–b   GRAMMAR

3. A school that is called Somewhere or Other College is one providing courses and awarding degrees in the liberal arts, and usually the sciences, at the bachelor's level.

4. Within a university, a "college" is one of a group of associated academic faculties; the "university" itself is the resulting association, the unity of diverse parts.

5. A "school" is a professional college, usually awarding advanced degrees.

6. A "division" may be a part of a college, or it may be a separate administrative unit; concerned with academic work, it nevertheless does not usually award degrees.

7. Schools and colleges have self-governing faculties under the direction of a dean, and an independent college also has a president, as does a university.

8. Departments are concerned with particular academic disciplines—like English, history, foreign languages, philosophy, chemistry—and the courses and major curricula in those disciplines, and are administered by heads, or chairmen.

9. Academic ranks commonly are instructor, assistant professor, associate professor, and professor.

10. Outside the academic group are numerous administrative officers, like the Director of Admissions, the Registrar, the Comptroller, the Bursar, the Business Manager, and all the others needed to keep house.

5. PRONOUNS

a. Definition

Pronouns are words that substitute for nouns, allowing us to avoid awkward repetition. Whatever meaning they have they take from the context. (See Chapter 1, **Ref.**)

b. Classes

There are eight classes of pronouns.

PERSONAL: I, you, he, they, and so on
RELATIVE: who, which, that, what (= that which)
DEMONSTRATIVE: this, that, these, those
INTERROGATIVE: who, which, what, and so on

PRONOUNS   Gr 5a–d

REFLEXIVE: myself, himself, themselves, and so on
INDEFINITE: one, you, they, it, everyone, and so on
INTENSIVE: myself, yourself, and so on
RECIPROCAL: each other, one another

The personal pronouns have different forms for case, person, number, and gender, and so do the reflexives, the indefinites, and the intensives, all of which resemble the personals. The relative *who, whose, whom* show changes for case.

Like nouns, personal, relative, and indefinite pronouns may function as Subjects, as Complements, or (in the possessive case only) as Modifiers. Interrogative pronouns function as Subjects. Reciprocal pronouns function as Complements. The rest function as Modifiers. Except for the relatives, which begin their word-groups, and the intensives (*I* MYSELF), pronouns take the same functional positions as nouns in the basic sentence pattern.

c. Troublesome Relatives

Fortunately, only the relative pronouns cause very much trouble. They are very common, appearing in most noun and adjective clauses, but students often do not recognize the relatives as pronouns in the way they readily recognize the personals as pronouns. Much of the difficulty some students have with clauses would disappear if they remembered that *who, which,* and *that* (and such compounds as *whoever*) are pronouns and may be Subjects or Complements in subordinate clauses.

d. *Who, Which, That*

Minor trouble with relative pronouns also occurs in choosing between *who, which,* and *that. Who* is used only to refer to persons, *which* to refer to nonpersons, and *that* to refer to either. Use: The person *who,* the thing *which,* the persons or things *that. That* is never used now with nonrestrictive adjective clauses. (See pages 116–118.)

EXERCISE

Underline the pronouns in the following passage and identify the function of each as Subject, Complement, or Modifier.

Gr 5a–e GRAMMAR

The wolf trotted into his den and flopped down in his favorite chair. (It was not a very comfortable chair, but it was one he liked, which is all that matters.) "I met the silliest girl today," he remarked to his wife as she brought him his pipe and slippers. "She was on foot, but was wearing a riding hood, for one thing. It was red, and not very appropriate for such a green child—." (His wife sneered at this pun, but he ignored her.) "She stopped me in the woods and carried on a long, pointless conversation about the contents of a basket which she was carrying. And then later I ran onto her again, and—." He paused to be sure he was getting his wife's full attention. "Here's the payoff, my dear. She decided I was her grandmother!" He smiled reminiscently and gently smacked his lips. "However," he added, "silly as she was, I rather liked her. She was a good girl."

e. Case

Case is the property of nouns and pronouns which shows by changes in the form of the words whether they are functioning as Subjects (subjective, or nominative, case), as Complements (objective, or accusative, case), or as Modifiers (possessive, or genitive, case).

For Modern English nouns, word order (position in the sentence) has largely replaced changes in form to indicate function. We place Subjects first, before the verb, and place Complements after the verb or the preposition they are completing; the same form of the noun is used for both functions. Possessives are formed by adding an apostrophe and usually an *s* to the common case forms. The only real difficulty with case in nouns, consequently, comes in the formation of the possessive case. For a discussion of that problem, see pages 148–149.

The case of pronouns causes more trouble. We use pronouns oftener than we do nouns, and consequently have retained a fuller declension for case, especially with the personal pronouns, which still have three case forms.

 SUBJECTIVE CASE (pronoun functioning as Subject or subjective Complement):
  I—we
  you—you
  he, she, it—they
 POSSESSIVE CASE (pronoun functioning as Modifier):
  my, mine—our, ours

58

PRONOUNS Gr 5e

        your, yours—your, yours
        his, her, hers, its—their, theirs

(Where possessive forms occur in pairs, as in *my, mine*, the first member is used when the pronominal adjective precedes the noun it modifies: *my, our, your, her,* or *their* book. The second member of each pair is used as a predicate adjective or as the object of the preposition in a phrasal possessive: This book is *mine, ours, yours, hers,* or *theirs*. He is a friend of *mine, ours, yours, hers,* or *theirs*.)

    OBJECTIVE CASE (pronoun functioning as Complement):
        me—us
        you—you
        him, her, it—them

In spite of the relatively full declension of the personal pronouns, they ordinarily cause little difficulty. But there are at least six fairly common situations which students do find confusing.

1) SUBJECTIVE COMPLEMENTS

    Use the *subjective* case for a subjective Complement.

    It is *I*. This is *he*.

This usage has all but vanished from conversational English. Even well-educated speakers commonly *say* "It is me" in ordinary conversation. But in written English, except that which is imitating speech, as in dialogue, you are expected to use the subjective case for a complement following the verbs of being, the "linking verbs." (See pages 65–66.)

2) WORDS IN PAIRS

    When words are used in pairs, use the case demanded by the function of the pronoun.

    This is between *you* and *me*. Give it to John and *me*.
    The class nominated *her* and *me* to represent it.
    She and *I* will be there.
    (*If such sentences seem awkward, they may always be rephrased to avoid the construction, as,* She and I were nominated to represent the class. She will be there, and so will I.)
    We Americans are proud of our country.

Gr 5e · GRAMMAR

Europe sometimes distrusts *us* Americans.
Let *us, you* and *me,* go. Let's *you* and *me* go.

In all such sentences, the function can be seen more readily if the pronoun is used alone. No one would say, "This is between I," "Me will be there," "Give it to he," or "Give it to I," "The class nominated I," "Us are proud," "Europe distrusts we," or "Let I go." (The mere existence of another word functioning in the same way should not be allowed to obscure the function of either member of a pair.)

3) AFTER *than* OR *as*

Normally, use the *subjective* case after *than* or *as*.

He is as tall as *I*. She is smaller than *I*.

Such constructions are considered to be parts of clauses the rest of which is merely "understood," as if you had said, for example, "He is as tall as *I* (am tall)." If the full clause, however, would demand the objective case, it should be employed.

I like her better than (I like) *him*.

4) MODIFYING GERUNDS

If the pronoun modifies a gerund, use the *possessive* case.

Imagine *his* singing being so pleasant. (Gerunds are *verbal nouns*. See page 75. It is the singing that is to be imagined; the pronoun merely modifies it. With nouns before gerunds the objective case is often used.)

5) SUBJECT OF INFINITIVE

Use the *objective* case for the subject of an infinitive. (See pages 75, 77, 90.)

They thought *him* to be the greatest general in the war.
I want *them* to go.

6) WITH THE INFINITIVE *to be*

The infinitive *to be* is followed by the same case as the case that precedes it.

They thought *him* to be *me*.
I was thought to be *he*.

f. *Who* and *Whom*

The relative or interrogative pronoun *who* probably causes more trouble with case than all the other pronouns put together. With nouns, position in the sentence has become relatively fixed, and we can tell the function of a noun by its position: If a noun comes before the verb, it is usually subject; after, it is usually object. But *who*, like all relatives, begins its clause; it may appear first in a sentence or a clause and still be an object of a verb or of a preposition. Or it may actually be the subject in its own clause and yet seem to be an object of a preceding verb or preposition that really has nothing to do with it. We are never quite sure when we should use *who,* and when we should use *whom*. In conversation, the problem does not worry us; most *speakers* say *who* when the pronoun comes at the beginning of the sentence, regardless of its function, as in, "Who did you invite?" "Who did you give it to?" But the educated *writer* still carefully distinguishes between the subjective case and the objective case, according to the *function of the pronoun in its own clause*. In written English, we need to be precise.

If you can identify the verb, the problem is not hard to solve. Ask Who? or What? before the verb; the answer will be the subject. If there is no other substantive as subject, use *who*. If there is some other subject, the relative must be a complement; use *whom*.

Fortunately, the difficulty occurs in relatively few constructions.

1) SUBJECT IN A CLAUSE

Use *who* when the pronoun is *subject* in its own clause.

He spoke to the man *who* was here yesterday.
Who told you that?

Do not allow a parenthetical clause coming between *who* and its verb to obscure the function of *who* as subject.

Who do you think will win? (*If the sentence were merely Who will win? there would be no confusion. The presence of a parenthetical clause does not affect the main clause.*)
He spoke to the man *who* (I thought) was here yesterday.

When the relative pronoun (usually *whoever, whichever,* and so on) is *subject* of a noun clause, the *subjective* case is used, regardless of the function of the clause as a whole.

The prize will be given to *whoever* calls the station first. (Whoever is the subject of calls. It is the whole clause which is the object of the preposition to.)

2) OBJECT OF A VERB OR VERBAL

Use *whom* when the pronoun is *object* of a verb or of a verbal.

Whom did you invite? (Did invite *is the verb, and* you *is its subject. The pronoun is object of the verb and in the* objective *case.*)
Tell me *whom* you really came to see. (*Cf.* You came to see *him.*)

3) OBJECT OF A PREPOSITION

Use *whom* when the pronoun is *object* of a preposition.

Whom did you give it to? (*A more formal sentence would be, "To whom did you give it?" Such a sentence is sometimes too formal for the prevailing tone of a paper, and seems stiff and pedantic. But the* objective *case would be used for the relative pronoun in either sentence.*)

g. Whose

When the pronoun *who* is used as a possessive Modifier, the form is *whose*.

Whose books are these?

Do not confuse *whose*, the possessive pronoun, with *who's*, the contraction for *who is*. In informal writing, *whose* is sometimes used as a possessive form for *which*, in place of the formal *of which*. In college writing, it is perhaps best to follow the formal usage.

Remember: The case of a pronoun is always determined by *its function in its own clause*. If the relative pronoun is Subject in its own clause, use the subjective *who*; if it is a Complement in its own clause, use the objective *whom*.

h. Person, Number, Gender

These three aspects of nouns and pronouns cause little trouble except as problems in pronoun agreement. See Chapter 1, **PAgr**, for a discussion.

VERBS Gr 5/6a

EXERCISE

In each of the following sentences, select the form which would be used in formal writing. Identify the function of each pronoun.

1. (We, us) students of grammar lead difficult lives.
2. I think (we, us) should study harder.
3. No matter how popular Professor Snodgrass is with the rest of the class, I like Professor Highfill better than (he, him).
4. (Who, whom) do you suppose I saw today?
5. (Who, whom) do you suppose was at the airport when I landed?
6. Although he is big, he is very graceful, and I admire (his, him) dancing.
7. (His, him) dancing is a pleasure to watch.
8. He is a man (whose, who's) integrity is unquestioned.
9. Kenney sent his best regards to Marjorie and (I, me).
10. You ask for the best candidate, and that is (I, me).
11. This is no time for (he, him) to be loafing.
12. I am sorry, but I cannot tell you (who, whom) the winner is.
13. It was (they, them) who called on us yesterday.
14. As delegates, the girls elected Mary, Martha, and (I, me).
15. Mary and Martha are not as wise as (I, me).

6. VERBS

a. Definition

The verb is the heart of the sentence. There is always a verb expressed in a full sentence, and implied in any minor sentence in which it is not explicit. Once you have found the verb, the rest of the sentence can be worked out easily.

Verbs are not easy to define. In meaning, they name actions, like *run, walk, sleep;* or "states of being," like *is, become.* They tell what the subject does or is, or what is done to it.

In form they are clearer. Verbs are words or (more often) word-groups with such forms as *to be, ran, walked, walking, to write,*

63

Gr 6a

written, sings, to shout. (A few auxiliary verbs—*can, must, shall,* and the like—lack some of these forms.)

In function, true verbs function only as Verbs. We shall presently need to distinguish verbs from verbals, but at the moment it is enough to know that true verbs may be inflected to show differences in person and number; verbals may not.

The position of verbs is determined by the basic sentence patterns.

      V
The snow *drifted* across the roads.

      V
The mountain passes *were choked.*

     V
Traffic *is going to be* delayed a long time.

  V
That *is* too bad.

Verbs have many forms, to indicate *number* (one or more than one), *tense* (time in relation to the writer's point of view), *mood* (*indicative,* stating fact; *subjunctive,* expressing doubt; or *imperative,* giving a command), and *voice* (*active,* with the subject doing the acting; *passive,* with the subject being acted upon). And there are related forms which are not true "finite" verbs at all, but *verbals,* functioning not as Verbs, but as nouns, adjectives, or adverbs, as Subjects, Complements, or Modifiers.

Each of these aspects of verbs causes trouble, and we must accordingly consider each in turn. For the verb is in a very true sense the heart of the sentence. Once you understand verbs, finding the Subjects, the Complements, and the Modifiers, and identifying clauses, will be relatively easy.

First, we will consider the finite verbs, the forms which function as Verbs in asserting action, condition, or state of being of the subject in a clause or a sentence. Then we will consider the infinite, unlimited forms, the troublesome verbals, which function as nouns, adjectives, or adverbs, that is, as Subjects, Complements, or Modifiers.

VERBS   Gr 6b

b. Kinds

There are three kinds of finite verbs: *transitive* verbs; *intransitive* verbs; and *linking*, or *copulative*, verbs.

1) TRANSITIVE

Transitive verbs name and assert the presence of an action and require an object which receives the action. The action of the verb is "carried across" to the object. We cannot, for example, say merely, "He installed." We must tell what or whom he installed, as in "He installed the furnace," or "He installed the new chairman in his office." When any verb has an object as a Complement, we call it a *transitive* verb.

2) INTRANSITIVE

Intransitive verbs are *not* transitive. They do not, that is to say, require an object as a Complement. They express ideas which are complete in themselves, so that we may have a sentence with no more to it than Subject and Verb alone: "Jesus wept." Intransitive verbs may be modified by adverbs, and they often are; but they do not take Complements. Some verbs, *rise* for example, are always intransitive. We do not say, "I rise the flag," or that anybody "rises" anything.

It should be noted that many verbs may be either transitive or intransitive, depending on the idea being expressed. Every sentence must be analyzed according to the way the words function in that sentence. We can, for example, say, "Jesus wept tears of compassion." In that sentence, *wept* is transitive precisely because it has an object, *tears*.

According to the use of the verb in the given sentence, a verb which requires an object as Complement is *transitive;* one which does not require an object is *intransitive*.

3) LINKING

Linking verbs (also called copulative verbs, "coupling" verbs, or copulas) might be considered a form of intransitive verbs. They express no action, and so cannot pass action on to a receiving object.

65

Gr 6b

But they do require a Complement. They are the verbs of condition or states of being, such as, principally, *be* in all its forms, and sometimes *appear, become, feel, look, seem, smell, sound, taste,* and some others, when these verbs express no idea of action. The Complement that linking verbs require is either a substantive which renames the subject (a predicate noun or predicate pronoun, word or word-group, that is, a subjective Complement), or an adjective which modifies the subject, a predicate adjective. (*To be,* especially, is occasionally completed by a predicate adverb.)

>It is I. (*It and* I *are the same person.*)
>George VI was King of England. (*George VI and King are the same person.*)
>She is charming. (*Charming modifies she.*)
>The roast smells good. (*Good modifies roast.*)
>I feel fine. (*Fine modifies I.*)
>John is here. (*Here completes the otherwise incomplete verb-idea and modifies* is.)

In the examples, these linking verbs express no action; they are, except in the last example, essentially equals-marks. (It = I. The roast = good.) If you remember that linking verbs are usually little more than equals-marks, you will not be distressed by the fact that the same verbs used in another way may express more active ideas. When we say, "The velvet feels soft," we are using *feels* as a linking verb. When we say, "My fingers feel the velvet," we have a transitive verb taking an object.

Linking verbs, then, take no objects because they express no action. They are rarely modified by adverbs, because adverbs customarily qualify or describe or limit actions. But linking verbs do require subjective Complements or predicate adjectives. The subjective Complement renames the subject; the predicate adjective modifies the subject.

Verbs, true verbs, whether transitive, intransitive, or linking, function in only one way, as Verbs. They assert that the subject is acting or is existing in a certain way. They are "finite." That is, they are limited to specific person and number. (If that term "finite verb" has puzzled you, remember that it means any verb functioning as a Verb.)

VERBS   **Gr 6b–c**

EXERCISE

Underline the finite verbs in the following sentences. Identify each as transitive, intransitive, or linking. Identify the objects of the transitive verbs and the subjective complements or predicate adjectives completing the copulas.

1. Old MacDonald had a farm and assorted livestock, and on top of that had to plow, plant, and harvest crops.

2. MacDonald must have expended a tremendous amount of energy.

3. Not everything is said in a song that could be said.

4. Every English sentence has a verb, whether the verb-idea is important or not.

5. We use the expletives (*it is*, or *there is* or *are*) when the verb-idea is of very minor importance, because the expletive pattern throws strong emphasis on the subject.

6. Avoid the expletive pattern, therefore, whenever a stronger verb would be useful.

7. A sudden burst of rain drenched the Saturday shoppers.

8. I have sat patiently for an hour, but I would like to know whether or not the doctor is really in the office.

9. Doctors know that time cures many illnesses, so they give patients time to be sure they are really sick.

10. One patient waited so long that he found an item for rent included in the doctor's bill.

c. Number

English recognizes two numbers: *singular,* when only one is involved; *plural,* when two or more are involved.

The chief trouble that occurs in the number of verbs arises from the fact that an *s* must be added to the stem of the verb to form the third person *singular,* present indicative.

I think	I run	I say
You think	You run	You say
He (or John) thinks	He (or John) runs	He (or John) says

Since in nouns an *s* indicates plural, some students have unnecessary trouble with verb agreement (see pages 22–24) because they fail to remember that an *s* ending in a verb is a singular ending. And since all nouns including noun phrases and clauses are third person, as well as the third person pronouns, that confusion can be serious.

d. Tense

Tense, with either verbs or verbals, means *time*, the time of the action or state asserted by the verb in relation to the time point of view of the speaker or writer.

1) THE SIX BASIC TENSES

It is usually said that English verbs have six tenses, formed by combining the "principal parts"—the infinitive, the past tense, and the participles: *begin, began, begun, beginning; wait, waited, waited, waiting*—according to systematic patterns. These key tenses are the *present*, now; *past*, a single time before now; *present perfect*, a recently completed action or sustained action begun in the past and carried up to the present; *past perfect*, sustained action begun and ended in the past: *future*, single action later than the present; and *future perfect*, sustained action later than the present. (*Perfect* means "completed," "perfected.")

On that simplified basis, our verb conjugations may be illustrated by following an irregular verb, first person singular, through its tense forms in the indicative mood.

PRESENT: I begin. (*Time, now.*)
PRESENT PERFECT: I have begun. (*Time, before but leading up to now.*)
PAST: I began. (*Time, before now.*)
PAST PERFECT: I had begun. (*Time, before some past time.*)
FUTURE: I shall (will) begin. (*Time, after now.*)
FUTURE PERFECT: I shall (will) have begun. (*Time, before some future time. The terminal future point is normally indicated by an adverbial modifier.*)

VERBS   Gr 6d

The same tense relation may be seen graphically.

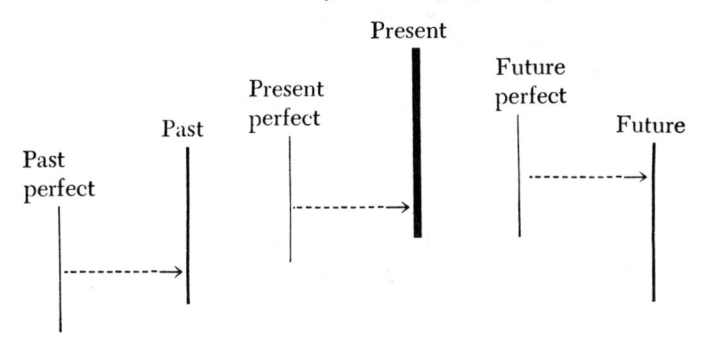

[Diagram showing tense relations on a timeline: Past perfect, Past, Present perfect, Present, Future perfect, Future]

2) OTHER TENSE FORMS

Actually, English verbs are far more flexible than that conventional classification suggests. We can and do express all sorts of time and mood relations beyond that simple six-tense system by varying our verb forms. This convenient flexibility arises from the way our verbs are constructed: We name the action we have in mind by the last member of the verb phrase and modify our tense and mood concept by combining "auxiliary" verbs or prepositional adverbs or adverbial phrases in varying patterns with that naming form.

In analyzing sentences, therefore, we must almost of necessity consider as a unit the whole verb-group. Unless you are trying specifically to identify the elements of such a verb phrase, call the entire unit a verb, without worrying about the number of words that may be involved. To appreciate the complex tense and mood concepts that English can express and to understand the use of verb phrases as units, consider the following:

> PRESENT: I *run*. (*But we seldom use this simple present to express present action. The two following are more common.*)
> I *am running*. (Called the "progressive present.")
> I *do run*. (Called the "emphatic present.")
> FUTURE (with modal overtones): I *shall run* in the 440 in next week's meet.
> I *am going to run* in the 440.
> I *run* in the 440 in every track meet.

69

Gr 6d–e

>   I *should run* in the 440, but I *would* rather *run* in the 220.
>   I *may run* in both the 440 and the 220.
>   I *plan to run* in the 440.
>   I *am to run* in the 440.
>   The coach wants me to change, but I *am going to go on running* in the 440.

And we use *can, could, did, have, had, might, must,* and *ought* as auxiliaries, too.

These complexities naturally are very confusing to foreign students of the language, but fortunately only a few forms cause the native speaker and writer any trouble.

e. Tense Problems

1) PAST FOR PAST PARTICIPLE

The educated dialect makes distinctions between the past tense and the past participle that some nonstandard dialects do not. Variations in the pattern grate on the educated ear. The trouble comes with the use of past tense forms with auxiliaries for other than simple past tenses, or the past participle as past tense. The problem occurs only with irregular, "strong" verbs, since regular verbs have identical past tense forms and combining forms.

>   I *went;* but I *have* or *had* or *am* or *was* or *shall be gone*
>   I *saw;* I *have,* etc., *seen*
>   I *did;* I *have,* etc., *done*

NEVER: *I have did,* or *I done; I have saw,* or *I seen.* Of the "principal parts" of a verb, the past tense form is used *only* for the past tense. Misuse of the past tense form with auxiliaries is the most obvious indication of uneducated speech or writing. Except in dialogue representing uneducated speakers, it has no place in college writing, and few instructors can bring themselves to pass a theme in which the slip occurs.

2) *Of* FOR *have*

A second glaring error is the use of *of* as if it were an auxiliary verb. In speaking, we often slur *have* in an unstressed position so that it sounds like *of.* But in writing we must use the verb. In dialogue, to reproduce the sound, use the contraction *'ve.*

WRONG: I would *of* come if I had known.
CORRECT: I would *have* come if I had known.
INFORMAL DIALOGUE: I would've come if I'd known.

3) Shall AND *will*

A great deal of time is wasted worrying about *shall* and *will* in future and future perfect tenses. British and American usages differ, and neither has ever consistently followed the patterns you may have struggled with—*shall* in the first person, *will* in the rest. Although it is scarcely worth much thought, some readers will worry about it, especially in formal writing. The same rules are said to apply to *should* and *would*. Actually, *should* and *would* often still carry their Old English meanings of obligation and willingness, respectively, with the result that the minute you begin to apply "rules" to them, you are liable to write something you do not mean at all. Use whichever form seems natural. It is probably also "correct."

I should go = *I ought to go*, and suggests *I do not really expect to go*.
I would go = *I am willing to go*, but often more than suggests *I am not going*.

With *should* and *would*, relax and be natural; it is safest.

4) OVERUSE OF *would*

Compound tenses with *would* now sometimes suggest, not willingness, but past habitual action, as in, "Each summer, we would spend two months at the seashore." But avoid a *would* phrase in sentences in which the simple past or the past perfect expresses your true point of view.

This would be easy if you *examined* (not *would examine*) your point of view as writer.

5) SPECIAL USES OF THE PRESENT

Three special uses of the present tense need to be mentioned: the present tense expressing *habitual* or *characteristic action*, the present tense expressing *universal truth*, and the *historical present* in narrative.

Gr 6e   GRAMMAR

HABITUAL ACTION

Habitual or characteristic action is often expressed by the present tense, regardless of the tenses of other verbs in the sentence.

He told the police that whenever he *comes* to town, I *call* on him.

UNIVERSAL TRUTH

Universal truth is expressed by the present tense.

He knew that five fives *are* twenty-five.
Galileo discovered that the earth *travels* around the sun.
In *David Copperfield,* Dickens *presents* a picture of his own boyhood.
Chaucer *says* that murder will out.

HISTORICAL PRESENT

The historical present uses the present tense in particularly exciting moments to make the reader feel that the action described is taking place before his eyes. Douglas Southall Freeman, for example, describing Pickett's Charge on the last day of the Battle of Gettysburg in *Lee's Lieutenants,* tells in the past tense of General Longstreet's reluctance to order the attack, of the beginning of the charge, and of the growing carnage. At the height of the advance, Freeman slips into the historical present:

> . . . On the left, where Mayo had no support, the ground was littered. Discouraged soldiers were turning back or were lying down among the dead.
> Garnett has halted to deliver his first volley. Kemper is doing the same thing. Faintly audible through the wrathful roar of a hundred Federal guns is the high quaver of the rebel yell. This time, where the smoke is swept away for a moment, the colors are higher on the hill but they are less numerous. . . .

Then as the tide rolls back, he returns to the past.

Because narrative recounts events that have already occurred, the past tense is the normal narrative tense. Unless the action is crucial, the use of the present tense in narrative suggests an uneducated speaker of the "So I says . . ., an' he says . . ." type. See Damon Runyan's short stories for a skillful use of the present tense to convey social comment about the speaker.

VERBS   Gr 6e–f

6) SEQUENCE OF TENSES

"Sequence of tenses" concerns the interrelations between the tenses of the verbs and the verbals in a sentence or a longer passage.

The tense of the verb in the first main clause governs the tenses of the other verbs and those of the verbals in a sentence. Assuming that your first main clause says exactly what you mean, it is taken as the starting point, and all other verb and verbal tenses are determined by the temporal relationships between them and the tense of the verb in the first main clause.

From one sentence to the next, keep the tenses of the verbs in the main clauses consistent. Do not illogically and unnecessarily shift from one tense to another. On the other hand, if the time relations among the things you are writing about change, you must change the tenses in main clauses accordingly.

Within a sentence, use the tenses in subordinate clauses that logically indicate the time relations to the action of the verb in the main clause. (See the tense chart, page 69.) Remember that there will often quite properly be differences between the tenses of the main clauses and those of subordinate clauses, or even between the tenses of two subordinate clauses.

> He *says* (present) that he *was* (past) there while she *was being questioned* (past passive progressive).

f. Mood

Mood (or mode) is a property of verbs which indicates the speaker's attitude toward the verbal idea, as fact or as contrary to fact, as command, as possibility, and so on. English uses the *indicative* mood of fact most of the time, but also uses the *imperative* mood for commands, expresses various modal overtones by verb phrases with *can* and *may*, *should* and *would*, and so on, and occasionally still uses the *subjunctive* mood of doubt. Only the *subjunctive* mood causes trouble, because it is rare and fading fast. We retain it in a few situations, chiefly involving the verb *to be*.

In conditions contrary to fact:

> If I *were* you . . . (which I am not).
> If it *were* true . . . (but it is not).

(Sometimes, as in the two examples following, the subjunctive seems archaic or very formal.)

> If this *be* treason . . . (but I do not think it is).
> *Were* I able . . . (but I am not able).

In parliamentary action:

> I move this *be* accepted.
> *Be* it enacted . . . .

In wishes, and after *demand, insist,* and so on:

> I wish I *were* going. I demand (or insist) that he *come*.

After *as if* or *as though:*

> He looks as if he *were* ill.
> I feel as though I *were* causing you too much trouble.

There are other moods—the potential, for example—that we express through regular forms of auxiliaries to indicate the possible, the permissible, or the obligatory. They cause us no trouble.

g. Voice

In the *active* voice, the subject does the acting or is in the condition asserted by the verb.

> He runs. He seems bored. I am giving the orders.
> We endorse these products.

In the *passive* voice, we follow a regular system in transforming the Complement of the transitive verb into the Subject, and use a verb phrase with some form of *to be* plus the past participle.

> These products are endorsed by us.
> The orders are being given by me.

The passive is used chiefly when the doer of the action is unknown or unimportant.

> A caricature of the teacher was scrawled on the blackboard.
> Cows are milked twice a day.
> The boy down the street was struck in the head by a baseball.

Use the active voice whenever possible. It is stronger and more emphatic than the passive voice, and consequently leads to more effective writing. Avoid the "weak passive."

VERBALS   Gr 6/Gr 7-7a

PREFER: We use and endorse these products.
AVOID: These products are used and endorsed by us.

EXERCISE

Correct all errors in number, mood, and tense sequence in the following sentences.

1. Had I a-knowed I could've rode, I would've went; but even if I had've went, I couldn't've et nothing.
2. Aldiborontiphoscophornio, how left you Chrononhotontologos?
3. When I go to the beach, I would sit at the edge of the tide and let the water purl around me.
4. I move that Senator Snort makes the nominating speech.
5. Mabel was kissed squarely on the end of her nose by Jim, by Jove.
6. Joan liked me ever since she was a child.
7. I should be grateful if you would fill my order promptly.
8. Whoever buys the tickets numbered in the even hundreds are to receive a door prize.
9. I did not know before I read it in the paper that until last week the President had been planning to go to England when Parliament next meets.
10. Casey was struck out.

7. VERBALS

Verbals are verb forms which do not function as Verbs—or, if you prefer, verbals come from verbs, look something like verbs, and have certain verb characteristics, but are not true finite verbs; instead, they are nouns, adjectives, or adverbs which name actions, but function as Subjects, Complements, or Modifiers. Because of their verbal ancestry, however, they may have Subjects or Complements of their own, as we shall see when we consider verbal phrases.

There are three kinds of verbals: *gerunds, participles,* and *infinitives.*

a. Gerunds

Gerunds function as Subjects or Complements. They (or the first member of a word-group verbal) always end in *-ing,* and they always function as substantives, that is, as Subjects or Complements.

75

>   S
> *Swimming* is good exercise.
>
>   C   C
> I prefer *sitting* to *standing*.
>
>   C
> He devotes his attention to *loafing*.
>
>   C
> One should be thankful for *having survived* the perils of adolescence.

The only trouble with gerunds comes in distinguishing them from present participles. Remember that gerunds are verbal *nouns*. (To associate the two, remember the *n* in *gerund* and the two *n*'s in *noun*.)

b. Participles

Participles function as Modifiers, and when they stand near substantives they readily attach themselves. Most of the time, in fact, they do modify substantives, but they sometimes modify whole clauses, adverbially. When they stand first in the sentence, however, they always seem to be modifying the Subject, and dangling participles may result. (See **Dng**.)

There are two basic participial forms, *present* and *past*. In more complex tenses, the basic participial tense form may be found in the first member of the verbal group.

1) PRESENT

Present participles always end in *-ing*. They look like gerunds, and are distinguished from gerunds only by the fact that they function as adjectives, whereas gerunds function as nouns. (To associate the terms, remember the *n*'s in *gerund* and *noun*, the *a*'s in *participle* and *adjective*.)

>   S
> GERUND: *Swimming* is good exercise.
>
>   M
> PARTICIPLE: The *swimming* horse seemed nearly exhausted.

VERBALS   Gr 7b–c

                       M
PARTICIPLE: *Having been swimming,* the boy had wet hair.

                                                M
PARTICIPLE (PREDICATE ADJECTIVE): The fish are *swimming.*

(If you wish to call the phrase *are swimming* the verb, many would agree.)

2) PAST

    Past participles end in various ways. Usually, they end in *-ed*, like simple past tenses, with which they are easily confused. (In "She burned the steak," *burned* is verb in the past tense. In "The burned steak had to be thrown away," *burned* is past participle, modifying *steak.*) Or they end in *-t*, as in "The burnt child shuns the fire"; or in *-en*, as in "A broken reed makes a poor staff." Or sometimes they are formed by an internal vowel change, as in, "Sprung rhythm is characteristic of Hopkins' poetry."

    Participles are verbal *adjectives.* (Again, remember the *a* in *participle,* and the *a* in *adjective.*)

c. Infinitives

    Infinitives function as Subjects, Complements, or Modifiers. They normally consist of *to* plus the "name form" of the verb, that is, the form you would look for if you were trying to find the verb in the dictionary (the name form is the first member in a phrase). The *to*, however, is not always present. We say,

    Allow me *to go.*

but

    Let me *go.*

In both sentences, *go* is an infinitive.

    Notice that the infinitive without *to* looks just like a present tense verb, and may be distinguished from the verb only by the fact that it functions, not as a Verb, but as a noun, an adjective, or an adverb, that is, as Subject, Complement, or Modifier.

                  S   C
NOUN: *To know* her is *to love* her.

Gr 7c–e

                      M

ADJECTIVE: The man *to elect* is the man who can best fill the office.

                      M

ADVERB: I went *to buy* a loaf of bread.

                      V

VERB: I *buy* bread frequently.

d. Split Infinitives

Aside from the problem of distinguishing infinitives from verbs, the chief trouble with infinitives occurs with "split infinitives." It would obviously be awkward to say.

I went *to* as cheaply as possible *buy* a loaf of bread.

Split infinitives are weak precisely because they are awkward, but it sometimes happens that it is still more awkward to avoid them. How else could one say, "We hope to more than double our enrollment"? Remember, however, that many readers have long been convinced that no infinitive should ever be split. Avoid the construction whenever you can.

Because of their derivation from verbs, verbals may show changes for tense and voice, they may have subjects or take objects or subjective complements, they may be modified by adverbs, and they always *name* actions, conditions, or states of being. But they do not function as Verbs, asserting that the action is going on. Instead, they function as nouns, adjectives, or adverbs, as Subjects, Complements, or Modifiers. They cannot be used without an accompanying finite verb.

e. Verbals in Fragments

It is failure to distinguish between verbs and verbals which leads to the writing of many *fragmentary sentences* containing one or more verbals, but without a true verb in a main clause to assert action or condition actually occurring. Do not allow mere length to fool you; a sentence must have a finite verb in a main clause.

FRAGMENT: John, being eager to work and always ready to do whatever he could find that needed doing.

Remember: Verbals look like verbs, but do not function as Verbs.

Gerund—ends in *-ing;* used as a noun.

VERBALS   Gr 7e–f/7

Participle—ends in *-ing*, or *-ed*, or *-t*, or *-en*, or shows an internal vowel change; used as an adjective.

Infinitive—"name form" of the verb, usually preceded by *to*; used as a noun, an adjective, or an adverb.

f. Tense Sequence with Verbals

The tense of a verbal is governed by its time relation to the main verb in its own sentence.

A *present participle* is used for action occurring at the same time as the action of the verb.

Sailing into the harbor, the captain sighed in relief.

A *perfect participle* indicates time prior to that of the verb.

Having weathered the storm, the sloop sailed into the harbor.

A *present infinitive* indicates the same time as the time of the verb, or a time later than that of the verb.

John wanted *to take* Mary to the dance.
I hope *to see* you next winter.

A *perfect infinitive* indicates time prior to that of the verb.

He was thought *to have been seen* near the accident.

EXERCISE

In the following sentences, underline the verbals. Identify each as a gerund, present or past participle, or infinitive. Identify each as noun, adjective, or adverb. Indicate the function (S or C) of the verbal nouns. Indicate the elements modified by the verbal adjectives and adverbs.

1. I am glad to be the one chosen to commend you for your fine work.

2. Students and professors alike seem to feel that there is somehow more virtue in having forgotten something than there is in never having learned it, though neither is eager to give the other much credit for virtue of that kind.

3. Both students and professors, being human beings, have a full share of human failings.

79

4. Building a building is more profitable than having one built.
5. Gerunds, being verb forms rather than true nouns, do not have plural endings.
6. Eating, quarreling, twittering, and roosting are among the starling's principal activities.
7. To dream, as Hamlet knew, is not always pleasant.
8. The nightmare is the dream to be feared by living dreamers.
9. In that sleep of death, what dreams may come to ramp across the soul-nerves of our souls.
10. I am sorry. I had not intended to think of that.

8. MODIFIERS

a. Adjectives

Adjectives function only as Modifiers of substantives, either immediately before the substantive or after a linking verb, as predicate Complementary Modifiers. They describe the substantive, or identify, designate, point out. They tell what the substantive is like, or which one it is.

They take many forms—*blue, successful, intense, happy, warm, tall*—and they show regular changes for comparison—*blue, bluer, bluest; successful, more successful, most successful.*

Single-word adjectives normally precede the substantive or follow a linking verb. The first is called an *attributive* adjective; the second a *predicate* adjective. Word-group adjectives (phrases and clauses) normally follow the substantive.

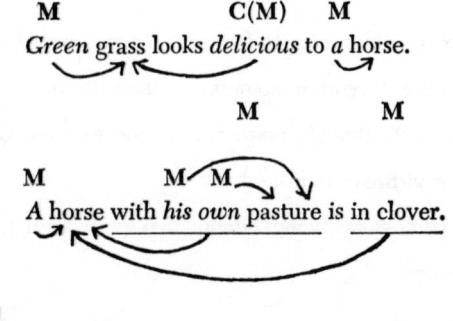

    M   C(M)   M
Green grass looks *delicious* to *a* horse.

                    M   M
M   M M
A horse with *his own* pasture is in clover.

MODIFIERS ───────────────────────────── Gr 8a–b

There was *a* man in *our* town who was wondrous wise.

Notice that the articles, *a, an,* and *the* designate which one and are adjectives.

If you can recognize substantives, that is, nouns and other naming words that function as Subject or Complement, and can recognize the limiting or describing function of Modifiers, adjectives should cause no trouble.

b. Adverbs

Adverbs indicate such diverse ideas as the time or duration of an action, the manner in which it is done, the degree of intensity of adjectives or adverbs, and many other things: *rapidly, slow, slowly, very, not very* (both are adverbs), *intensely, actively.*

Many adverbs are formed by adding the suffix *-ly* to adjectives: *rapidly, intensely, successfully,* though when *-ly* is added to nouns it produces adjectives, as in *manly.* (The *-ly* comes from *like: intense-like.*) They are usually inflected to show comparison: *rapidly—more rapidly—most rapidly.*

Adverbs function as Modifiers, and serve to qualify verbs, adjectives, other adverbs, and whole predications. Perhaps the easiest way to identify them is to recognize that they are Modifiers but are not modifying substantives.

Single-word adverbs normally precede adjectives or other adverbs. When they modify verbs, they often follow them or split word-group verbs. But many adverbs, especially the word-group adverbs, move around freely.

> Phrase ideas *carefully;* a *well-*chosen word; thinking *deeply; no,* I will *not* do it; *usually* truthful.

MODIFYING VERBS: He ran *awkwardly*

MODIFYING ADJECTIVES: It is *very* warm.

81

Gr 8a–b GRAMMAR

M   M   M

MODIFYING ADVERBS: It is *not* very warm.

TELL HOW: It rained *hard* (*Adverb of manner.*)

TELL WHERE: He is *here.* (*Adverb of place.*)

TELL WHEN: Registration begins *tomorrow.* (*Adverb of time.*)

TELL WHY: He dieted *to reduce.* (*Adverb of purpose.*)

TELL WHY: He won *because the judge is his brother.* (*Adverb of cause. Such adverbs are normally clauses.*)

TELL WITH WHAT RESULT: He won, *so he was given the prize.* (*Adverb of result. Normally clauses.*)

TELL UNDER WHAT CONDITIONS: We will come *if it doesn't rain.* (*Adverb of condition. Normally clauses.*)

TELL WITH WHAT CONCESSIONS: *Even though you forbid it,* I will do it. (*Adverb of concession. Normally clauses.*)

TELL TO WHAT DEGREE: He is *very* lazy. (*Adverb of degree.*)

COMPARE: I am not as tall *as you.* (*Adverb of comparison. Normally clauses.*)

REVERSE A VERB OR A MODIFIER: He is *not* lazy. (*Adverb of negation.*)

AFFIRM OR DENY: *Yes, no.* Yes, I did it. (*Adverb of affirmation or negation.*)

CONNECT EQUAL CLAUSES: I go; *however,* I shall return. (*Conjunctive adverb. Other common conjunctive adverbs are* consequently, nevertheless, moreover, therefore, accordingly, so, yet, then.)

INTRODUCE QUESTIONS: *Where* are you going? (*Interrogative adverb.*)

EXERCISE

Identify the adjectives and the adverbs in the following passage. Include all possessive nouns or pronouns. Indicate what each modifies.

The little old lady laid her old-fashioned string bag carefully on the counter and nervously plucked off her lace mittens. Tentatively, she peered into the dim recesses at the back of the cigar store, quickly counted the all-male sales force, and cleared her throat timidly. "I am," she announced to the burly, straw-hatted clerk who had brusquely asked if he could help her, "a professional babysitter. In my time I have watched many television shows, and I have carefully observed the sly, or audacious, or misguided, or successful techniques employed by many a slippery customer. I believe I am," she smirked proudly, "one of the nation's foremost experts on skullduggery, shrewdness, and sheer violence." The store clerk gaped uncomprehendingly. "I see," she continued hastily, "that you do not quite realize the inner purport of my comments." A glint of light along the nickeled barrel of a .32 momentarily distracted the clerk's attention. The little old lady purred, not very gently, "This is a stick-up, Bub."

c. Verb-Adverb Phrases

One very common use of adverbs is to form entirely new verb-ideas. This would cause no trouble if the adverbs concerned did not look so much like prepositions. These prepositional adverbs are essentially parts of the verb and might best be so regarded. *To put*, for example, means one thing; *to put up* means something else; *to put up with* means something else still. These verb-adverb phrases may take objects, but those objects are not the objects of prepositions, at all, and such phrases may not require objects. Yet many readers are deeply disturbed if what looks like a preposition comes at the end of the sentence, and if you end a sentence with a verb-adverb phrase, they will be distracted from what you are saying to worry about the way that you say it. Do not worry unduly if you must use the construction, but try to avoid using it at the end of the sentence. Few will ever notice it if it comes anywhere else.

These verb-adverb phrases are most common in informal and colloquial usage. *To put up with* means essentially the same thing as *to tolerate*. If the overall tone of your paper is formal, harmony of tone and exactness of diction both may suggest that you avoid a verb-adverb phrase and use a more formal verb instead.

d. Confusion of Adjectives and Adverbs

Be careful, too, not to confuse adverbs and adjectives. If you are in doubt as to whether a given word is properly adverbial, consult the grammatical classification given it in your dictionary. Sometimes the problem arises because of different usages in conversational English and most written English. Thus, many say, "It *sure* was hot," or "That was a *real* nice party"; but we are more likely to use *surely* and *really* when we write. Written English nearly always needs to be more precise than spoken English.

9. CONNECTIVES

a. Prepositions

Prepositions function only as Connectives. They connect substantives to some other part of the sentence and show the relationship involved. The resulting prepositional phrase functions as a Modifier, but we will postpone consideration of such phrases until we can consider the functioning of groups of words.

Prepositions are usually little words, and they indicate such abstract relations as direction, position, duration, and so on. They are most easily identified by the fact that they are invariably accompanied (usually followed) by substantive Complements, as in *in* town, *under* the rug, *during* the storm, *to* Tom, *between* the dark and the daylight, *at* the party, *concerning* your objection.

Prepositions normally stand first in the phrase, and consequently precede the substantive headword. But it has never been true in English that they may not follow the substantive on occasion, as in "Tell me what you are thinking *about.*" The latter usage, however, is rare in formal writing; and as with the verb-adverb construction, you might avoid it at the end of a sentence whenever you can gracefully do so.

Notice that the substantives which are objects of the prepositions may be and often are modified by adjectives, but that fact need not obscure the essential relation between the preposition and the object. Ask the question Whom? or What? after the preposition; the substantive that answers the question is the object, and the whole word-group is a modifying phrase.

b. Conjunctions

Conjunctions function only as Connectives. They connect words or groups of words (phrases or clauses), and they work chiefly to provide grammatical information about the relations of other words in the sentences. They are not, however, interchangeable in meaning. *And* is not *but; unless* is not *until.*

CONNECTIVES   Gr 9b

There are two kinds of conjunctions that we need to consider: *coordinating* and *correlative conjunctions,* connecting only grammatically equal elements; and *subordinating conjunctions,* which usually introduce adverb clauses and indicate their relation to the main clause.

1) COORDINATING AND CORRELATIVE CONJUNCTIONS

For all practical purposes, we can say that there are five coordinating conjunctions: *and, but, or, nor, for.* A few other connectives are sometimes loosely used as coordinating conjunctions, such as *while* when it means *and* or *but,* as in "I am going to town, while you may do as you please," but they cause little trouble. Remember that *and, or* and *nor* always connect equal elements. *But* always does unless it is a preposition meaning *except,* as in "Anyone but John would know that," or an adverb meaning *only,* as in "But little good can come of such action." *For,* the conjunction, is not quite a coordinating conjunction, but it is punctuated as if it were (see page 107), so that we may treat it as a coordinating conjunction in considering the one aspect in which it might give trouble. Use *and, but, or, nor,* and *for* to connect only grammatically equivalent elements, and remember that they are the coordinating conjunctions. They stand between the elements they connect.

Coordinating conjunctions connect equal words.

> John *and* Mary danced *and* sang.
> John, *but* not Mary, sang.
> John *or* Mary will call you.

They connect equal phrases.

> He went around the house *and* down the cellar stairs.
> He went into the house, *but* not up the stairs.

They connect equal clauses.

> If it rains *and* if we can't get the car, we won't go.
> This little pig went to market, *but* this little pig stayed home.
> You may go, *or* you may stay here.

A subtype works in pairs, called *correlative* conjunctions, with compound subjects, complements, or modifiers: *either . . . or . . . , neither . . . nor . . . , not only . . . but (also) . . . .* Each member of the pair stands before one member of the compounded element. (See also //Cst.)

> You will *either* do the work of the course, *or* fail.
> It is *not only* dark, *but also* late.

2) SUBORDINATING CONJUNCTIONS

Subordinating conjunctions connect subordinate clauses to main clauses and show the relation between them.

Most subordinating conjunctions introduce adverbial clauses and connect them to the main clause. The most common are *if, because, unless, until, though, although, even though, when, while, where,* and so on.

> *If* it rains, I won't go. I won't go *even though* you ask me. Come *when* you please.

When *that* introduces a noun or adjective clause having some other subject, *that* may be a subordinating conjunction, or it may be a relative pronoun and object of the verb.

> I know *that* he will do it. (*Subordinating conjunction.*)
> There is a view *that* you will never forget. (*Object and therefore a relative.*)

c. Conjunctive Adverbs

Finally, a number of transitional words are at least partly adverbial, though they connect first and modify second. They are the *conjunctive adverbs: however, moreover, nevertheless,* and so on. Unlike the other connectives, they may stand at many points in any given sentence.

10. INTERJECTIONS

Interjections function only as Absolutes, that is, they do not function in a sentence at all; they are merely there. They are always thrown into a sentence parenthetically. The emotion they express may be violent, or may be very mild indeed.

> *Oh,* that I were a glove upon that hand.
> She said, *alas,* that she could never love me.
> *Well,* perhaps it is better so.
> *Why,* how can you say such a thing?

FORMAL GROUPS

11. PHRASES

A phrase is a group of words without an essential subject and verb, functioning as a unit.

As we are well aware, there are many kinds of phrases, but we need to consider only three or four kinds. From the point of view of form, we will examine *verb phrases, prepositional phrases,* and *verbal phrases.* From the point of view of function, the same phrases may be called *verb phrases, noun phrases, adjective phrases,* and *adverbial phrases.*

a. Verb Phrases

Verb phrases are very common, because Modern English normally indicates changes in tense, mood, and voice by combining verbs and verbals (by combining a basic form naming the action with various auxiliary, or "helping" verbs). And Modern English creates many new verb-ideas by combining verbs with prepositional adverbs. In most sentences, consequently, the verbs consist of more than one word; they are word-groups built of verbs and adverbs, or of verbs and participles and infinitives. Consider, for example, such verb phrases as *had been going, had gone, have gone, was going, am going, do go, shall go, can go, am going to go, shall have been going, should have been going, am willing to go, am going to go on going, would have gone*—and so on, almost *ad infinitum.*

Treat these verb-groups as single verbs. If you wish to break down such a phrase as *should have been going* into verb, infinitive, past participle, and present participle, you may do so, of course, but since that particular verb-idea can be expressed in no other way, the exercise will have little effect on your understanding of the sentence. Call such phrases *verbs* and be done with them.

b. Prepositional Phrases

Every preposition has an object; as a result, every preposition introduces a prepositional phrase. Prepositional phrases consist of the preposition, plus its object, plus any modifiers of that

Gr 11b–c   GRAMMAR

object. The object itself may be a phrase or even a clause, and the modifiers may be phrases or clauses. No matter. The word or the group of words that answers the question Whom? or What? after the preposition comprises, with the preposition itself, a prepositional phrase.

> He went *down town.*
> He went *into the city.*
> He walked *from school to the center of town.*
> She went *to the dance which promised to have the longest stag line.*
> Give it *to whoever comes to that door which opens directly on the street.*

Prepositional phrases function as Modifiers—as adjectives or as adverbs.

ADJECTIVE: They bought the house *on the hill.* (*Tells which house.*)

ADVERB: He went *down town.* (*Tells where; adverb of place.*)

ADVERB: *In 1800,* the federal government moved *to Washington.* (In 1800 *tells when; adverb of time.* To Washington *tells where; adverb of place.*)

c. Verbal Phrases

Since there are three kinds of verbals—gerunds, participles, and infinitives—there are three kinds of verbal phrases: *gerund phrases, participial phrases,* and *infinitive phrases.* Each kind of verbal phrase functions in exactly the same way as the verbal headword. Gerund phrases function as nouns; participial phrases function as adjectives; infinitive phrases function as nouns, as adjectives, or as adverbs.

The verbal phrase, of whatever kind, consists of a verbal plus a subject or an object, plus (perhaps) modifiers. The modifiers or subjects or objects may be single words or phrases or clauses, but the resulting word-group functions as a unit. The key headword of the phrase is the verbal, and the phrase functions in whatever way that headword functions.

PHRASES ───────────────────────────── **Gr 11c**

1) GERUND PHRASES

Gerunds are verbal nouns ending in *-ing*. Gerund phrases, then, function as nouns, that is, as Subjects or Complements.

    S
Doing swan dives is fun.

    S
Hitting the ball over the fence is unfair to the fielders.

      C
I enjoy *eating too much dinner*.

      C
My chief pleasure is *eating good food*.

          C
Professor Snodgrass persists in *grading papers for English as well as for history*.

2) PARTICIPIAL PHRASES

Participles are adjectives, and participial phrases function as adjectives, that is, as Modifiers of substantives. (From a slightly different point of view, participial phrases sometimes seem to modify the whole predication and consequently to be adverbial. See, for example, the second sentence below—and also see **Dng**.)

       M
Douglas, *swimming the turbulent stream,* was nearly exhausted.

    M
Swimming the turbulent stream, Douglas was nearly exhausted.

           M
The ball went over the fence *surrounding the ballpark.*

3) ABSOLUTE PHRASES

One special form of participial phrase, consisting of a noun plus a participle, modifies the following main clause and so functions as a rather loose adverb—so loose that it is called an *absolute phrase.*

 The rain having stopped, the game was continued.
 The game being over, we left the stadium.

Gr 11c
GRAMMAR

The construction is well established in English, but many readers find it stilted. Consequently, it should be used chiefly in formal writing, and then sparingly.

4) INFINITIVE PHRASES

Infinitives may be nouns, adjectives, or adverbs, and so infinitive phrases function as nouns (S or C), adjectives (M), or adverbs (M).

          S   C

To keep one's nose to the grindstone is to limit one's view of life.

     C

I want *him to come to the party.* (Him *is subject of the infinitive. The whole phrase is object of the verb.*)

     M

The best place *to catch the biggest fish* is under the noses of scoffing witnesses. (*Adjective: modifies* place.)

     M

He came *to see what he could see.* (*Adverb of purpose: tells why he came.*)

Infinitives, in fact, do many things, not all of them as easy to classify as these. Like adverbs, they cover a great deal of ground for us.

EXERCISE

In the following sentences, underline all phrases. Identify each as verb phrase, prepositional phrase, gerund phrase, participial phrase, or infinitive phrase. Indicate the function of each as noun, verb, adjective, or adverb. Indicate the function of each as Subject, Verb, Complement, or Modifier.

    1. To Washingtonians, as to all Americans, the majesty of the government of the United States is awe-inspiring despite occasional grumbling.

    2. But that awe is somewhat dented by the realization that the

FBI, or the Department of State, or the Treasury is a man across the street or the fellow next door.
3. To be a lieutenant colonel or a commander in the Navy is great in the outposts of the service, but in the Pentagon it is merely to be one more worker in the swarm.
4. In directing traffic consisting of swarms of lieutenant colonels, a policeman who served in the army as a private sometimes succeeds in getting his revenge.
5. In the opinion of some Washingtonians, it is not at all difficult to explain the frustrations of rush-hour traffic.
6. Substantives answering the question Whom? or What? after participles are objects of the participles in participial phrases.
7. Having identified a participle, you need only to determine whether or not it has an object to decide whether or not it is part of a participial phrase.
8. Identifying participles and distinguishing them from gerunds depends on recognizing the functions of the verbals.
9. Include all word or word-group modifiers of the headword to identify a complete phrase, not forgetting modifiers of modifiers.
10. After having identified the complete phrase, it is often useful to work backward from the end of it to determine the separate elements of which it is composed.

12. CLAUSES

A clause is a group of words containing both a subject and a verb and functioning as a unit. In one sense, any subject-verb combination is a clause, but as a rule we use the term *sentence* (simple sentence) if a predication has only one such combination.

There are two kinds of clauses: *independent clauses* (also called *main clauses*, or *principal clauses*) and *dependent clauses* (also called *subordinate clauses*).

a. Independent Clauses (Main Clauses, Principal Clauses)

Independent clauses are little trouble to anyone who can recognize complete sentences. They contain a subject and a verb and are not introduced by any subordinating word. They express a grammatically complete thought and could stand alone as complete sentences. All that distinguishes an independent clause from a sentence, indeed, is the fact that the writer did not choose to let it stand alone.

Three sources of difficulty arise. First, a given utterance may express a complete thought in context and still scarcely be called a clause: "I am going to do it." "Why?" (*Why*, with neither subject nor verb, is not a clause.) Second, an independent clause may well contain noun clauses as Subjects or Complements, or adjective or adverb clauses as Modifiers, as in, "Whoever demands guidance may follow a guide who knows as little as he does himself; and both may go astray." There are four subject-verb combinations in the first main clause; yet there is only one independent predication: "A may follow B." The other three clauses within the main clause are subordinate. Third, grammatical completeness may not be logical completeness. In "He was here" we have a grammatically complete statement, even though clarity of meaning depends on knowing who *he* is. The test is always, Could this group of words stand alone, in this context?

b. Dependent Clauses (Subordinate Clauses)

Dependent clauses contain subjects and verbs and are introduced by a subordinating word (which is not always explicitly expressed). They function as nouns (S or C), as adjectives (M), or as adverbs (M). We shall consider each kind in turn.

1) NOUN CLAUSES

Noun clauses are substantives and function as Subjects or as Complements. They are usually introduced by relative pronouns (*who, which, that, whoever, whichever, whatever,* and so on).

        S
Whoever calls the station first will get the prize.

CLAUSES   **Gr 12b**

      C
 I will take *whichever you reject.*

      C
 Give it to *whatever charity you select.*

When *that* is used to introduce a clause having some other subject, *that* may be a subordinating conjunction.

 He always knew *that* something would turn up.

After a few verbs, notably *tell* and *know,* noun clauses functioning as objects may be introduced by *when, where, why,* and so on. These noun clauses look like adverbs, but they answer the question What? after the verb, not When? or Where? or Why? They are objects, not Modifiers.

      C
 Tell Mother *where you have been.*

      C
 I know *when he came in last night.*

Compare

      C
 I know *whom you mean.*

      M
 I heard him *when he came in last night.*

To determine whether a subordinate clause is a noun clause, there are several tests you can apply. First and best, does it function as a noun, as Subject or Complement? If so, it is a noun clause. Second, if you find it hard otherwise to identify Subjects and Complements, does the clause answer the questions Who? or What? before the verb, or the questions Whom? or What? after a verb or preposition? If it does either, it is a noun clause, Subject or Complement. Third, can it be moved to any other position in the sentence? Subjects normally come before the verb, and objects normally follow the verb. If the clause cannot be moved easily, without rephrasing the sentence altogether, it will be either a noun clause or an adjective clause; the other tests will settle the question.

Gr 12b

GRAMMAR

EXERCISE

Underline the noun clauses in the following sentences. Identify the subject, the verb, and the introductory word of each noun clause. Identify the function (as S or C) of each noun clause.

1. "Who steals my purse steals trash."
2. Do you suppose Iago really carried trash in his purse?
3. Perhaps that apparent admission demonstrates that Iago was deceitful in all things, small as well as large.
4. Eight o'clock in the morning is an hour when no man should be abroad, let alone in class.
5. Registration clerks seem to believe that every student should have at least one eight o'clock class every term.
6. The administration argues that classrooms must be used at all suitable hours.
7. To say that eight o'clock in the morning is "suitable" is ridiculous.
8. It would be just as sensible to say that eleven o'clock at night is suitable, or that three in the morning is.
9. Don't say anything like that where anyone can hear you. The administrators might forget when they had decided to begin the school day and schedule a class for three in the morning.
10. If any such proposal is made, address your protests to the chaplain or to whoever else may have influence with the powers that be.

2) ADJECTIVE CLAUSES

Adjective clauses do nothing but modify substantives. They are usually introduced by relative pronouns. They usually follow the substantive they modify.

He is the man *who spoke so persuasively.*

He is the man *that you told me to meet.*

Occasionally, the pronoun is omitted, especially in informal writing. But it can be readily supplied.

He bought the house (*that* or *which*) *he had long wanted.*

Rarely, some introductory element other than a relative pronoun will be used with adjective clauses. The clauses still modify substantives.

>There comes a time *when all must work.*
>This is a period *in which cooperation is essential.*

Unlike single adjectives, which usually precede the nouns they modify, adjective clauses follow their nouns, coming immediately after the noun unless another modifier intervenes.

>He is a man *who should go far.*
>There was a man in our class *who knew all the answers.*

If you have a sentence containing a substantive immediately followed by *who, whom, which,* or *that,* plus a verb, you can be sure you are dealing with an adjective clause.

As a further test, notice that adjective clauses, like noun clauses, cannot be moved around in the sentence. They must follow the substantive they modify, and the position of that substantive is determined by its function.

EXERCISE

Underline the adjective clauses in the following sentences. Identify the subject, the verb, and the introductory word of each clause. Identify the substantive each adjective clause modifies. Identify the independent clauses in each sentence.

1. Adjective clauses are subject-verb combinations which modify substantives.
2. Substantives are nouns or other words or word-groups which function the way nouns function.
3. The words which introduce adjective clauses (relative pronouns or subordinating conjunctions) stand at the beginning of the clause.
4. A student who cannot recognize adjective clauses needs to

Gr 12b

GRAMMAR

learn to recognize subjects and verbs, relative pronouns, and subordinating conjunctions.

5. The most common relative pronouns in adjective clauses are *who, which, that, whichever, whoever,* and *whomever.*
6. Whenever a sentence contains a noun which is followed by a relative pronoun and a verb, you can be sure that it contains an adjective clause.
7. In an adjective clause which is introduced by a subordinating conjunction (most often *that* or such combinations as *in which*), a substantive following the conjunction functions as the subject.
8. Do not overlook such adjective clauses, in which the subordinating conjunction looks like a relative but is not the subject.
9. Any sentence containing a noun that is followed by either a relative pronoun and a verb or a subordinating conjunction, a substantive, and a verb probably contains an adjective clause.
10. As you are no doubt aware, the sentences in this exercise indicate some of the means by which you can identify adjective clauses.

3) ADVERB CLAUSES

Adverbial clauses, like adverbs, are Modifiers. They tell How? Why? When? Where? Under what conditions? With what result? and so on, about another clause, or they complete a comparison of an adjective or adverb.

They are introduced by subordinating conjunctions, among the most common of which are *if, because, unless, until, though, although, as, than, where, wherever,* and so on.

If it is too hot, the picnic will be canceled.
Unless you tell me, I'll never know.
If you study *whether or not you are in the mood,* you should be ready for surprise quizzes. (*Whether or not you are in the mood* modifies *if you study.* Together they modify the main clause.)

CLAUSES Gr 12b

I was doing fairly well *until she began to help.*
Whenever you are ready, we can begin.
He is stronger *than I am.*
Hercules worked harder *than most people do.*

Adverbial clauses are often placed at the beginning of the sentence, because the end is a more emphatic spot and should not be wasted on a mere Modifier. But notice that the adverbial clause, alone among subordinate clauses, often *may be moved around in the sentence.* It may come first, before the main clause, or it may follow the main clause. We can say either

Because you are here, I am happy.

or

I am happy *because you are here.*

You may, consequently, recognize adverbial clauses by their function as Modifiers of a clause or of an adjective or adverb; by the presence of an introductory subordinating conjunction like *if, as, because, until,* and so on; or by the fact that they may usually be moved around in the sentence without necessitating major rephrasing of the sentence-idea.

EXERCISES

A. Underline the adverbial clauses. In each adverbial clause, identify the subject, the verb, and the introductory word. Identify the element each adverbial clause modifies. Identify the independent clause in each sentence.

1. Students should be especially careful early in a term to keep up their work, because the end of any term is always busier than anyone expects it to be.

2. Have you seen Mabel since she was operated on for appendicitis late last term?

3. Because Mabel was in the hospital at the end of the term, she had to take an Incomplete in all her courses.

97

Gr 12b _____ GRAMMAR

    4. Not all students who fall behind in their course work are as lucky as Mabel was last term.

    5. Roger, when he failed Chemistry 2, took Chemistry 1 over again as an auditor.

    6. Professor Fetterwate announced that he was resigning as head of the Physics Department because of his health.

    7. Wherever there is a college, there is at least one popular coffee and coke joint.

    8. Whatever *do* you suppose became of Judge Crater?

    9. If you can recognize subordinating conjunctions, you can tell adverbial clauses from noun clauses; if you can identify the word or word-group that a clause is modifying, you can tell adverbial clauses from adjective clauses—always assuming that you can recognize a clause.

    10. Unless you can find subjects and verbs readily, understanding clauses will be very difficult.

  B. Identify the phrases and subordinate clauses in the following sentences. Explain the form and the function of each.

    1. Many students who are quite willing to learn the special terminology of a science course rebel at learning grammatical and rhetorical terms.

    2. "So long as I can correct a sentence," they complain, "there is no sense to my learning to label mistakes, to memorizing what different kinds of mistakes are called in the textbook."

    3. One answer to that is that knowing the labels leads to understanding the mistakes, because the labels serve to classify common errors and thereby group many errors under a single, manageable category.

4. Another reason is that every sentence is unique, so that only the ability to classify and label mistakes will allow the student to consult a handbook for guidance when he knows that a sentence is faulty but does not know how to correct it.
5. If he can look at a sentence and say, "There is a dangling participial phrase," he can consult any handbook and discover what to do to correct it.
6. If he can recognize nonrestrictive adjectives or adverbs, he can quickly learn how to punctuate the sentence in which they appear.
7. Without a knowledge of terminology, however, he and his teacher are nearly helpless in the task of trying to correct habitual errors.
8. All the teacher can say is, "That sentence is wrong, and so is that one, and so is that one."
9. If, in addition to this traditional terminology, he knows something of the terms and the methods of the structural linguist or the transformational grammarian, he can greatly increase his understanding of English and can further refine his control of the writer's medium.
10. But one who understands the terms we have been using, as we have used them, can work readily with almost any grammatical reference book he may later consult.

3—

Punctuation

P   Punctuation

The importance of punctuation, 104
Two fundamental principles, 105
    1. Not separating related elements, 106
    2. Separating unrelated elements, 106
*The Comma: The four troublesome sentence patterns, 107
  * 1. Two independent clauses, 107
      a. With coordinating conjunctions, 107
         1) Semicolon with internal commas, 108
         2) The dash rarely used, 108
      b. Without coordinating conjunctions, 108
      c. Comma splices (See also Cs, P5e.), 109
         1) Conjunctive adverbs, 109
         2) *So*, 109
         3) Test to prevent comma splicing, 110
      d. Run-on sentences, 110
      e. Possible subordination of one clause, 111
  * 2. Introductory elements, 112
      a. Adverbial clauses and verbal phrases, 112
      b. Prepositional phrases, 113
  * 3. Parenthetical elements, 114

* There are exercises for items marked with an asterisk.

a. Absolutes, 115
   1) Interjections, 115
   2) Transitional words and phrases, 115
   3) Nouns of address, 115
   4) Nominative absolutes, 115
   5) Adverbs of affirmation or negation, 115
b. Nonrestrictive modifiers and appositives, 115
   1) Nonrestrictive modifiers and appositives: illustration, and graphic depiction of restrictive and nonrestrictive adjective modifiers, 116
   2) Nonrestrictive adverbial modifiers: definition, illustration, graphic depiction of restrictive and nonrestrictive adverbial modifiers, and test for adverbial modifiers, 118
   3) Nonrestrictive appositives, 119
c. Elements out of order, 120
d. Tests, 120
   1) Remove parenthetical elements from the sentence, 120
   2) Read the sentence aloud, 120
e. Reminder: Set off parenthetical elements at both ends (See also P6a, b.), 121
f. Rule, 121
g. Modifications, 122
   1) Slight parenthesis, 122
   2) Elements to be minimized, 122
   3) Elements to be emphasized, 122
   4) With internal commas, 122
* 4. Coordinate elements in series, 123
   a. A, B, and C series, 123
   b. Adjectives in series, 124
      1) Tests for coordinate adjectives, 125
      2) Note: No comma before the noun, 125
   Graphic summary of the four troublesome sentence patterns, 126
* 5. Miscellaneous uses of the comma, 129
   *a. Prevent misreading, 129
   b. Contrasted elements, 129

P   PUNCTUATION

      c. Dates, 129
      d. Addresses and geographical items, 130
      e. Quotations (including comma splices and fragments in dialogue) (See also P1c, P7a.), 130

* 6. Overuse of the comma, 132
      a. Separating subject and verb (See also P3e.), 132
      b. Separating verb and complement (See also P3e.), 132
      c. Separating restrictive modifier and modified word, 133
      d. Separating words and phrases connected by *and* or *or,* 133
      e. Separating coordinating conjunctions from elements they introduce, 134

Other marks of punctuation, 135

* 7. Period, 135
      a. Marking the end of a sentence, 135
      b. With abbreviations, 136

* 8. Question mark, 136
      a. Direct questions, 136
      b. Indicating doubt, 137
      c. Not used to label irony, 137

* 9. Exclamation point, 137
      a. Marking the end of a sentence, 137
      b. Not to be overused, 137
      c. Not to be doubled up, 137

10 Semicolon, 138
     *a. Compound sentences without coordinating conjunctions, 138
      b. Compound sentences with coordinating conjunctions and internal commas, 139
      c. Between members of an A, B, and C series with internal commas, 139

11. Colon, 139
      a. In compound sentences, 140
      b. Between a generalizing statement and a particularizing series, 140
      c. Between a formal orientation phrase and a formal quotation, 140
      d. In formal correspondence, 140
      e. Between titles and subtitles, 140
      f. In Biblical references, 140

PUNCTUATION ─────────────────────────────── **P**

    g. In numerical references to time, 140
*12. Dash, 141
    a. With a sentence broken off, 141
    b. With an emphatic appositive, 141
    c. With digressions, 141
    d. With an emphatic parenthetical element, 142
    e. Indicating decided and emphatic hesitation, 142
    f. Between a series and a summarizing passage, 142
    g. Setting off parenthetical elements with internal commas, 142
    h. In place of colons in informal writing, 142
    i. The dash splice in compound sentences, 142
13. Parentheses, 143
    a. To minimize a parenthetical element, 143
    b. With other punctuation, 143
    c. Misuse with material to be deleted, 143
    d. Parentheses always in pairs, 144
14. Brackets, 144
    a. To enclose material inserted in a quotation, 144
    b. With other punctuation, 144
*15. Quotation marks, 144
    a. Double quotation marks except with internal quotation, 144
    b. With direct quotations, 144
    c. With a quotation of more than one consecutive sentence, 145
    d. With a quotation of more than one paragraph, 145
    e. With nicknames, 145
    f. With words as labels or in an unusual sense, 145
    g. With words as words (now rare), 145
    h. With titles, 146
    i. With other marks of punctuation, 146
        1) With periods and commas, 146
        2) With colons and semicolons, 147
        3) With question marks and exclamation points, 147
16. Apostrophe, 148
    a. To indicate the possessive case, 148
        1) *Note:* When to use the apostrophe alone, when to use apostrophe and *s*, 148
        2) In compounds, 149

      b. In contractions, 149
      c. To indicate the plural of symbols, 149
  17. Suspension points (ellipsis marks), 149
      a. In quotations, 149
      b. In dialogue, 150

THE IMPORTANCE OF PUNCTUATION

The living language is the spoken language, which the written language reflects. When we speak, we have much besides words to help us communicate our ideas. We have facial expressions—our own and our listeners'. We have gestures, ranging from the lifting of an eyebrow or the tilting of the head through a shrug of the shoulders and a flick of the fingers to violent pounding on a desk or the stamping of a foot. The one word *yes* can be said in a way that will mean vigorous affirmation, coy and hesitating consent, dubious willingness to suspend disbelief, or scornful rejection. A *lighthouse keeper* and a *light housekeeper* are quite different. *John will do it* is a comforting statement; *John will do it?* may be hopeful or despairing. In addition to facial expressions and gestures, which are themselves systematic, we can give many shades of meaning to a spoken phrase by systematic variations of the tone or the emphasis of our voices or by pauses of varying length—and usually by combinations of all three. These oral devices for conveying grammatical information, and consequently meaning, are known as *pitch, stress,* and *juncture*. We have found these concepts useful in considering basic grammar. They are at least as useful in learning conventional punctuation. We need not worry about the details of the four meaningful degrees of stress, of pitch, and of juncture, since they are difficult to distinguish. But we do need to know that they exist and are important to us.

    When we write, we are trying, somewhat clumsily, to put into black marks on white paper all the kaleidoscopic richness of the human voice and oral delivery. The experienced and skillful writer varies his sentence patterns to achieve shifting emphasis. He chooses words that reflect his meaning, words that will produce soft sounds, strong sounds, melodious sounds, or jarring cacophony—and he still has black squiggles on white paper. But even the least experienced writer has at his command the major device which helps convey the tone, pace, vehemence, interrogation, and pauses of oral

PUNCTUATION

delivery. For these effects, all writers must depend heavily on twelve marks of punctuation. One little mark alone, in shifting combinations, manages to do very nearly 85 percent of the work. Next to words, the comma says most to your readers—if you use it skillfully. But if you use commas in a way your readers do not expect, commas can do almost as much as misused words to make your writing confusing. The other eleven marks of punctuation, too, give your readers clearly defined signals as to how you would have spoken the lines if you had been speaking instead of writing. If you use any of the marks of punctuation in a way your readers do not expect, you are depriving yourself of the standard device which helps the writer represent the flexibility of the human voice.

In other words, it is extremely important to you to learn the commonly accepted conventions of punctuation.

Fortunately, English sentences fall into one or another of certain limited sentence patterns. The skilled and practiced writer can vary the basic combinations widely. But even the beginning writer can learn to give his reader the most important elementary clues to his meaning. As a matter of comforting fact, an understanding of the conventional punctuation of four troublesome sentence patterns will solve many of your punctuation problems. Those four sentence patterns comprise the following:

1. The sentence with two independent clauses
2. The sentence with an introductory modifier
3. The sentence interrupted by parenthetical elements
4. The sentence containing elements in series

In the discussion that follows, we shall be concerned first with those four troublesome sentence patterns. Their punctuation is largely a matter of comma usage, though one or two other marks are also involved. Then we shall examine the miscellaneous uses of the comma and the overuse of the comma. Finally, we shall consider the other marks of punctuation, which cause relatively little trouble.

TWO FUNDAMENTAL PRINCIPLES

Modern English punctuation chiefly indicates the pitch and juncture patterns of spoken English, and they in turn usually indicate the grammatical structure of the sentence. Once in a while the structures and the pitch-juncture signals are at odds (as they are when we say "Yessir" but write "Yes, sir"), so that we need to be aware of them both. Whenever our standard punctuation practices seem illogical, we can only accept them as established conventions which give our readers the signals they are used to.

Two common practices reflect the relationship between punctuation and structural patterns:

1. **WE DO *NOT* NORMALLY USE PUNCTUATION TO SEPARATE SENTENCE ELEMENTS THAT BELONG TOGETHER STRUCTURALLY**

Subjects and verbs and complements, for example, belong together structurally. Essential modifiers standing in normal positions belong structurally to the elements they modify. Even though slight pauses may occur between such elements, they are normally not separated.

2. **WE *DO* NORMALLY USE PUNCTUATION TO SEPARATE ELEMENTS THAT DO NOT BELONG TOGETHER STRUCTURALLY**

Most introductory elements, like introductory adverbs, belong logically and structurally to the predicate or to the whole main clause, but they stand before the subject, and we separate the two. Nearly all elements out of their normal positions are set off. Nonessential (nonrestrictive) modifiers are set off. Absolutes are set off. And so on. Accompanying changes in the pitch of voice, and decided pauses, usually mark the spots at which punctuation belongs.

These two principles underlie not only the conventional punctuation of the four troublesome sentence patterns, but many of the other "rules" of punctuation as well.

Those "rules" are at best codifications of what most reputable writers do in certain conventional situations to suggest how they would speak their sentences if they could talk to you. To begin with, learn these basic punctuation conventions and follow them. Your reader expects you to give him conventional clues. Do not worry if you observe variations in the punctuation of experienced writers. After you have become thoroughly familiar with the conventions and know what your reader expects and what your punc-

TWO INDEPENDENT CLAUSES **P 1a**

tuation says to him, you too may make skillful variations from the standard forms to suggest subtle nuances of meaning. But while you are learning, follow the rules.

THE COMMA: THE FOUR TROUBLESOME SENTENCE PATTERNS

1. SENTENCES WITH TWO INDEPENDENT CLAUSES

a. With coordinating conjunctions: Two independent clauses which are connected by *and, but, or, nor,* or *for* are usually separated by a comma.

> Every writer should revise his work carefully, for even Homer nods.
> He entered the grounds by the garden gate, and the full glory of the garden in spring burst upon him.
> He proposed to Jane, and Mary has not spoken to him since.

Read those sentences aloud and listen to what you do with your voice at the comma. At *carefully, gate,* and *Jane* your voice rises, then drops to a level tone or a little below, and there is a perceptible pause before you go on to the conjunctions that follow. You have warned the listener that more is to follow in the sentence, but that the first major part is finished. The reader interprets the comma at that point as the same kind of signal.

The failure to use a comma in such a sentence often misleads your reader. The function of coordinating conjunctions is to connect grammatically equal words, phrases, or clauses. If you do not use the comma between clauses, your reader may be momentarily confused, since he may assume that the conjunction is connecting two nouns in a compound object and may have to back up and reread the sentence when he finds himself deep in a new, unannounced predication. See, for instance, the last example above. It could be very confusing without the comma.

The inclusion of the conjunction *for* perhaps should be explained. It is not, strictly, a coordinating conjunction. But to avoid confusion with the preposition *for,* conventional writers customarily set off *for* clauses.

107

P 1a–b   PUNCTUATION

Compare the following examples:

I did it for you. (For *is a preposition.*)
I did it, for you told me to. (For *is a conjunction.*)

We can depict graphically the rule for the punctuation of such sentences with a coordinating conjunction.

| (Independent | (Con- | (Independent |
| clause) | junction) | clause) |

────────────── , & ──────────────

1) SEMICOLON WITH INTERNAL COMMAS: IF THE INDEPENDENT CLAUSES CONTAIN POTENTIALLY CONFUSING INTERNAL COMMAS, USE A SEMICOLON INSTEAD OF A COMMA BETWEEN THE CLAUSES TO INDICATE THE GREATER IMPORTANCE OF THE MAJOR BREAK IN THE SENTENCE EVEN THOUGH THE CLAUSES ARE CONNECTED BY A COORDINATING CONJUNCTION.

He rode madly up hill and down dale, through forest, field, and stream; and still the fox eluded him.

2) THE DASH RARELY USED

Only rarely should independent clauses be separated by a dash. Study the primary functions of the dash (P12) and be sure you are using the dash properly before you use one in a compound sentence.

b. Without coordinating conjunctions: Two independent clauses *not* connected by coordinating conjunctions (*and, but, or, nor, for*) are separated by a semicolon.

No one spoke to him as he walked through the village; no one seemed to recognize him. (*Two independent clauses, no conjunction.*)

The surroundings seemed thoroughly familiar; however, he did notice some changes. (*Two independent clauses connected by a conjunctive adverb, not by a coordinating conjunction.*)

Washington weather is much maligned; even though other regions have a similar climate, Washingtonians are fond of insisting that their weather is worse. (*Two independent clauses, the second preceded by an adverbial clause. There is no coordinating conjunction.*)

TWO INDEPENDENT CLAUSES P 1b–c

If you read these sentences aloud, you will hear a more distinct change in pitch between the clauses, and a maximum juncture at the main break in the idea, as if the clauses were separate sentences— which, indeed, they could be, so far as structure goes.

In such sentences, a comma would be adequate only if the clauses were short and no confusion could result. Often, a subordinate clause intervenes between the independent clauses. Use the semicolon, still, to indicate the main break in the sentence, as in the third example just above.

c. Comma Splices (See also **Cs.**)

The use of a comma instead of the heavier semicolon between the independent clauses of such sentences results in the *comma splice* (also called the *comma fault* or the *comma blunder*), which can be very confusing to the reader. As we shall see, the comma is used to set off many lesser elements from the central main clause. If you use one between two independent clauses, the reader may be confused until he stops to analyze your sentence.

> CONFUSING: After the storm, cracks appeared in the bridge pavement, the piers and the cables, however, were undamaged. (If the main break in the sentence, after *pavement,* had been indicated by a semicolon, no confusion would have resulted.)

Listen to your voice, first as it stumbles through the confusion caused by the comma, then as it marks the main break in the sentence that a semicolon after *pavement* would indicate. Notice that the term "comma splice" refers only to this misleading use of a comma between independent clauses.

1) CONJUNCTIVE ADVERBS

The same rule enables you to handle the punctuation of sentences connected by conjunctive adverbs like *however, moreover, nevertheless, consequently, then,* and sometimes *yet* and *so.* They are not coordinating conjunctions and may in fact be used along with coordinating conjunctions. Unless *and, but, or, nor,* or *for* is present, use semicolons between independent clauses.

2) *So*

So is a special problem. In the first place, students grossly overuse it. Avoid it on general principles. If you must use it as a connective between clauses, ask yourself just what it means. If it is synonymous with *consequently*, it is a conjunctive adverb and connects clauses that probably should be separated by a semicolon. If it means *so that*, the succeeding clause is not an independent clause at all, but an adverbial clause of purpose or result, and the punctuation falls under P3b.

3) TESTS

Could the clauses stand alone? If so, they are independent and equally important. The reader expects to be warned that one clause does not modify the other. Commas are not enough warning, and a comma between independent clauses not connected by *and, but, or, nor,* or *for* splices the clauses together with insufficiently heavy punctuation.

Read the sentences aloud, comparing the pitch and juncture signals for commas and for semicolons.

d. Run-on sentences

If you are so little conscious of your own meaning that you run together two independent clauses without any punctuation at all and consequently without giving your reader even the slightest warning, you commit the cardinal sin of writing a **run-on** or a **run-together sentence,** which is worse than a comma splice because it confuses your reader still more thoroughly.

> WRONG: His sunburn was painful for a week he was in agony.
> WRONG: He is a stimulating teacher everybody says there is none better.
> WRONG: He wrote steadily for an hour the results were terrible.

Correct such sentences by applying the principles discussed in both **a** and **b** above. Wherever you think the main break in the sentence should come, indicate it to the reader by using the proper punctuation.

We can depict graphically the rule for punctuating compound sentences without a coordinating conjunction.

(Independent (Independent
clause)   clause)

———————— ; ————————

TWO INDEPENDENT CLAUSES ———————— **P 1e–P 1**

e. Possible subordination of one clause

Before we leave the punctuation of compound sentences, we might consider one final point. Should those sentences be compound sentences at all? Remember that the form of the compound sentence says to the reader, "Here are two distinct and independent ideas, neither modifying the other, yet both belonging in one sentence because together they express a single, unified idea." That is not a very common rhetorical or logical necessity. If your themes frequently contain comma splices or run-on sentences, stop and consider. Are your sentences really reflecting your thought? Should the compound sentences have been broken up into two simple sentences, or should one independent clause have been reduced to a subordinate clause or a modifying phrase or even a single modifying word?

Graphic Summary

The punctuation of sentences with two independent clauses is normally handled in one of these ways:

With *and, but, or, nor, for*:

(Independent clause)   (Conjunction)   (Independent clause)

——————— , & ———————

Without *and, but, or, nor, for*:

(Independent clause)   (Independent clause)

——————— ; ———————

EXERCISE

Punctuate the following.

1. There is a great deal of good expository writing in English but most of it is topical and goes out of date quickly.

111

P 1/2a

2. We are all firmly convinced that men possess certain inalienable rights however it requires uncommon tolerance to recognize that our own rights are also the rights of other men.
3. The first of our troublesome sentence patterns concerns compound and some compound-complex sentences comma splices and run-ons do not occur in other kinds of sentences.
4. The usual practice of educated writers serves to establish a convention which readers expect you to follow failure to follow it, therefore, may confuse your readers badly.
5. My lawn is composed of bluegrass chickweed and sorrel also thrive in it.
6. Two of Rachel Carson's books attracted wide attention: *The Sea Around Us* made us sit up and think of Rachel Carson, *Silent Spring* made us sit up and think.
7. Law is the ethical minimum to be merely legal is to be morally sleazy.
8. The FDA reported, as the main deleterious side effect, heart damage, kidney, liver, and other visceral damage and damage to the nervous system sometimes resulted also.
9. Ruth flirted outrageously with Kenney and Caleb and Dick flirted with her.
10. The careers of most men are decided by chance, choice in comparatively few cases is the determining factor.

2. INTRODUCTORY ELEMENTS

a. Adverbial clauses and verbal clusters: Introductory adverbial clauses and verbal clusters are usually set off from the main clause by a comma.

> As soon as the sun came out, the sidewalks began to steam.
> If you wish to see a doctor's excuse, I can get one.
> To find your way around in the city, get a good map.
> Having dragged himself out of bed, he decided he might as well go to class.

Your voice, again, will warn you by signals of pitch and pause that there is a break in the construction of the sentence. A comma signals that break to the reader.

We can depict graphically the rule for the punctuation of sentences introduced by an adverbial clause or a verbal cluster.

INTRODUCTORY ELEMENTS ——————————— **P 2b**

    (Clause or verbal)   (Independent clause)

~~~~~~~~~~~~~~~~ , ————————————————

b. Prepositional phrases: An introductory prepositional phrase is often *not* separated from the main clause. If the phrase is long, requires special emphasis, or might be misread, it may be set off by a comma.

    NO COMMA NECESSARY: To the right of the door is the drinking fountain.
    In a troubled world personal peace of mind is hard to secure.
    COMMAS PROBABLE: In every examination throughout the entire semester, Professor Snodgrass flunked Gertrude.
    In short, she failed the course.

Usage here is divided. The best test is provided by your own voice. If you read your sentence with a decided pitch-pause signal after the prepositional phrase, use a comma; if not, leave it out. The same test can be applied to single introductory adverbs, though they seldom cause trouble either way.

We can depict graphically the rule for the punctuation of sentences containing introductory prepositional phrases.

    (Prepositional   (Independent clause)
      phrase)

                   ?
~~~~~~~~~~~~~~~~ , ————————————————

(Long or emphatic prepo-   (Independent clause)
  sitional phrase)

~~~~~~~~~~~~~~~~ , ————————————————

EXERCISE

Punctuate the following sentences containing introductory modifying elements. Be prepared to explain why you use or do not use a comma in each sentence.

P 2/3   PUNCTUATION

1. For the latest weather forecast dial 936-1212.
2. Until we get a heavy rain the forest will be tinder dry.
3. To prevent disastrous fires the governor has closed the state parks by executive order.
4. As you no doubt already have discovered when you are asked to write a theme during a class hour it is useful to have a list of interesting topics filed in your notebook.
5. Many places, like banks, still provide convenient counters at which to write checks, but since the triumph of the ball-point pen few places now provide blotters.
6. Occasionally one can substitute Kleenex for a blotter, but the result is seldom a happy one.
7. To the student who is concerned only with his grade a satisfactory grade will probably come; to the student who is concerned only with how much he can learn will probably come not only a satisfactory grade, but also satisfaction.
8. Pausing after the delivery of a ringing phrase the mayor awaited applause.
9. To a surprising number of otherwise well-taught students dashes and hyphens are virtually identical.
10. After all there is but one race—humanity.

3. PARENTHETICAL ELEMENTS

Any element which does not vitally modify the sentence or which is out of its normal order in the sentence may be considered parenthetical or interpolated (that is, "stuck in"), whether it comes in the middle of the sentence, at the end, or even at the beginning, like the special cases discussed in P2 above. Any such element, since it is not essential to the elements it stands by, is separated from the rest of the sentence, "set off," by commas.

The voice signals of pitch and pause are normally clear with all such parenthetical elements. The pitch rises before the interpolation and again at the end of it, and there is a decided pause, after which the pitch is markedly lowered. With essential modifiers, on the other hand, neither pitch change nor pause occurs. With a parenthetical element at either end of the sentence, of course, only one set of signals occurs, but in any position the signals are unmistakable in the spoken sentence. Commas signal the break in writing.

Notice the signals in the following sentences.

> Dr. Bradley, who tries to keep abreast of new discoveries, spends a great deal of time reading medical journals.

PARENTHETICAL ELEMENTS — P 3a–b

>Any doctor who tries to keep abreast of new discoveries must spend a great deal of time reading medical journals.
>Come out, wherever you are.
>John, is this clear?

The problem in punctuating, when the elements come in the middle of the sentence, usually lies in forgetting to set off the element at *both ends*. One comma merely separates the subject from the verb or the verb from the complement. Two commas give the reader the structural signals he needs.

The most common types of parenthetical interrupters may be considered separately.

a. Absolutes: Absolutes are set off by commas.

Absolutes are words or phrases, rarely clauses, that do not grammatically affect the sentences in which they appear. Interjections, transitional words or phrases, nouns of address, nominative absolutes (absolute phrases), adverbs of affirmation or negation (*yes*, and *no* when it is not directly modifying a word in the sentence) —all these are absolutes and are set off by commas. All can be removed from the sentence without affecting the sense of the sentence, and all are set off by commas.

>Oh, why do you say that?
>I say it, of course, because I believe it to be true.
>I say it, as you might have known, because I believe it to be true.
>Tell me, John, when you expect to go.
>Yes, I'll go with you.

b. Nonrestrictive modifiers and appositives: Nonrestrictive modifiers and nonrestrictive appositives are set off by commas.

Since *nonrestrictive* is a negative term, here and in each subsequent discussion under this general rule it will be necessary to consider the restrictive elements first, in order to understand the nonrestrictive elements.

A *restrictive* element is one that is so vital to the understanding of the sentence that it could not be omitted without seriously disturbing the clarity of the sentence. It restricts (limits) the meaning so sharply that it cannot be removed. It belongs to the sentence, and we do not separate elements that belong together. We read them together without a change in pitch and without pause, and we do *not* set them off in writing.

A *nonrestrictive* element, on the other hand, may add useful information, but it does not so sharply restrict the meaning that it cannot be removed without materially changing the meaning of the sentence. In reading or speaking, our voices separate it from the rest of the sentence. It is, consequently, parenthetical and is set off from the rest of the sentence by commas.

1) NONRESTRICTIVE ADJECTIVE MODIFIERS: NONRESTRICTIVE ADJECTIVE MODIFIERS ARE SET OFF BY COMMAS.

To understand the nonrestrictive adjective modifier, we need first to consider the restrictive adjective modifier.

A *restrictive* adjective modifier is a phrase or a clause that particularizes, limits, points out, designates, *identifies* the noun it modifies. *It tells which one of several possible things the sentence is about, and it is not separated from its noun either by the voice or by punctuation.*

> RESTRICTIVE: The man in the tweed suit is not listening. (*There are several men present, but only one is in tweeds, and only he is not listening.*)
>
> RESTRICTIVE: The book I borrowed from Budd was very interesting. (*There are many books. I am talking now about the one Budd lent me.*)
>
> RESTRICTIVE: The click of the light switch woke me up. (*Clicks occur often. It was that one click that disturbed me.*)

We can depict graphically the function of the *restrictive* adjective modifier.

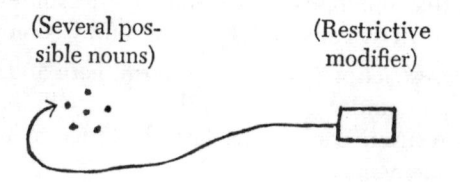

(Several possible nouns)   (Restrictive modifier)

A *non*restrictive adjective modifier, as the name suggests, is *not* restricting, not identifying. It does add useful or interesting information, or it would not be there at all, but *it could be left out without destroying the sense of the sentence,* and both our voices and our punctuation separate it accordingly.

PARENTHETICAL ELEMENTS — P 3a–b

NONRESTRICTIVE: Mr. O'Neill, who is wearing a tweed suit, is not listening. (*There is only one Mr. O'Neill in the group, and he is already identified by name. The tweed suit is incidental. The sentence would be clear without that modifier.*)

NONRESTRICTIVE: *Europe since 1914,* which I borrowed from Budd, was interesting. (*The title identifies the book. Where I got it is merely additional information, not necessary to the sense of the sentence.*)

We can depict graphically the function of the *nonrestrictive* adjective modifier.

(Identified noun)   (Nonrestrictive modifier)

•   +   ▱

Compare these examples:

                         Several men   The one in the tweeds

RESTRICTIVE: The man in the tweed suit is asleep.

                         O'Neill   A tweed suit

NONRESTRICTIVE: Mr. O'Neill, who is wearing a tweed suit, is asleep.

                         Several eggs   The egg I broke

RESTRICTIVE: The egg I broke was no good anyway.

                         Eggs   Protein

NONRESTRICTIVE: Eggs, providing protein, are welcome at breakfast time.

117

P 3a–b _____ PUNCTUATION

Nonrestrictive adjective modifiers could be omitted without destroying the sense of the sentence, and consequently are parenthetical and are set off by commas—*two* commas if the element comes in the middle of the sentence.

Very often, however, the modifier, as an adjective phrase or clause modifying an object, comes at the end of the sentence. Your voice will give the same pitch-pause signal at the beginning of the element; one comma clarifies the pattern for the reader.

Please awaken Mr. O'Neill, who is wearing a tweed suit.

We can depict graphically the punctuation of sentences containing *nonrestrictive* modifiers,

| (Part of main idea) | (Nonrestrictive modifier) | (Rest of main idea) |

——————— , ~~~~~~~~~~~~ , ———————

| (main idea) | (nonrestrictive modifier) |

——————— , ~~~~~~~~~~~~

2) NONRESTRICTIVE ADVERBIAL MODIFIERS: NONRESTRICTIVE ADVERBIAL MODIFIERS ARE SET OFF BY COMMAS.

The distinction between restrictive and nonrestrictive adverbial modifiers is less clear-cut than that between restrictive and nonrestrictive adjectives and appositives. Sometimes only the writer can be sure of the exact degree of separation he wishes to indicate, and the reader must hope that the punctuation is dependable and that the modifiers which have been set off were really meant to be nonrestrictive. If the writer is careless here, confusion will inevitably result. Your voice provides the best guide. Read the sentence aloud as you would speak it, and use a comma where pitch and pause signal a break.

Sometimes the adverbial modifier is clearly necessary to the sense of the sentence and therefore could not be omitted. Such modifiers are not set off.

RESTRICTIVE: I have not seen her since yesterday morning.
RESTRICTIVE: I will not do it unless there is no one else for the job.

PARENTHETICAL ELEMENTS ——————— **P 3a–b**

Sometimes the adverbial modifier merely adds a useful but nonessential idea and could be omitted without vitally changing the central thought. Such modifiers are set off by commas.

>NONRESTRICTIVE: I will do it, unless you can find someone else who wants the job.

The two may be represented graphically.

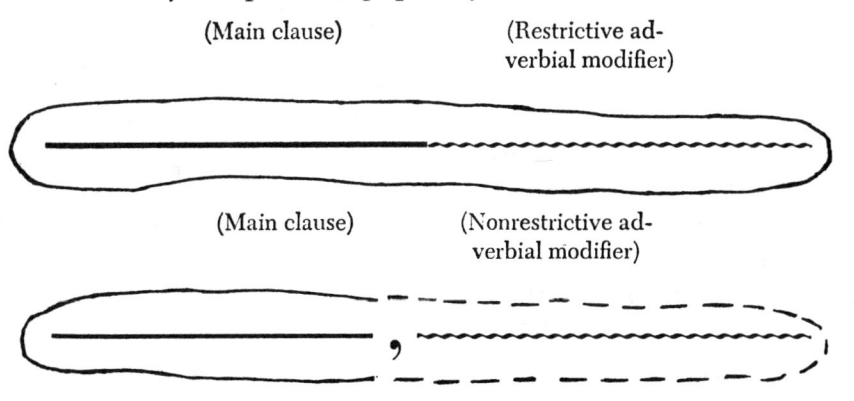

   (Main clause)   (Restrictive adverbial modifier)

   (Main clause)   (Nonrestrictive adverbial modifier)

3) NONRESTRICTIVE APPOSITIVES: NONRESTRICTIVE APPOSITIVES ARE SET OFF BY COMMAS.

An appositive is a noun repeating another noun and making it more specific. A restrictive appositive identifies. A nonrestrictive appositive, like the nonrestrictive adjective modifier, merely adds interesting information; it does not identify which one of several possibilities the sentence is about. Since the appositive follows another noun, it never begins the sentence, though it may end the sentence. The same signals of pitch and juncture (pause) that mark the nonrestrictive modifier will warn you to set off nonrestrictive appositives.

Examples should make the distinction between restrictive and nonrestrictive appositives clear.

>RESTRICTIVE: The poet Keats died young.

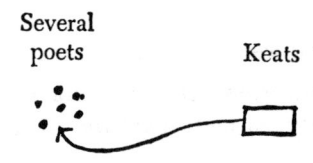

119

P 3a–d PUNCTUATION

NONRESTRICTIVE: Keats, the poet, died young.

Keats • + Poet ▨

RESTRICTIVE: I visited my brother Martin.

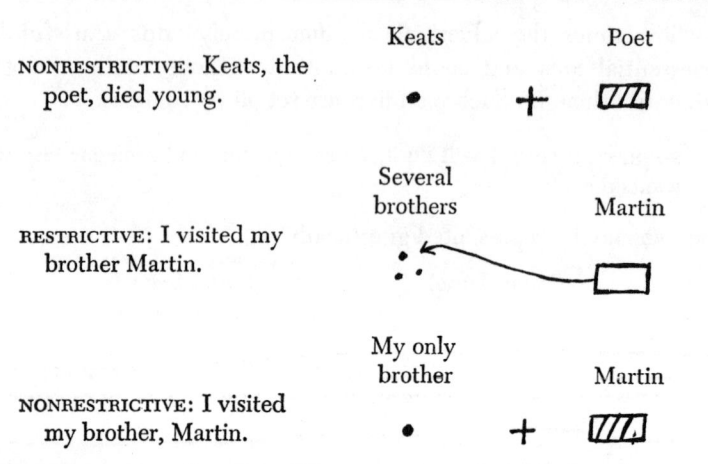

Several brothers ⠶ ← Martin ▭

NONRESTRICTIVE: I visited my brother, Martin.

My only brother • + Martin ▨

c. Elements out of order: Elements out of normal order in the sentence are set off by commas.

> Happily, he sang all through his bath.
> The horse, old and infirm, was retired to pasture.

Many elements in English can be shifted into a slightly unusual order for changes in emphasis. Adverbs, for example, may precede the main clause; adjectives may follow nouns instead of precede them; conjunctive adverbs, like *however*, may go into the middle of a clause instead of between clauses. All such elements may change the normal flow of thought; when they do, they are parenthetical and are set off by commas.

d. Tests

1) REMOVE PARENTHETICAL ELEMENTS FROM THE SENTENCE.

To determine whether an element of any sort is parenthetical and should be set off, try removing it from the sentence. If the remainder of the sentence is grammatically and logically complete and essentially the same without it, the element is parenthetical and should be set off by commas.

2) READ THE SENTENCE ALOUD.

An even better test, for *most* parenthetical elements, we have already learned. *Read the sentence aloud and listen to your voice.*

PARENTHETICAL ELEMENTS — P 3d–f

If you pause, before and after the element, if the tone of your voice rises and falls, if you "read around" the element, the element is parenthetical and should be set off by commas. This "pause test" is not valid for all questions of punctuation, and of course is of no help at all to anyone who reads in a stumbling monotone; but with a few exceptions, such as *sir* in "Yes, sir," it will work in determining whether or not a given element is parenthetical. Listen for the commas. If your voice inserts them, insert them in the written sentence.

e. Reminder: Set off parenthetical elements at both ends.

If the parenthetical element comes in the middle of the sentence, *be sure to set it off at both ends of the element*. Only rarely do students fail completely to recognize that an element is parenthetical. What they often do fail to do is indicate clearly to the reader where the parenthetical element both begins and ends. *One comma with a parenthetical element merely chops the sentence confusingly in two, separating subject from predicate or verb from complement. Two commas are essential if the parenthetical element comes anywhere except at the beginning or the end of the sentence.* (See also P6a, b.)

f. Rule

The rule for the punctuation of sentences containing parenthetical elements may be represented graphically.

(Part of main idea)	(Parenthetical element)	(Rest of main idea)
——————— , ~~~~~~~~~ , ———————

(Parenthetical element)	(Main idea)
~~ , ———————————

(Main idea)	(Parenthetical element)
——————————— , ~~~~~~~~~~~

121

P 3a–g

g. Modifications

Four modifications of the rule should be mentioned.

1) SLIGHT PARENTHESIS: ELEMENTS THAT ARE ONLY SLIGHTLY PARENTHETICAL ARE USUALLY NOT SET OFF.

I am indeed pleased to be here.

2) ELEMENTS TO BE MINIMIZED: PARENTHETICAL ELEMENTS THAT ARE TO BE MINIMIZED ARE ENCLOSED IN PARENTHESES, NOT COMMAS.

She is sure (I talked to her yesterday) that he will do it.
Chaucer (1340?–1400) held court positions under three kings.

3) ELEMENTS TO BE EMPHASIZED: PARENTHETICAL ELEMENTS THAT ARE TO BE STRONGLY EMPHASIZED ARE SET OFF BY DASHES, NOT COMMAS.

Conventional punctuation—and this you must believe—helps your reader understand your sentence.

4) WITH INTERNAL COMMAS: PARENTHETICAL ELEMENTS THAT WOULD NORMALLY BE SET OFF BY COMMAS ARE OFTEN SET OFF BY DASHES IF THEY CONTAIN INTERNAL COMMAS.

The three youngest boys—John, Elmer, and Stanley—ran home crying.

The pitch and juncture signals given by the voice when such sentences are spoken differ, subtly but distinctly, from each other and from the signals that call for commas in the patterns we have been considering under P3. They are difficult to describe without special training, but all of us use them constantly in speaking and listening; they can just as successfully be used in punctuating.

EXERCISE

Punctuate the following sentences to set off parenthetical elements conventionally. Be prepared to justify your punctuation.

1. A comma most of the time represents a change in the pitch of the voice and a distinct pause in the breath both of which can easily be heard in a spoken sentence.

2. It is precisely these pauses and changes in pitch the comma signals that make it unwise to break up a sentence by using too many parenthetical elements.
3. Spoken a style with too many interrupters is called "roller coaster prose"; read silently it seems more like briar patch prose because the reader's mind is snagged by the commas.
4. Omitting the commas however merely ignoring the problem is to force your reader unwillingly to determine if possible the structures underlying your sentences and to guess at the degrees of separation between them.
5. It is better instead to learn to give the conventional signals which can be done by paying attention to both structure and sound.
6. Throughout the country the growth of populations and of industries in addition to increasing use of air conditioning in towns and irrigation on our farms is producing a potential inadequacy of water supplies.
7. Increasingly men look to the ocean for future resources whether of food, of water, or of minerals.
8. Man races for the moon and the stars lest he outgrow the earth.
9. Already the moon long a symbol of romance and happy-ever-afters has become a symbol of man's greed instead.
10. What fools as Puck remarked these mortals be.

4. COORDINATE ELEMENTS IN SERIES

There are two common patterns involved in this item: the A, B, and C series, and coordinate adjectives modifying the same noun but not affecting each other.

a. A, B, and C series: Coordinate words, phrases, or clauses in an A, B, and C series are best separated by commas.

Here, admittedly, usage varies. Many reputable writers do not use a comma before the *and* when the elements of the series consist of words or short phrases. But because the function of *and* is to connect, it is safest in college writing to indicate clearly to the reader that B and C are no more closely related than A and B. Almost all writers use the comma before the *and* in a series of long phrases or of clauses. When *or* is used, most conventional writers use the comma in all cases.

Both the structure of the sentence and the pitch and juncture signals of the voice suggest the use of commas between all the members of the series, as you can confirm by listening to your reading of the following examples.

> Toast, coffee, and eggs are common foods for breakfast.
> Toast and coffee, bacon and eggs, and ice cream and cake are three combinations often found together.

It is perhaps the double pull of both these criteria that leads many readers to object to the omission of the comma before the *and* at the end of the series. Justification for the omission lies in the modern tendency to reduce the amount of punctuation. The clarity of the series is the ultimate guide.

Until you are certain that your writing is skillful enough to guarantee perfect clarity, use

$$A, B, \text{ and } C.$$

> John, Elmer, and Stanley were the three youngest boys.
> He looked in the closets, behind the bureau, and under the bed.
> If my work is done, if Mary will go, and if the weather is cool, I'll go to the Bay with you on Saturday.
> We chose an excellent day for the picnic, the girls provided excellent food, and we all enjoyed ourselves thoroughly. (*This example, containing a series of independent clauses, represents a special problem. If the clauses had been so long that the reader might have become confused, the use of commas would have resulted in an apparent comma splice. To prevent confusion, semicolons might be used in a series of long independent clauses: A; B; and C.*)

b. Adjectives in series: Coordinate adjectives modifying the same noun but not affecting each other are separated by commas.

> The exhausted, miserable child sobbed herself to sleep.
> The excited, happy rooters cheered the team.
> The old, infirm horse was retired to pasture.

It is not always easy to decide just when such adjectives cease to be coordinate (that is, performing equal functions in the sentence) and begin to have more or less subtle effects on each other, so that one functions adverbially. Often, too, the final adjective and the noun form a virtual compound, so that the earlier adjective modifies both words together and not the noun alone.

COORDINATE ELEMENTS IN SERIES   P 4b

> The dress was too youthful for the little old woman who bought it. She should never have purchased a yellow silk evening gown.

1) TESTS FOR COORDINATE ADJECTIVES

Insert an *and* between the adjectives. Since *and* will connect only equal elements, if the *and* will fit, it follows that the adjectives are coordinate. If the *and* will not fit comfortably, it must follow that the adjectives, instead of being coordinate, are actually affecting each other in some way. Therefore they belong too closely together to be separated.

> He cut a switch from the sour apple tree. (*No one would say, "The sour and apple tree." The adjectives are not coordinate and should not be separated.*)
> The exhausted and miserable child sobbed herself to sleep.

Try the adjectives in some other order. If they are truly coordinate, any order should be possible, though one may be logically preferable.

> The miserable, exhausted child . . . .
> (*But no one would say:* The apple, sour tree . . . .)

Read the sentence aloud and listen to your voice. The pitch and juncture signals of *the old, infirm horse* are quite different from those of *the little old lady* or *the sour apple tree*.

2) NOTE: NO COMMA BEFORE THE NOUN

The final adjective is *not* separated from the noun.
This is the pattern:

> Adjective **,** adjective noun

Coordinate adverbs are less common than coordinate adjectives. When they occur, they are punctuated as adjectives are punctuated.

> The crowd cheered excitedly, happily.

EXERCISE

Punctuate elements in series in the following sentences according to the practice of strictly conventional writers.

125

P 1–4   PUNCTUATION

1. The wind blew the windows rattled the thunder rolled and the rain beat upon the huddled houses.
2. John and Mary danced sang and ate hamburgers.
3. The old gray mare does not look much like Man o' War.
4. Think on this doctrine: that reasoning beings were created for one another's sake that to be patient is a branch of justice and that men sin without intending it.
5. How can I marry such a pretty little girl when I have a wife and three children at home?
6. Through the valleys down the mine shafts and beneath the cabins the wind raged.
7. The captain on the bridge the engineer in the depths of the ship and the steward chasing cups across the galley floor knew that the ship was pitching heavily.
8. The battered leaking vessel lurched head-on into the waves.
9. Presently almost abruptly, the ship passed out of the storm, and the sea was amazingly calm.
10. Before a storm, a calm oily sea is a frightening portent.

GRAPHIC SUMMARY

The conventional punctuation of the four common troublesome sentence patterns has been depicted graphically as each was discussed. It is helpful to see those graphic representations all together.

1. TWO INDEPENDENT CLAUSES

(Independent clause)   (Coordinating conjunction)   (Independent clause)

───────────── , & ─────────────

(Independent clause)   (Independent clause)

───────────── ; ─────────────

2. INTRODUCTORY ELEMENTS

(Adverbial clause)   (Independent clause)

∼∼∼∼∼∼∼∼∼∼ , ─────────────

ELEMENTS IN SERIES — P 1–4

(Verbal cluster) , (Independent clause)

(Prepositional phrase) ? (Independent clause)

,

3. PARENTHETICAL INTERRUPTERS

(Part of main idea)　(Parenthetical element)　(Rest of main idea)

———————— , ~~~~~~~~~~ , ————————

(Parenthetical element)　(Main idea)

~~~~~~~~~~ , ————————

(Main idea)　(Parenthetical element)

———————— , ~~~~~~~~~~

4. ELEMENTS IN SERIES

A, B, and C

Adjective, adjective noun

EXERCISE

Punctuate the following sentences, illustrating the four most troublesome sentence patterns, according to the practice of strictly conventional writers.

1. When I am punctuating sentences that someone else wrote I can do very well.
2. The trouble comes with sentences of my own I know exactly how the sentences should be read and can't see when my punctuation has been misleading.
3. You must learn of course to punctuate your own sentences correctly.
4. Other people's sentences other people's punctuation and other

127

people's meaning are problems the other people must solve for themselves.
5. America broke away from England in the eighteenth century and as a result many American idioms reflect eighteenth century British practice.
6. The British often object to "Americanisms" but as a matter of fact many of the expressions they object to merely represent older to them outmoded British usage.
7. Not every Tom Dick and Harry can manage to occupy the White House.
8. Considering the difficulty of securing the nomination by a major political party for the presidency we have succeeded in electing an astonishing number of good Presidents and an incredibly small number of poor ones.
9. To a reasonable being that alone is insupportable which is unreasonable.
10. Neither death nor exile nor pain nor anything of this sort is the true cause of our doing or not doing any action, but our inward opinions and principles.
11. As a man thinketh in his heart so is he.
12. The human voice is an elaborate flexible instrument capable of lending many shades of meaning to a spoken English sentence written English a far less flexible instrument must depend on precise diction careful control of the form and position of sentence elements and a sensitive handling of the conventions of punctuation.
13. It is little wonder therefore that writing well is difficult and reading well is demanding.
14. Unfortunately the more exactly one knows what he wants to say, the more dissatisfied he is likely to be with his best efforts to say it.
15. Writing revising rewriting—these must be stopped at some point as time and deadlines pass.
16. A dialect is a system of speech peculiar to a region a class and a time in sounds words and constructions.
17. The written English of the educated American is a dialect a minority dialect indeed from one region to another dialect differences occur even within educated written English.
18. Without intensive study no one can say though many do say even many who should know better that a particular locution is the only standard pattern.
19. There are of course many locutions that are not used in educated

MISCELLANEOUS USES OF THE COMMA   P 5a–c

writing unless that writing represents nonstandard usage as in dialogue.
20. There are many locutions too that many readers object to even though they are well established the writer uses them at his own risk.
21. No student of language maintains that "anything goes" the rhetorical effect of one's language must always be considered.
22. Ideally your thought should flow without distraction into the reader's mind your sentences should be so carefully controlled that they are read exactly as you wish them to be read.
23. Punctuation is a matter of major importance it helps determine how easily the reader can read your sentence as you wished it to be read.
24. There are many ways in which a practiced writer can suggest subtle variations of thought by varying the basic punctuation patterns but even the inexperienced writer who studies the basic patterns can be fairly sure that he will not lead his reader badly astray.
25. If you believe it is easy to say exactly what you mean think of all the successful lawyers you know who make a practice of breaking each other's carefully drawn wills and contracts.

5. MISCELLANEOUS USES OF THE COMMA

a. Prevent misreading: Elements that might be mistakenly read together are separated by commas.

Occasionally, to say what we want to say, we are forced to put side by side elements that might be confusingly read together. To warn the reader of the separation, we use a comma between such elements.

Whatever is, is right.

b. Contrasted elements: Contrasted elements are separated by commas.

Not John, but Peter, was given the most responsible duty.
Peter, not John, was the older.

c. Dates: Commas are used to separate the month and the year, and the day of the month from the year when the day is given.

October, 1492
October 12, 1492

Commas are customarily omitted, however, if the form *12 October 1492* is used.

When the date occurs in the middle of a sentence, most writers use a comma also after the year.

> Columbus arrived in America on October 12, 1492, and opened the New World to European exploration.

d. Addresses and geographical items: **Commas are used to separate the parts of an address or other geographical item.**

> His address is 110 Kenner Avenue, Indianapolis, Indiana.

When the address occurs in the middle of a sentence, most writers use a comma also after the name of the state.

> If 110 Kenner Avenue, Indianapolis, Indiana, is no longer the right address, write in care of his parents.
> He once lived in Washington, D.C.

When the geographical item occurs in the middle of a sentence, most writers also use a comma after the last element.

> Paris, France, is a beautiful city.

e. Quotations (including comma splices and fragments in dialogue): **Commas are used to separate such orientation phrases as *he said* from the *direct* quotations they introduce.**

> He said, "I am ready for the exam."

When the orientation phrase occurs in the middle of the quotation, punctuate the entire passage according to the sentence pattern of the whole.

> "I will do as you ask," he said. "It would be foolish to disobey."
> (*The first clause and the orientation phrase make a full sentence; the following clause makes a full sentence. They are punctuated accordingly.*)
> "She denies it," he pointed out; "however, the evidence is clear."
> (*The quoted sentence, exclusive of the orientation phrase, is a compound sentence without a coordinating conjunction and requires a semicolon. The orientation phrase does not change the pattern.*)
> "Give me liberty," he cried, "or give me death." (*The first part of the quotation, with or without the orientation phrase, could*

stand alone as a sentence, but the second part could not. It must be included in the basic sentence.)

Avoid **comma splices** (see **P1c** and **Cs**) in sentences like the first and second examples above. Avoid **fragmentary sentences** (see **P7a** and **Frag**) in sentences like the third example above.

With these miscellaneous conventions, pitch and juncture signals are subtle and may be missed. It is perhaps best merely to learn the half-dozen constructions involved.

EXERCISE

Punctuate the following sentences illustrating the most common miscellaneous uses of the comma. If necessary, adjust the capitalization.

1. What a piece of work is a man how noble in reason how infinite in faculty in form and moving how express and admirable in action how like an angel in apprehension how like a god.
2. Two miles above the sky was laced with clouds.
3. Huntsville Alabama should not be confused with Huntsville Texas.
4. Dorothy is a Texan not only by birth but also by choice.
5. One's choices not one's innate characteristics are one's own responsibility.
6. Beyond the railing on which he leaned fifteen feet below the water foamed and tumbled.
7. "Tell me" she said "why you look at me so curiously."
8. "I was wondering what kinds of people invent new styles of make-up" he answered "what a fiendish sense of humor they all must have."
9. His address is 2029 G Street Northwest Washington D.C.– 20006.
10. On October 11 1492 Columbus sailed the ocean blue.
11. By 13 October 1492 he had discovered not the continent the Vikings had long known nor the continent the Polynesians traded with but a rather small island.
12. As a result of the voyages of Columbus and the subsequent reports both continents are named not Columbia but America.
13. What a wonderful thing is publicity writers make history.

P 6a–b PUNCTUATION

14. "What is so rare as a day in June?" the poet asked and was answered by the calendar "any day in February is rarer."
15. For the right answer the right question is important.

6. OVERUSE OF THE COMMA

Since we do not separate elements that belong together, the overuse of commas can be as confusing as the omission of commas where your reader expects to find them. Remember, too, that commas signal pitch and juncture patterns and that consequently excessive commas produce a distractingly bumpy prose.

It is not quite true that the foregoing rules cover all the possible sentence situations in which commas may be useful, but in your college writing it might be well to avoid using a comma which cannot be justified by one of those rules.

Avoid unnecessary commas, particularly in the following five situations.

a. Do not use a comma to separate subject and verb.

No idea is expressed unless both subject and predicate are present. The two "belong together" as much as any two grammatical elements can. Even when the subject is a long noun clause, or a noun modified by a long restrictive phrase or clause, avoid a comma after the subject and before the verb unless confusion will result without it.

> Whoever comes to the office to claim this package may have it.
> The little old man who came every day to feed the pigeons was a friend of mine.

Note: Parenthetical elements coming between subject and verb are set off by *two* commas; they do not affect the syntax of the main clause. (See also P3e.)

> Old Mr. Saunders, who came every day to feed the pigeons, spent a great deal of money on cracked corn.
> Horatio Hornblower, the incomparable naval officer, won every war he entered.

b. Do not use a comma to separate verb and complement.

An incomplete subject-verb idea demands a complement; consequently that complement belongs to the verb and should not be separated from it.

OVERUSE OF THE COMMA — P 6b–d

> The answers are clear and comprehensive.
> He told us that he would surely be there.

Note: Parenthetical elements coming between verb and complement are set off by *two* commas; they do not affect the syntax of the main clause. (See also P3e.)

> I shall explain, as clearly as I can, all I know about the problem.

c. Do not use a comma to separate restrictive modifiers from the words they modify, nor to separate restrictive appositives from the words with which they are in apposition. (See P3b.)

This rule may be applied not only to restrictive adjective and adverb phrases and clauses, but also to the last member of coordinate adjectives in series before a noun and to the first in a series of coordinate adverbs after a verb.

> The man who answered first was wrong.
> The girl's shrill, petulant voice echoed through the house.
> She spoke harshly, stridently.
> Shakespeare the poet only rarely took suggestions from Shakespeare the businessman.

Note: Since the relative pronoun *that* is now used only with restrictive adjective clauses, or with noun clauses functioning as subject or complement, the punctuation of *that* clauses is simple. *Do not set off* that *clauses,* except in A, B, and C series.

> This is the book that I told you to read.
> The charity that begins at home arouses our greatest interest.
> That you can do it if you try is unquestionable.
> He said that he would think about it, that he would call me, but that I should not call him.

d. Do not normally use a comma before *and* or *or* connecting words or phrases, except in A, B, and C series. (Such a comma may be used if the degree of separation is distinct or if confusion might result from its omission.)

> He was uncomfortable and cross.
> He will do all that he can for you and will let you know what happens.
> You will pay that bill by tomorrow or be sued.
> John, Tom, and Mary went to the movies.

P 6a–e

e. Do not separate coordinating conjunctions (*and, but, or, for, nor*) from the clause, phrase, or word they introduce.

> The clouds gathered, and the rains came. (*A comma after* and *lends entirely too much emphasis to the connective.*)

Conjunctive adverbs, like *however* and *nevertheless*, may or may not be set off, depending on how formal the rest of the punctuation is in the passage.

EXERCISE

Correct the punctuation of the following sentences by removing unnecessary commas. Insert any commas that are required.

1. Driving inland from the East Coast, one passes, the Tidewater, the Piedmont (or foothill region), and a relatively low range of mountains before one comes to the Appalachians.
2. To the true Easterner, the area between the Atlantic, and the Appalachians is the only one, which is of any consequence, for, beyond the Appalachians the West begins.
3. It is amazing, how many people, in this country, would be surprised, to think of Ohio—or Nebraska—as, "the West."
4. Lord Dunsany, an English scholar and critic, once invented a sentence to illustrate excessive punctuation: "Moreover, Jones, who is, also, of course, Welsh, is, perhaps, coming, too, but, unfortunately, alone."
5. The pitches and junctures in Lord Dunsany's sentence, are enough, to make a reader seasick.
6. Despite the length of time it has taken scholars to classify the uses of pitch, stress, and juncture in English, children have long been aware of it, and just for fun read the wrong signals into passages of prose, roaring with laughter at the results.
7. Experts in double-talk, too speaking rapidly give, the right signals but, for, the wrong structures and listeners, puzzled, wonder why they do not quite understand.
8. A foreigner speaking English may get the words and the forms of words and the order of words perfectly and still be difficult to understand because he misses the signals of pitch, stress, and juncture and consequently misses the English tune.
9. From time to time and place to place the system of signals

changes, but it is always systematic, and understood by all, who speak the dialect.
10. The signals, that are understood by a group of speakers, constitute the system for that group.

OTHER MARKS OF PUNCTUATION

In the foregoing discussion of the four troublesome sentence patterns, the miscellaneous uses of the comma, and the dangers of the excessive use of the comma, we have considered about eighty-five percent of all punctuation. There remain to be considered eleven other marks of punctuation (some few uses of which have been treated as we worked with the troublesome sentence patterns). Fortunately, these other marks of punctuation are chiefly employed in clearly defined and stereotyped situations. Once their functions are understood, they give very little trouble.

7. PERIOD (.)

a. Marking the end of a sentence: The period is used to mark the end of a declarative sentence, an imperative sentence (unless it is very emphatic), and many exclamatory sentences which express only mild emotion.

> Many coeds regard classes as annoying interludes separating weekends.
> Shut the outside door.
> How tired we all were after the party.

Note: The period should not be used to create **fragmentary sentences.** Except in very unusual circumstances, be sure that everything you write as a sentence expresses a complete thought. (For full discussion, see **Frag** [Chapter 1], and pages 41–42. See also P12e.)

> WRONG: My brother, who everybody knows is far more energetic than I and who has developed a native resourcefulness by a strenuous career as a newspaperman.
> WRONG: I will gladly do it for you. After you have paid me for the three previous jobs.

b. With abbreviations: The period is used after abbreviations and after initial letters representing words.

> Etc., Mrs., *ibid.*, A.D., J. L. Smith.

Exceptions: Periods are not used with initials representing government agencies, with an increasing number of other organizations, or with abbreviations (clipped forms) which have become recognized words in their own right. (Such clipped forms are usually very informal.)

> TVA, AEC, CIA, MLA, AAUP, exam, ad, taxi

8. QUESTION MARK (?)

a. Direct questions: The question mark is used after an interrogative sentence, one which asks a direct question. It is not used after a declarative sentence reporting an *indirect* question.

> Where did you get that notebook?
> He asked where I got this notebook.

The use of question marks is especially important in two situations, chiefly because many students fail to use them and thereby mislead a reader. The first is at the end of a long sentence which has been made interrogative by the inversion of the subject-verb order of declarative sentences.

> Did you read the story in the paper which told of the discovery by archaeologists of one of the earliest cities in the Fertile Crescent, the presumed area of the birth of civilization?

The other is at the end of a sentence which does not invert the declarative subject-verb order, but depends instead on the interrogative pitch and juncture signals.

> John will do it?

The question mark is used after a sentence rendered interrogative by a parenthetical question coming at the end of the sentence. It is usually not used if the parenthetical question comes elsewhere in the sentence.

> I wish I knew how he can afford to date her, don't you?
> You think, don't you, that I never study.

EXCLAMATION POINT   P 8b–c/P 9a–c

b. Indicating doubt: The question mark, usually in parentheses, is used to indicate doubt about the accuracy of some statement.

Chaucer was born in 1340(?) and died in 1400.

c. Not used to label irony

Do *not* use the question mark to call attention to ironic remarks. If your jokes are so feeble that they need to be labeled, you are perhaps better off if your reader overlooks them.

WEAK: He is a scholar (?) and a football player.

9. EXCLAMATION POINT (!)

a. Marking the end of a sentence: The exclamation point is used after an emphatic exclamatory sentence, after a strong interjection, or after an exclamatory question.

Your house is on fire!
Whew!
How can you stand it!

b. Not to be overused

Do *not* overuse exclamation points. They are known as "screamers." Save them for occasions when you want to scream.

c. Not to be doubled up

Do *not* attempt to show that this time you really need an exclamation point by using two or three at once. Use them sparingly, and one will be enough.

WEAK: Honestly! I was so mad! ! He was late! ! !

EXERCISE

Punctuate the following sentences conventionally.

1. Who, me
2. Has it really occurred to you that I might have meant someone else
3. Be reasonable enough, won't you, to admit your guilt
4. Brutus is an honorable man
5. He asked Father William why he continually stood on his head

137

6. The President is unquestionably the greatest living American, don't you think
7. Look out We're going to hit him
8. She glared at him angrily "You're crazy"
9. He replied, inquisitively, "You think so   Why"
10. He asked why she thought so

10. SEMICOLON (;)

The semicolon (not to be confused with the colon) functions as a heavy comma, but is used principally between elements which are grammatically equal. Overuse of the semicolon between unequal elements confuses the reader. The pitch and juncture signals for semicolons, particularly between independent clauses where they most often appear, are essentially the same as those for a period: a sharp dropping of the voice, followed by a full stop of the breath, that is, the maximum juncture. Only the logical unity of the resulting sentences distinguishes between periods and semicolons, and valid differences of opinion are usually possible.

a. Compound sentences without coordinating conjunctions: The semicolon is used to separate independent clauses not connected by a coordinating conjunction. (See also P1b and Cs.)

> Professors tend to stress theory rather than practice in their courses; they realize how much more stable theories are than the variable methods by which theories are applied.
>
> We wish that we could accept your invitation; however, we have a previous engagement.

As the second example above indicates, conjunctive adverbs (like *however, nevertheless, accordingly, therefore*) may connect independent clauses. But they are not coordinating conjunctions; they are primarily adverbs. When they occur between clauses without an attendant coordinating conjunction, separate the clauses with semicolons. (See also P1b, c.)

Note: Do *not* assume that semicolons always precede conjunctive adverbs. If the conjunctive adverb is inserted parenthetically within a clause, it is set off by commas as a parenthetical interrupter. (See also P3.)

He has studied hard all semester; therefore he has little need to cram for exams. (*A comma after* therefore *would be more formal.*) He has studied hard all semester; he has little need, therefore, to cram for exams.

EXERCISE

Punctuate the following sentences conventionally.

1. The Dean was present however he slept all through the meeting.
2. That was not the first important meeting moreover in which he had been caught napping.
3. He was a man of action at the same time he was a man of dreams.
4. There is no history there are only the interpretations of events by historians.
5. The farther into the past an event recedes, the more likely historians are to reach agreement while we might as well accept their opinions we should realize that probability is involved rather than certain truth.

b. **Compound sentences with coordinating conjunctions and internal commas:** The semicolon is used instead of the comma between independent clauses connected by a coordinating conjunction whenever internal commas might obscure the importance of the main break in the sentence.

After swimming, riding, dining, and dancing, they retired to their rooms; and being somewhat wearied by their exertions, they slept soundly till the following noon.

c. **Between members of an A, B, and C series with internal commas:** Semicolons are used instead of commas to separate the members of an A, B, and C series whenever commas within the members might confuse the reader.

Abel, Martha; Ambrose, Murray; Berger, Henry—these names led the class roll.

11. COLON (:)

The colon (not to be confused with the semicolon) is used between a formal introductory passage and that which follows. Unlike the semicolon, which is used between grammatically equal elements, the colon separates elements which are logically equal but are often grammatically quite different.

a. The colon is used between independent clauses when the second clause repeats or develops the idea of the first.

> The Duke of Wellington was a perfect example of the strictly honorable English gentleman: after a long separation and without any intervening indication of interest on either side, he married his youthful sweetheart because he believed he had once led her to expect him to do so.

b. The colon is used between a generalizing statement and the formal series of details which particularizes it.

> Three types of governmental functions are carefully distinguished in the Constitution: administrative functions, legislative functions, and judicial functions.

c. The colon is used between a formal orientation phrase and a formal quotation.

> Jean Jacques Rousseau long ago observed: "If children are not to be made to do things merely for the sake of their obedience, it follows that they will learn nothing until they recognize in it a real and immediate profit or pleasure."

d. The colon is used between the salutation and the body of the letter in formal correspondence.

> Dear Sir:
>   Your very interesting suggestion has been referred to . . . .

e. The colon is used between titles and subtitles.

> *Middlemarch: A Study of Provincial Life*

f. In Biblical references the colon is used between chapter and verse.

> Ecclesiastes 12:12

g. The colon is used between hours and minutes numerically represented.

> 10:45 P.M.

12. DASH (—)

The dash (not to be confused with the hyphen) is a useful and quite legitimate mark of punctuation, but with two exceptions it does not substitute for any other mark of punctuation. (See P12g, h.) Indiscriminate use of the dash, therefore, is not only an indication of the writer's unwillingness to learn conventional punctuation, but is an imposition on the reader, since it forces him to decide what kind of punctuation was intended. A dash in the wrong place is always annoying and often confusing.

Remember that the dash is an emphatic mark. It suggests sharp and often sudden breaks in thought, and it is marked by very distinct pitch, stress, and juncture signals, characterized chiefly by abrupt and emphatic shifts. It is sometimes considered more appropriate in informal than in formal writing, because formal writing tends to be more measured and more calm than a dash will permit.

In print, a dash is at least twice the length of a hyphen. To indicate a dash in typing, use two hyphens with no space between them and the preceding and succeeding words, or space-hyphen-space.

a. With a sentence broken off: The dash is used to suggest that a sentence has been sharply broken off.

> I tell you—. But, no, I will not tell you after all.

b. With an emphatic appositive: The dash is used to emphasize an oppositive.

> There is one room the sovereign of England may never enter—the chamber of the House of Commons.
> Only one man—the President—can appoint justices to the Supreme Court.
> [Notice that commas would be normal in both sentences if emphasis were not required; see P3b(3).]

c. With digressions: The dash is used to set off an emphatic digression.

> You must not—and I mean this—use dashes indiscriminately.
> It was last Thursday—no, it was the Tuesday before—that I wrote to Henry about it.

d. With an emphatic parenthetical element: The dash is used to emphasize a parenthetical element which might normally be set off by commas. (See P3.)

> Unlike the public figure, if an ordinary man should undergo a nervous breakdown—which, under certain circumstances, could happen to anybody—he could at least secure a reasonable privacy.

e. Indicating decided and emphatic hesitation: The dash is used in informal writing to suggest a decided and emphatic hesitation before adding an afterthought.

> I will gladly do it for you—after you have paid me for the three previous jobs.

Note: This punctuation will provide, legitimately, the effect student writers often attempt to secure by putting the afterthought into a **fragmentary sentence.** (See P7a and **Frag.**) Use it, however, sparingly; overuse is distracting.

f. Between a series and a summarizing passage: The dash is used between a series and a summarizing passage.

> Beauty, family background, wealth, an excellent education, a prosperous and happy marriage—all these explain her arrogant self-assurance.

g. Setting off parenthetical elements with internal commas: Dashes are used as substitutes for commas to set off parenthetical elements containing internal commas.

> Considering the manifold blessings of civilization, everyone—man, woman, and child—should know as much as possible about first aid.

h. In place of colons in informal writing: Dashes sometimes substitute for colons in informal writing.

> FORMAL: Bacteria fall into two groups: aerobic and anaerobic.
> INFORMAL: Bacteria fall into two groups—aerobic and anaerobic.

i. The dash splice in compound sentences

Avoid the dash in place of the semicolon between independent clauses not connected by coordinating conjunctions. (See P1c and P10.)

PARENTHESES ——————————— P 13b–c

On rare occasions the clauses of a compound sentence may be held tightly enough together by logic to provide a unified sentence in spite of the abrupt separation of the dash, but normally such a dash destroys unity. If you need the emphasis of the dash, it may legitimately be used between two sentences.

13. PARENTHESES ( )

a. To minimize a parenthentical element: Parentheses are used to enclose elements interrupting a sentence when that material is to be minimized, providing the reader with necessary information but offering the least possible distraction from the main idea. The pitch patterns of parentheses and dashes do not differ greatly, but the stress is light with parentheses and the junctures are less abrupt. The effect is much less emphatic.

> John Keats (who died at the age of twenty-six) was perhaps the most promising young poet that England has ever produced.
> Parenthetical (interpolated) material may be set off by commas, parentheses, or dashes, depending on the degree of emphasis desired.

b. With other punctuation: When parentheses occur at a point in the sentence which requires other punctuation, place the other mark of punctuation *inside* the final parenthesis if the other mark belongs to the parenthetical material, *outside* if it does not.

> Enrollment in English courses will take place in Monroe Hall (Room 103).
> The 1920's were a period of roaring prosperity. (But the farmer even then was in trouble.)
> If tomorrow is a windy day (and the weather report suggests that it may be), there will be little passing in the football game.

c. Misuse with material to be deleted: Do *not* use parentheses to enclose material you wish to delete from a manuscript. Instead, draw a line completely through the material to be omitted.

> WRONG BECAUSE CONFUSING: He accepted the offer (although) in spite of the fact that it was disappointing.
> RIGHT: He accepted the offer ~~although~~ in spite of the fact that it was disappointing.

d. Parentheses always occur in pairs. Do not forget to close the parenthesis by inserting the) at the end.

> CARELESS: Solomon was given to thoughtful meditation (he had many, many wives.
> RIGHT: To avoid comma splices, you must first memorize the five coordinating conjunctions (*and, but, or, nor,* and *for*).

14. BRACKETS [ ]

a. To enclose material inserted in a quotation: Brackets are used primarily to insert explanatory or connective material of your own in passages quoted from another writer.

> "For this story [*A Study in Scarlet*] which first introduced Sherlock Holmes, the most famous and the most profitable detective of all time, Dr. Conan Doyle received exactly £25 [then worth $125]."

b. With other punctuation: When brackets occur at a point in the sentence requiring other punctuation, place the other mark of punctuation *inside* the final bracket if the other mark belongs to the bracketed material, *outside* if it does not.

15. QUOTATION MARKS (" ")

a. Double quotation marks except with internal quotation: Quotation marks in American practice are double (" ") except when a quotation occurs within another quotation. Do not attempt to distinguish between quotations of varying importance by using single quotation marks (' ') in anything other than an internal quotation. (Because British practice reverses American practice, you have sometimes seen single quotation marks where you expected double ones.) Follow American practice when writing for American readers.

b. With direct quotations: Double quotation marks enclose all material directly quoting the exact words of a speaker or writer. They are *not* used with indirect quotations.

> "I can't do the impossible," he said. "What do you take me for, a marine?"
> Lincoln began quietly: "Fourscore and seven years ago. . . ."
> "I will be there," he promised.
> He promised that he would be there.

"On November 6, 1817, died the Princess Charlotte, only child of the Prince Regent, and heir to the crown of England."
Lytton Strachey

c. **With a quotation of more than one consecutive sentence:** When a quoted speech or passage consists of more than one consecutive sentence, use quotation marks to enclose the entire quotation, *not* to enclose separate sentences.

> WRONG: "I will gladly go with you." "I was going that way anyway."
> RIGHT: "I will gladly go with you. I was going that way anyway."

d. **With a quotation of more than one paragraph:** When a quoted passage consists of more than one paragraph, *begin* each paragraph with double quotation marks, but do not use closing quotation marks until the end of the quotation.

e. **With nicknames:** Double quotation marks are used to enclose nicknames, unless the nicknames are already familiar to your reader.

> "Butch" Cabot, "Spike" Lowell, and "Ladyfingers" O'Toole shared the leadership of the segment of Boston society I knew as a child.
> Stonewall Jackson was one of America's greatest generals.

f. **With words as labels or in an unusual sense:** Double quotation marks are used to enclose a word used as a label or a word used in an unusual way. In both usages, the quotation marks have the same effect as the phrase "so-called."

> A word or phrase in which the sounds reflect and reinforce the meaning is called "onomatopoetic."
> Elmer's "industry" is closely akin to other people's idea of laziness.

g. **With words as words (now rare):** Rarely, double quotation marks are used to enclose a word used as a word, that is, as a combination of letters without reference to the meaning. More commonly now such a word is put in italics (underlined).

> OLD-FASHIONED: You have too many "and's" here.
> BETTER: You have too many *and*'s here.

Note: Avoid "apologetic quotation marks" to enclose slang or colloquial phrases inappropriately employed in formal writing. The use of quotation marks in such situations is now old-fashioned. Modern writers will use a slang or colloquial term without apology *if it is appropriate* (that is, if the intended reader will understand it and if it is in harmony with the tone of the whole). If it is not appropriate, do not use it.

> OLD-FASHIONED AND INEPT: We did the best we could with the job, and even if the result wasn't "top notch," at least it would "come pretty high up" on anybody's scale.
> VERY INFORMAL: We did the best we could with the job, and even if the result wasn't top notch, at least it would come pretty high up on anybody's scale.
> FORMAL: We gave our best efforts to the task, and even though the result fell short of perfection, it was not a result of which we needed to be ashamed.

h. With titles: Double quotation marks are used to enclose the titles of works which are parts of larger wholes, such as stories from a collection, articles from a magazine, chapters from a book, poems from a collection, and so on. Titles of complete works are now commonly put in italics (underlined). (See also **Ital.**)

> "The Adventure of the Empty House" (a story from the volume entitled *The Return of Sherlock Holmes*), "Cheap Clothes for Fat Old Women" (an article from the magazine entitled The *Atlantic Monthly*), "Matter Prefatory in Praise of Biography" (a chapter from the novel entitled *Tom Jones*), "My Last Duchess" (a poem from the volume entitled *Dramatic Romances*)

i. With other marks of punctuation: American practice, followed by all but a few American writers and publishers, is easy to learn. British practice is more complex, but since you are writing for American readers, learn and follow the American practice.

1) WITH PERIODS AND COMMAS: PERIODS AND COMMAS GO INSIDE QUOTATION MARKS, REGARDLESS OF THE LENGTH OR THE NATURE OF THE QUOTATION.

> "Butch," "Spike," and "Ladyfingers" led the gang.
> "Speak to me of my beauty," she purred.
> "Aw, go on," he responded brusquely.
> The reaction is technically known as "reduction."

QUOTATION MARKS ⎯⎯⎯⎯⎯⎯⎯⎯⎯⎯⎯⎯⎯ P 15h–i

2) WITH COLONS AND SEMICOLONS: COLONS AND SEMICOLONS GO OUTSIDE QUOTATION MARKS, REGARDLESS OF THE LENGTH OR NATURE OF THE QUOTATION.

"Some books are to be chewed and digested": Bacon's essays themselves are not to be read hastily.
"Give me liberty or give me death"; that spirit is not dead in twentieth-century America.

3) WITH QUESTION MARKS AND EXCLAMATION POINTS: QUESTION MARKS AND EXCLAMATION POINTS GO INSIDE QUOTATION MARKS IF THEY BELONG TO THE QUOTED MATERIAL; OTHERWISE THEY GO OUTSIDE QUOTATION MARKS.

He asked, "Are you going?"
Did he say, "I am going"?
Did he ask, "Are you going?"
"Help!" he cried. (*Notice that we usually do not double up punctuation. The exclamation point replaces the normal comma before the orientation phrase.*)
He said, of all things, "No comment"!

EXERCISE

Punctuate the following sentences illustrating the uses of quotation marks.

1. He spoke with quiet exasperation. You have neglected to hand in five themes. You have missed nearly half of the meetings of the class. You made a score of fifty-three on the final examination. And you complain because you failed the course!
2. But I've got to get a B, or I can't be initiated, the boy insisted.
3. I would suggest, the professor replied, that you consider that point somewhat earlier in the next term, if you are still in school.
4. Professor Snodgrass is just an old meany.
5. That chapter called Oxidation and Reduction is the hardest one in the book.
6. The American Way is harder to define than many people realize.
7. Stonewall Jackson was one of Lee's principal generals; Old Pete Longstreet was another.
8. Where were you on the night of June the third? the prosecutor thundered.

147

P 16a — PUNCTUATION

9. I was at home, she answered, reading a story entitled Injured Innocence, from a book called Perilous Pitfalls.
10. Her own definition of innocence was what interested the jury.

16. APOSTROPHE (')

a. To indicate the possessive case: The apostrophe is used to indicate the possessive case of nouns and of indefinite pronouns. It is *not* used in the possessive case of personal pronouns nor with the relative pronoun *who-whose*.

boy—boy's   boss—boss's
man—man's   bosses—bosses'
men—men's   Moses—Moses'
everybody—   one—one's
   everybody's   one's self *or* oneself

NOT: hi's, her's, it's, who's
USE: his, hers, its, whose
It's is a contraction of *it is*.
Who's is a contraction of *who is*.

1) NOTE: WHEN TO USE THE APOSTROPHE ALONE, WHEN TO USE APOSTROPHE AND "S."

To decide when both an apostrophe and an extra *s* are needed to form the possessive case of nouns and indefinite pronouns, remember that the apostrophe is *always* needed. If, when you pronounce the possessive case, you add an extra *s-* (or *z-*) *sound* to the form of the common case, use an extra *s* in addition to the apostrophe.

man + *s-sound* = man's
boss + *s-sound* = boss's
bosses + no *s-sound* = bosses'
Moses + no *s-sound* = Moses'

The man is here. The man's coat is torn.
He is the boss. John married the boss's daughter.
They are the bosses. To marry the bosses' daughters would be bigamous.
Moses led the Children of Israel out of Egypt. Moses' writings are well known.

148

SUSPENSION POINTS　　　　　　　　　　　P 16b–c/P 17a

You can trust your own pronunciation. Proper names about which you are in doubt probably have alternate forms.

> I went down to St. James' Infirmary.
> He is our ambassador to the Court of St. James's.

2) IN COMPOUNDS: IN COMPOUNDS, THE POSSESSIVE FORM USUALLY APPEARS IN THE LAST WORD.

> The King of England's horse
> Everybody else's opinion
> The man in the street's opinion

b. In contractions: The apostrophe is used in place of an omitted letter in a contraction.

> cannot—can't
> do not—don't
> it is—it's
> could have—could've (not *could of*)

c. To indicate the plural of symbols: The apostrophe is used to form the plurals of letters, words used as words, numerals, or other symbols. It is *not* used to indicate plurality in ordinary nouns.

> You have too many *and*'s in that sentence.
> Add two 2's and the result is 4.
> He sprinkles *&*'s throughout his writing as if it would exhaust him completely to write *and*.
> WRONG: They are leader's of the movement.
> RIGHT: They are leaders of the movement.

17. SUSPENSION POINTS (ELLIPSIS MARKS) (. . .)

a. To indicate an omission from a quotation: Suspension points (*three* dots) are used to indicate that something has been omitted from a quoted sentence.

> You cannot make a philosophic individualist into a good citizen. As the world is constituted at present, . . . probably it would be better to have hundred-percenters and A-1 patriots than to have reasonable individuals living reasonable lives.
> *Lin Yutang*

You are under a moral obligation, when using suspension points this way, to omit nothing which would change the sense of what

149

you are quoting. In the example above, an expansive detail, "with fierce national conflicts," was omitted. The omission did not distort the original. When the omission comes at a point in the original which requires other punctuation, add the other punctuation to the three dots, before them or after them according to the position of the omitted material in the original.

> Germany's payments, moreover, were fixed . . ., and the *de facto* relationship between war debts and reparation was clearly recognized.
>
> F. Lee Benns

> Then with a spilling, tumbling rush of water falling down into its trough, it [a wave] dissolves . . . .
>
> Rachel L. Carson

b. In dialogue: Suspension points are used, most commonly in dialogue, to indicate a decided but not emphatic hesitation, or to indicate that an uncompleted sentence trailed away into silence. (See also P12a, e.) These uses are rare, and suspension points should be used sparingly.

> "Mary. . . ." He spoke with soft embarrassment. "I . . . I missed you, . . . Mary."
> "The treasure is hidden in. . . ." But the feeble old voice had faded away. My father was dead.

EXERCISES

A. Punctuate the following sentences according to strictly conventional usage. Capitalize where necessary. Be prepared to defend your decisions.

1. This is an exercise reviewing all that we have studied about punctuation consequently you must be alert for any sort of problem may occur
2. There will be no trick sentences or at least not many
3. Any sentence which lacks the normal aid that conventional punctuation provides is to some extent tricky
4. How sweet the moonlight sleeps upon that bank Sandra quoted meaningfully Harold clutched his fraternity pin firmly and ran

EXERCISES

5. Many people who have lived for years in Washington D C maintain residences in another state where taxes are lower
6. Death taxes and clichés these no man can escape
7. Three may keep secrets if two be away
8. If sweet are the uses of adversity civilization is getting sweeter by the minute or should I say by every tick of the scientists' clocks
9. Our food is denatured pasteurized and reinvigorated and all of it tastes like old wallpaper paste
10. Wallpaper half of the time is plastic and paste as likely as not is a glutinous fraud
11. In the 1930s we laughed at the Germans *ersatz* materials how proud we are of our own synthetics many of which were developed from German patents incidentally
12. We fire rockets at the moon and flash madly around the inner reaches of space all the time dodging the left over junk from dead but still orbiting bric-a-brac
13. Many cities like Baltimore Maryland can boast mile after mile of rusting junk piles so perhaps space is as good a place to throw new junk as any other
14. Meanwhile although man has been going in and out through the rain for many millennia no one yet has invented a convenient comfortable way to go out in the rain without getting wet
15. Why doesnt some scientist think about some of the important problems of life
16. Names on the Land by George R Stewart is an excellent history of American place naming
17. The History of New York is one of its most interesting chapters
18. I will contribute upon one condition that my name not be made public
19. The time has come gentlemen to what time is it anyway
20. America needs you and I do mean you to preserve her institutions whenever they are threatened and to improve them wherever they are faulty
21. How long ago it was that Wordsworth said The world is too much with us
22. Life comes before literature as the material always comes before the work
23. He rushed into the room crying the house is on fire

24. Do not I said to him icily say the house is on fire tell us specifically what part of the house and inform us clearly of the seriousness of the conflagration before you stampede us into making utter fools of ourselves by calling the fire department quite unnecessarily

25. He said that he was sorry and that he would do better when we got another house

B. Punctuate the following passage.

One of the things that cannot be too often emphasized as you perhaps have heard before is the importance of writing about subjects you are interested in. If you will stop for a moment before you start work on a theme to think of the topics offered to twist those topics to fit subjects that you know something about to consider whether or not the theme can be made more to you than a mere exercise if you will do this until you have hit on an idea you really know about and are interested in your theme assignments will be easier to fulfill and your themes will be more interesting to read. Also you are quite likely to discover that somehow you have written better and more accurate English than you knew you could. Not even Shakespeare could have written his best when he was bored. Why should you try You may complain But the topics themselves seem dull. The only answer is that they shouldnt. Many students have written well on similar topics many times before. The topics are designed to fit your knowledge and your interests they were selected for those reasons. Remember three things you cannot learn to express yourself clearly unless you sincerely constantly try; unless you see your effort as useful to all the rest of your work in college and after unless you are interested in what you are saying and eager to say it well.

4

Spelling

Sp   Spelling

Historical background, 154
The importance of spelling, 157
Improving spelling deficiencies, 157
    1. Personal spelling list, 158
    2. Diagnosing the trouble, 158
    3. Using the dictionary, 160
        a. Syllabic division, 160
        b. Pronunciation, 160
        c. Derivation, 161
        d. Entry in personal spelling list, 162
    4. Visual spelling, 162
        a. The image in longhand, 162
        b. Fixing the image, 162
    5. Finger spelling, 163
    6. Memory aids, 163
    7. Regular patterns, 165
        a. Length of vowel, 165

  b. *un-, dis-, mis-,* 165
  c. *in-, com-,* 166
  d. *-ly, -ness,* 166
  e. Shifts in parts of speech, 166
  f. Plurals, 166
  g. Troublesome prefixes and suffixes, 167
 8. Spelling rules, 167
  a. *Ie* and *ei,* 167
  b. Doubling final consonants, 168
  c. Final silent *e* before consonants, 169
  d. Final silent *e* before vowels, 169
  e. Consonant plus *y* before suffixes, 169
  f. SEED words, 169
 9. Spelling lists, 170
  a. Words often misspelled because of careless pronunciation, 170
   1) Syllables and letters omitted, 170
   2) Syllables and letters added, 170
   3) Sounds changed or letters transposed, 170
  b. Similar words often confused, 171
  c. General spelling list, 172

HISTORICAL BACKGROUND

 Correctness in spelling, as in any aspect of the language, is established by *current, national,* and *reputable* usage. Fortunately for twentieth century users of English, the standard of correctness in English spelling is clear cut: Most English words are properly spelled in only one way, and that way can be learned and used confidently. Neither the audience you address, the tone of your writing, nor the level of language you adopt has to be considered in spelling.

 Even so, English spelling offers many complicated problems. It is not as illogical as it seems, but the logic behind it is the logic of history, and the history of our language has been very complex indeed. Many of our words, for example, came from the language our Anglo-Saxon forefathers spoke. Many other words came to us from Latin through the French of the Normans who conquered England in 1066 and formed the ruling class for some three hundred years thereafter. Other words came directly from classical Latin as still later borrowings. Others came from Parisian French, or were taken from classical Greek, or were borrowed from one or another of the many languages the far-ranging English have been in contact with over the years. And the spelling of all these words has been affected by the way the English-speaking peoples have pronounced them.

The effect of the changes in the sounds English speakers have given to their words can be seen in such a word as *priest*. Christianity touched the Angles and Saxons soon after they left their homeland in the north of Germany, fifteen hundred years ago, and the Greek word *presbyteros* was adopted to signify the spiritual elders of the tribes who taught the new doctrines. Over the centuries, that word wore down to *preost*, and that to *priest*. Then when the sixteenth century reformers of the faith wanted a new word to signify the leaders of the new sects, they went back to Greek and borrowed the same word all over again, and we have the priest on one side and the presbyter on the other. Similar changes have taken place in far shorter periods. In such words as *brought*, or *thought*, the *gh* was pronounced (somewhat like the Scottish *ch* in *loch*, or the German *ch* in *achtung*) in Chaucer's day, less than six hundred years ago. Two hundred years ago, all reputable speakers pronounced *deaf* to rime with *leaf*, and some grandmothers still pronounce it that way. Yet as the sounds have changed, the spelling has often remained the same.

There have been, also, other complicating factors. The scholars do not like the illogicalities of spelling any more than students do, and they have made many attempts (often misguided ones) to introduce order and simplification to the confusion. Sometimes they have attempted to go back to the "original word." Latin scholars, for example, decided that since Chaucer's word *dette* had made its way into English from the Latin *debitus*, it would be simpler and more "proper" to spell it *debt*. Other scholars decided that the perfectly good Anglo-Saxon word *iland* must have been derived from the same root as the word *isle*, which came into the language later from Norman French; so they spelled *iland* as *island*. In another sort of change, after the settlement of America, Noah Webster decided that American writers should drop the *u* from such English spellings as *colour* or *labour,* and spell the words *color* and *labor.* Although it is usage alone that establishes correctness, these particular prescriptions took hold; the best writers began to use the prescribed forms; and because those forms are now used by the best writers, they are now correct.

Not all attempts to simplify spelling have been so successful. As recently as the turn of the present century, Theodore Roosevelt threw all the weight of his tremendous energy and all the prestige of the presidential office behind a new effort to "simplify" English spelling. The federal government, many colleges, and some publishers adopted such spellings as *tho, thru, altho,* and *thoro.* But the reputable writers, the court of final appeal in such matters, simply refused to use them, and now they are rarely or never seen in books or carefully edited periodicals.

Nor are current schemes to simplify English spelling likely to be any more successful. The problem is more complex than it seems at first glance. Ideally, words should be spelled phonetically, that is, as they are pronounced. Yet even so apparently simple a solution is complicated. We have already seen that sounds change, sometimes quite rapidly. (We all know people who still meticulously retain the French pronunciation of the word we all spell as *garage,* carefully saying GA·RÁHZH where most of us say GA·RÁHDG and where the lower-class Englishman says frankly GÁRE·IDG.) Our spelling was almost phonetic when Chaucer was writing, just before the introduction of printing tended to fix spellings; and then the sounds changed, and have kept on changing. If we are to spell words as they are pronounced, the first question is: As they are pronounced when? Shall we be constantly changing spelling as our sounds change? It is hard enough now to learn a fixed spelling, much less to try to keep up with constant changes. Another question arises: As words are pronounced by whom? The Englishman, the Australian, the Bostonian, the Mississippian, the Chicagoan—all pronounce words differently. Whose pronunciation shall be taken as the standard? And who shall decide when an accepted spelling is to be changed? With all these considerations in mind, it should be clear that there is not much chance that spelling will be made easier. It will be necessary for you, rather, to improve your spelling to conform to standard practice.

THE IMPORTANCE OF SPELLING

Nothing is more obvious to the educated reader, nothing brings quicker scorn, than poor spelling, at least partly because everyone has some trouble with spelling and consequently few have patience with what seems to be lazy unwillingness to improve. The educated writer is expected to spell as others do, and no excuses are accepted.

And improvement can certainly be made, even though improvement is harder for some people than for others. (If you are a really bad speller, if you genuinely try but still have trouble with common, little words, if you literally cannot see the difference between such words as *trial* and *trail,* you have a special problem that needs expert help. But you can still improve. Your college Reading Clinic may be qualified to help you, or in large cities special remedial centers—some better than others—are available. You cannot go to them too soon.) Most poor spellers have merely never taken the trouble to learn to spell the comparatively few words they miss. As long as they were given *A*'s and *B*'s for their work, there really seemed to be no need to learn.

But your college instructors may prove less lenient. Since most students can spell conventionally, and since most poor spelling is merely a sign of laziness and indifference, college instructors, in English or any other subject, have little patience with it. Unless the instructors are unusually charitable, the day of *A*'s and *B*'s is over for the careless speller. And after college, the handicap imposed by poor spelling grows. At all stages of your career, poor spelling will brand you as ignorant, and will amuse as well as confuse your reader.

IMPROVING SPELLING DEFICIENCIES

Learning to spell, as late as your college years, is hard. It will require constant, individual effort for a long period, because your habits—bad habits here—are firmly fixed, and it will take determination and persistence to correct them. Fortunately, however, hard as the job is, it is not as hard as you think. You already spell most

Sp 1/2   SPELLING

words and most types of words correctly. Even a word you habitually miss is usually correct except for one or two letters. Further, your misspellings fall into discoverable groups and can be corrected by groups. To improve your spelling, you need first to learn what words you misspell and how you misspell them, second to learn the patterns of English spelling which will help you determine the proper forms, and third to discover ways to fix especially difficult words in your memory.

1. PERSONAL SPELLING LIST

Before you can begin to improve your spelling you must know where the trouble lies. What words and what types of words do you misspell and how do you misspell them? To discover where your trouble lies, keep a personal spelling list in your notebook. From every theme, from every other piece of writing you do, record the words you miss. Write out, this one more time, the misspelled form of the word as well as the correct spelling. (If you are a really bad speller, keep the list on three-by-five-inch cards, so that you can easily look to see if a given word has already been entered. If it has, make a check mark for each recurrence.) Any words you find yourself missing three or four times should be given particular attention. This list of your own problem words has a number of advantages. One of them is that it warns you to *doubt* your handling of particular words as you write, for obviously until you doubt your present practice, you can scarcely begin to form new habits. Not less important is the fact that it teaches you which words or types of words to doubt, so that you need not any longer regard the whole problem with numb despair.

2. DIAGNOSING THE TROUBLE

After a few themes have provided you with a representative sample of your mistakes, examine your misspellings, if necessary in consultation with your instructor. What kind of mistake are you making? You may find—and you should be embarrassed if you do—that practically all your errors result from sheer carelessness. If you can spell all the words that you use when you are thinking about spelling, your problem is easily solved: *Think about spelling* as you revise your themes, or even as you write them. There is no conceivable excuse for carelessness in a matter that can have such immediate bad effects.

The chances are, however, that the difficulty will not be so easily removed. An intelligent student who spells badly is more likely to have something besides carelessness to cope with. You may find that you do not know when to double consonants before suffixes, or when to use *ei* instead of *ie*, or when to drop or retain a final *e*. If some such confusion troubles you, most of your misspellings can be corrected by using the "spelling rules" you have repeatedly met but never mastered. They will frequently give you a clear path to follow, particularly if you remember that they are not "rules" at all, but very useful generalizations about what happens in large classes of words.

You will probably discover, though, that the trouble lies deeper than that. You may confuse the vowels in unaccented syllables, which we do not normally pronounce clearly, so that your ear is no guide even if you pronounce words properly. Or you may find that you misspell because you do *not* pronounce words properly, that you omit or add syllables unconventionally; that is, you spell what you say, but do not say what your readers assume you are trying to write. *Canidate* for *candidate* is a ready example; others are *strickly* for *strictly*, or the dropping of *-ed* from past participles. Or you may confuse similar words, even such common words as *to* and *too*.

Currently, the most frequent difficulty of all arises from the way you were first taught to read. (It is not always your fault if you are a poor speller, but it will be if you remain one.) If you were taught to read from the first by recognizing whole words at once, instead of by syllables—if in the first grade you saw and recognized *cat* instead of *c-a-t*, and later *separate* instead of *sep-a-rate*—you may never really have seen the words you misspell. Thousands of students, even when they are writing common words, begin and end with confidence and glory, but slither through the middle as best they can. All they know of a given word is that it begins and ends with certain letters, that it takes up approximately an inch on the page, and that there are no conspicuous letters, like *k*'s or *x*'s, anywhere in it. So they write *convience*, call it *conveni-ence*, and think, "I just can't spell."

Examine your misspellings carefully and try to identify your personal difficulty. The examples just given do not exhaust the possible kinds of trouble, but they do include the most common ones, and they should suggest the diagnostic method that will make it possible for you to work intelligently at the task of improving. Once you learn where your trouble lies, work on that trouble, in recurring words or in new words that bother you. Remember that *you never miss a whole word;* without making careless mistakes anywhere, concentrate on the parts of the word you do miss.

3. USING THE DICTIONARY

Whenever you enter a word in your spelling list, go to your dictionary for the correct spelling. Do not guess; *know* that you are entering it correctly. And do not just glance at the word, then write it down and forget it. You know already that that method will do no good, since you now have to turn to the dictionary again and again for certain words, without ever learning them. Instead, make intelligent use of the dictionary; it is one of your strongest allies.

a. Syllabic division

Look at the word carefully, syllable by syllable, with particular attention to the syllables you misspell. (If you are uncertain about the system your dictionary uses to indicate syllabic division, consult the explanations at the front of the book.)

b. Pronunciation

Pronounce the word carefully, syllable by syllable, stressing the troublesome part.[1] (If you are uncertain about the system your dictionary uses to indicate pronunciation, study the detailed discussion.) Our spelling is far from phonetic, but in a sense most of our words are spelled as they are pronounced. If a word contains a "long *a*" sound, for example, the vowel may be spelled any one of several ways (as in *gate, hail, day, steak, rein, obey, fiancée,* or even *gauge*), but you can be sure it is not spelled *ow* or *ck*. The letter *a*

[1] This careful, syllabic pronunciation, stressing the syllables which may cause trouble, is a device to use in studying spelling, not in normal speech. Overprecise pronunciation in speaking is no solution to anything. In fact, since many troublesome syllables are troublesome because they are not stressed in normal speech, misapplication of this advice might merely lead to confusion.

USING THE DICTIONARY ——————————— **Sp 3c**

in a word may not represent the long *a* sound of *gate*. It may represent the *a* of *arm*, or *can*, or *bath* (however you pronounce that), or *raw*, or any one of four or five other sounds. But it will not represent the sound in *foot*. Some of our consonants are "hard," like the *g* of *rag*, or "soft," like the *g* of *rage*. Some are "voiced," like the *s* of *lose*, or "voiceless," like the *s* of *loose*. A few consonantal sounds may be spelled several ways, like the *f* sound of *fish* and the *f* sound of *enough* or of *philosophy*. But most of our consonants represent fairly definite and identifiable sounds, and those sounds call for definite and dependable letters. Within these limits, and in this sense, most of our words are spelled as they are pronounced.

Pronounce the word carefully, *by syllables,* when you look up the spelling, and much of your difficulty may vanish. If you adopt such careful pronunciation as a regular practice when you are checking spelling, you should in time begin to recognize familiar letter combinations as they recur, and you will begin to be able to predict what combinations may be possible. Our later discussion will suggest the ways by which you can learn to choose the right combinations for any particular word.

There is at least one further way in which careful pronunciation by syllables as you check the spelling of a word will help. If you habitually leave out certain syllables, if you write *convience* for *convenience* or *rember* for *remember,* you can spot the difficulty readily by pronouncing the troublesome word as you revise your paper. In each of the examples just given, you would find yourself a syllable short. It should be no great trouble then to insert the missing syllable.

c. Derivation

It is often helpful to know something about the ancestry of a word. For one thing, it helps you to understand the presence of letters no longer pronounced, like the *gh* in *thought* or even like the *b* in *debt,* which has never been pronounced in English. It helps you to see relations between words you might not otherwise recognize as members of a word family. *Anthropology* and *philanthropy,* for example, share the Greek root word for man, *anthropos.* Recognizing such roots will help fix a shaky spelling. Also there are many classical or Anglo-Saxon prefixes and suffixes which constantly reappear, *in-, -ible, -ness*. Recognizing them in a new word,

Sp 3d/4a–b   SPELLING

and knowing something of how they affect spellings, will often help. Whenever you can, use the derivation of a word to help you remember its present form.

d. Entry in personal spelling list

After you have taken these three steps, enter the word in your personal spelling list.

4. VISUAL SPELLING

a. The image in longhand

As you enter the word in your spelling list, correctly spelled and in your own handwriting, *look at it.* Look at the whole word, but focus your attention particularly on the syllables you misspell. If it is a word you habitually misspell, this will be the first time you ever saw the word as it should look in your own handwriting. You have seen it frequently in print, but the visual patterns made by a word in print and in your own longhand are quite different things. Fascinate and *fascinate* do not look very much alike, and seeing the word in print a thousand times will do little to make you realize you have done something wrong if you read over your own themes and see *facinate* on the page.

b. Fixing the image

Look at the word you have just written (correctly, remember) for a full minute. Now close your eyes and see if you can visualize it. You will not be able to see it as clearly as you can see your own signature, the specimen of your handwriting you have seen most often, but you should be able literally to see the word. If the image is vague, look at the word again and again until you can see it clearly. (Inability to form such visual images may be a sign of a special problem. Bad spellers who cannot form visual images should seek expert help, beginning with the college Reading Clinic or special classes in spelling.)

Fixing such a visual image of the correct form will at least help to warn you, as you revise a paper, that a given word is wrong, and it may well help you to get it right. You already use the method, in an unmethodical sort of way. How many times have you turned to a sheet of scratch paper and tried out various combinations "to see which looks right"? If you have given yourself clear visual images of the correct form of these troublesome words, you can very easily pick out the correct combination.

5. FINGER SPELLING

We usually do not realize how much of our spelling is done by our fingers, without much prompting from our brains. When you want to write the conjunction *and,* for example, you never think *a-n-d.* You just write *and.* Again, how often do your thoughts get ahead of your hand? You are writing, say, "I plan to explain my opinion," and the *pl* of *plan* gets mixed up with the *pl* of *explain;* when you revise you wonder how on earth you came to write, "I plain my opinion," as if you were your own two-year-old nephew just learning to talk. In the same way, *rember* for *remember* is probably a finger mistake, the first *em* carrying over into the second. If your misspellings often contain such slips as *thought* for *though, throught* for *throughout, posses* for *possesses,* much of your trouble may lie in bad finger habits—that, and carelessness in proofreading. Some students, too, have trouble with different words when they type than when they write in longhand. Fingers again.

In order to teach the muscles and nerves of your fingers to write a word correctly, *make them write it correctly.* After you have fixed the visual image of the word, practice writing it. Write it out ten or a dozen times. The next day, do it again. *Do not* try to increase the dosage. If you set out to write the word twenty times or a hundred times instead of ten or a dozen, you will soon cease to concentrate, and your fingers will fool you by reverting to their old habits until you are actually practicing your mistakes. It is better by far to write a word correctly ten times a day for ten days than a hundred times at a single sitting.

6. MEMORY AIDS

In spite of all your efforts to follow these directions diligently, a few words will get by you. Or perhaps you are fortunate enough to be bothered by only a few words to begin with. There are ways to learn even these words. If you find that certain words are causing trouble again and again, throw your dignity away and invent memory crutches to help you. It doesn't matter how ridiculous they are.

Sp 6   SPELLING

In fact, the more ridiculous they are, the easier it will be to remember them. The pun involved in "The cemetery is full of ease" may be painful, but that pain will keep you from writing *cemetery* with an *a*. "The end of *friend* is *end*" may make little sense, but it will help you spell *friend*. "There is *a rat* in *separate*" may be sheer nonsense. What of it? It is useful. The word *lice* may help you remember the *li* of *relieve* and *believe* and the *ce* of *receive, deceive, conceive, perceive*.

The more you know about languages, of course, the easier the problem becomes. If *license* bothers you, and you know Latin, remember *licentia;* the second consonant could only be a *c*. If *discipline* bothers you, a medieval collection of rules to be followed by monks was called *Disciplina Clericalis*. The student who knows Latin can be sure of the spellings of *license* and *discipline* if he remembers the pronunciation of *licentia* and *disciplina*. Many other words can be similarly fixed in mind. You must, however, work at this consciously, or you will find yourself using English spellings in French class and French spellings in English themes, and being wrong both times.

But even if you know only English, there are many devices you can use. Try capitalizing trouble spots; write *con-VEN-i-ence*. Try mispronouncing for spelling alone. Does *separate* cause trouble? When you have to write it, say SEP-AY-RATE to yourself. Or shift a word from one part of speech to another. If you are uncertain of the third vowel of *definite* and habitually write the syllable with an *a*, remember that we clearly pronounce accented vowels and slur unaccented ones. (Really we pronounce most unaccented vowels about alike, as *uh*, like the last sound in *China*.) Shift the doubtful word into another part of speech, one in which suffixes shift the accent. You can never identify the third vowel in *definite*, but in *definition* the accent falls on the doubtful syllable; the letter could only be an *i*. Even the difficult *-able, -ible, -ance,* and *-ence* words can be managed, particularly since you will probably find that very few of them bother you. The shifted stresses of *dispensable—dispensation, existence—existential,* and such words can often help. Verbs ending in *-hend* go to adjectives in *-sive* or *-sible: comprehend—comprehensive —comprehensible*. One you can remember because it seems odd: *resistance* BUT *resistible*. Visual images, finger spelling, memory aids, and regular patterns all help.

7. REGULAR PATTERNS

It was suggested earlier that most words are spelled according to their sounds, as those sounds are represented by limited letter-combinations which follow regular patterns. Some of those patterns you know already, and many others cause you little trouble even though you are not consciously aware of them. Wherever such patterns will help you in learning to spell troublesome words, make use of them. Think of other words of similar sound and spelling, words you spell correctly already. They may help you see the pattern they are following.

A few patterns may be pointed out, to suggest the method or to indicate combinations you might not easily discover for yourself.

a. Length of vowel

In such words as *rate, secede, stripe, rope, brute,* the long vowel is followed by a single consonant and a silent *e*. When the *e* is dropped before certain suffixes (see also Spelling Rules 8c, d, and e, page 169), the vowel sound remains long and the consonant remains single, as in *rating, seceded, striping, ropy, brutish.*

Short-vowel sounds often occur before single consonants without a final, silent *e*, as in *brag, bed, drip, drop, rut.* Followed by vowels, as in many suffixes, the consonants are usually doubled: *bragging, bedding, dripping, dropped, rutted.*

Become is one of the few words that trip you here. It has a shortened vowel, but a single consonant and a silent *e*; with the suffix, it does not, as many students suppose, double the *m*. It is *becoming,* not *becomming.* (Notice that you will tend to pronounce those two with slightly different vowel sounds, if you really stop to think.)

b. un-, dis-, mis-

Such common prefixes as *un-, dis-, mis-* do not affect the spelling of the root word to which they are added. There is one *s* in *dis-,* one initial *s* in *satisfy,* and the two, joined, provide a double *s: dissatisfy.* But *appear* has no *s*, and so when *dis-* is added, only one *s* can be needed: *disappear.* The same principle applies to *unnatural, unappetizing, misspell, mistake.*

Some other prefixes cause trouble of a somewhat different kind. They often appear with roots that are less easily recognized, and they may themselves vary slightly in spelling. The pronunciation of the words offers the best guide: *homogeneous* but *homeopathic, archbishop* but *architect.*

c. *in-, com-*

A difficult variation of that pattern occurs with *in-, com-,* and a few other prefixes that are less common. As before, the prefixes do not affect the spelling of the roots, but the roots often affect the spelling of these prefixes. Before Latin roots beginning with *l, m,* or *r,* the *n* of *in-* is changed to the same letter as the initial of the root. Thus there are two *l*'s in *illuminate* (*in* + *luminare*), two *m*'s in *immediate,* two *r*'s in *irresistible.* (Before Anglo-Saxon roots the change does not occur: *inlet, inmate, inroad.*)

Com- becomes *con-* before most consonants: *concave, confess, conjugate,* and so on. Before *l* and *r,* the *m* becomes *l* or *r,* like the *col-* and *cor-* in *collaborate* and *corroborate.*

Among the others we might mention *ad-,* which accounts for the doubled letters early in such words as *account* itself, *affiliate,* and *aggression.* (See also Spelling Rules 8c, d, and e.)

d. *-ly, -ness*

Such suffixes as *-ly,* or *-ness* are simply added to the root. The chief troublemaker is *-ly.* Does the root word end in *l*? If so, when you add *-ly,* you will have two *l*'s as in *real* + *ly* = *really, cool* + *ly* = *coolly,* and so on. Similarly, *barren* + *ness* = *barrenness.*

e. Shifts in parts of speech

A *b* in a verb often becomes a *p* in a noun, as in *describe–description.* A *d, r,* or *t* in a verb often becomes *s* in a noun, as in *decide–decision, inquire–inquisition, convert–conversion.* The *c* in *-ence* nouns often becomes *t* in adjectives: *influence–influential, difference–different–differential, confluence–confluent.*

f. Plurals

Do plurals bother you? We usually add an *s* to the singular: *boy–boys.* If the singular ends in an *s* (or *z*) sound, or in a *ch, sh,* or *dg* sound, we add a syllable when we pronounce the plural, and we spell it *-es: classes, matches, brushes, judges.*

SPELLING RULES   Sp 7g/8a

When a noun ends in *y* preceded by a consonant, we change the *y* to *i* and add *-es*: *lady—ladies*, *baby—babies*. When a noun ends in *o*, we usually add *-es*: *Negro—Negroes*, *hero—heroes*, *potato—potatoes*, *tomato—tomatoes*. (Be careful to remember why the *e* appears. Do not pull it back into the singular and write *heroe*, or *potatoe*.) There are many nouns ending in *o*, however, which add only *-s*. They are likely to be musical terms from Italian sources, like *sopranos, pianos, solos;* but there are some others, like *silos*. If your visual image of the word or a memory crutch does not help, doubtful words ending in *o* had better be checked in the dictionary.

g. Troublesome prefixes and suffixes

Some troublesome prefixes and suffixes remain. It is easy to confuse *ante-* and *anti-*, *de-* and *di-*, *dis-* and *dys-*, *hyper-* and *hypo-*, *inter-* and *intra-*, *per-* and *pre-*. The only cures lie in studying the derivations of the words and the meanings of the prefixes, and in pronouncing the words carefully. Fortunately, only a few words may bother you. Your own spelling list will tell you which words recur, and your clear visual images of those words will serve to keep them straight.

8. SPELLING RULES

Last in the devices which will help you improve your spelling are the spelling "rules." They are like the regular patterns in spelling we have just been considering in that they indicate what usually happens in certain common spelling situations. They are unlike them in that they are extremely, even excessively, familiar to you, and so far they may not have helped very much. But if you really try to use them, they will help a great deal. (The "rules" are not rules, of course, but merely codifications of what is done most of the time, hence the "exceptions" that have long plagued you.)

Actually only about half a dozen of the rules are really helpful. You have seen them often before, but this time, perhaps, you mean business.

The following six rules are the most useful.

a. *Ie* and *ei*

When a word with an *ie* or an *ei* is pronounced with a long *e*, the most frequent form is *ie*. The *ei* usually follows a soft *c*. You know the rhyme,

167

Sp 8a–b SPELLING

I before *e*
Except after *c*.

Use it.

Many people find the code word *lice* more useful (*i* follows *l*, as in *relieve, believe,* and *e* follows *c,* as in *receive, conceive.* In *lice* itself, *i* comes before *e*, as it most often does). If that method seems more memorable, use the code word *lice.* If you remember that *the rule applies only to the long* e *sound,* there are nine fairly common exceptions—or perhaps only six: *either, financier, inveigle, leisure, neither, seize, sheik, species, weird.* (They can be put into a sentence of sorts: *Neither financier could inveigle the sheik to seize either species of weird leisure.*) But some people pronounce *either* and *neither* with a long *i*, not a long *e*, and the British pronounce *leisure* to rime with *pleasure,* so none of these three can be called a universal exception: If the word is pronounced any other way than with a long *e*, the spelling is usually *ei.* Some examples of words pronounced other ways: *weigh, neighbor, counterfeit, foreign, reign.* Some exceptions: *fiery, friend, mischief, view.*

After all that discussion—and all the times you have read similar discussions—it scarcely seems reasonable to remark that only four words ever bother you, and only two bother you often. It might be simplest just to learn them:

receive, deceive, perceive, conceive

b. Doubling final consonant

When a word ends in a single consonant preceded by a single vowel, with the accent on the final syllable (or on the only syllable, if there is only one), the final consonant is doubled before a suffix beginning with a vowel.

strip + *ing* = *stripping*
whip + *ed* = *whipped*

The rule is important. Every sentence has at least one verb, and by far the greater number of our verbs form their past tenses and past participles by adding -*ed.* All of them form their present participles and their gerunds by adding -*ing.* So those two endings alone, on verbs alone, bring this rule into play over and over. And other forms occur, as in

SPELLING RULES   Sp 8b–f

    begin—beginner   occur—occurrence
    bid—bidder   quiz—quizzes

Remember that the rule applies only to words of one syllable or to words accented on the last syllable. If the accent falls earlier, or if the accent shifts to an earlier syllable when the prefix is added, the final consonant is *not* doubled. Thus:

    bénefit, bénefited
    prefér, preférred, but préference

c. Final silent *e* before consonants

When a word ends in silent *e*, retain the *e* when adding a suffix beginning with a consonant, as in *achievement, arrangement, completely, desperately.*

Some common exceptions: *argument, awful, probably, truly, wholly.*

In such words as *development, developement, judgment, judgement,* the first form is more common in American usage, the second in British. For an American audience, prefer the American spelling.

d. Final silent *e* before vowels

When a word ends in silent *e*, drop the *e* when adding a suffix beginning with a vowel, as in *achieving, arranging, completing.*

Some exceptions:

After soft *c* or *g* before *a* or *o*, as in *advantageous, courageous, noticeable.*

To prevent mispronunciation or confusion with other words, as in *hoeing, shoeing, dyeing, singeing.*

e. Consonant plus *y* before suffixes

Words ending in a consonant plus *y* change the *y* to *i* before any suffix not beginning with *i*. The suffixes *-es* and *-ed* are especially common. The suffix *-ing* provides the chief exceptions.

    baby, babies; city, cities; dry, dries; try, tries
    happy, happily, happiness; duty, dutiful, dutiable
    BUT: *study, studying; cry, crying; try, trying* (Both the *y* and the *i*
        are pronounced.)

f. SEED words

Words that end in the sound SEED usually spell the final syllable *-cede,* as in *concede, precede, recede, secede.*

Sp 8f/9a SPELLING

Three words use -ceed: *exceed, proceed, succeed.*
One word uses -sede: *supersede.*

9. SPELLING LISTS

The following lists are made up of words that students often use and often misspell. Examine all of the lists carefully and learn the spelling of any words in these lists that you are unsure about. Since these are common words, your instructor will be very unfavorably impressed by inability to spell them correctly.

a. Words often misspelled because of careless pronunciation

SYLLABLES AND LETTERS OMITTED

accidentally	laboratory	really
Arctic	length	recognize
boundary	liable	representative
candidate	library	sophomore
curiosity	literature	strictly
everybody	mathematics	superintendent
February	miniature	surprise
generally	occasionally	temperament
geography	probably	usually
government	quantity	valuable
history		

SYLLABLES AND LETTERS ADDED

athletics	height	privilege
disastrous	hindrance	remembrance
drowned	lightning	similar
elm	mischievous	suffrage
entrance	momentous	translate
grievous	prejudice	umbrella

SOUNDS CHANGED OR LETTERS TRANSPOSED

accurate	formerly	perform
description	introduce	preparation
despair	irrelevant	restaurant
divide	optimistic	sacrilegious
existence	particular	separate

170

SPELLING LISTS — 8p 9b

b. Similar words often confused

accent, ascent, assent
accept, except
advice, advise
affect, effect
aisle, isle
all ready, already
all together, altogether
allowed, aloud
allusive, elusive, illusive
altar, alter
angel, angle
aught, ought
baring, barring, bearing
berth, birth
born, borne
breath, breathe
Britain, Briton
buy, by
canvas, canvass
capital, capitol
choose, chose
cite, sight, site
close, clothes, cloths
coarse, course
complement, compliment
conscience, conscious
core, corps, corpse
council, counsel, consul
dairy, diary
desert, dessert
device, devise
dual, duel
dyeing, dying
fair, fare
finally, finely
formally, formerly
forth, forty, fourth
hear, here
heard, herd
hole, whole
holy, wholly

huge, Hugh
human, humane
instance, instants
irrelevant, irreverent
it's, its
knew, new
know, no
later, latter
lead, led
lessen, lesson
loath, loathe
loose, lose
luxuriant, luxurious
material, matériel
medium, media (*pl.*)
mind, mine
moral, morale
of, off
passed, past
peace, piece
personal, personnel
plain, plane
planed, planned
precede, proceed
precedence, precedents, presidents
presence, presents
principal, principle
prophecy, prophesy
quiet, quite
respectably, respectfully, respectively
reverend, reverent
right, rite, wright, write
sense, since
shone, shown
staid, stayed
stationary, stationery
statue, statute, stature
steal, steel
straight, strait

171

than, then
their, there, they're
therefor, therefore
threw, through
till, until
to, too, two
track, tract

troop, troupe
waist, waste
weak, week
weather, whether
which, witch
who's, whose
you're, your

c. General Spelling List

(This list does not necessarily include all the words or all the forms of words in the specialized lists. Study all three lists carefully.)

absence
absurd
accept
accidentally
accommodate
accompanied
accumulate
accustomed
achieved
acquainted
across
address
advantageous
advice
advise
aerial
affect
aggravate
aggression
agreeable
aisle
alley
allotted
all right
already
altar
alter
altogether
alumna(ae)
alumnus(i)
always

amateur
among
amount
analysis
analyze
angel
angle
annual
answer
anxiety
apartment
apology
apparatus
apparent
appearance
appreciate
appropriate
Arctic
argument
arithmetic
around
arouse
arrangement
arrival
article
ascend
assassin
association
athlete
athletics
attacked

attendance
attractive
audience
auxiliary
awkward
bachelor
balance
banana
barbarous
baring
barring
battalion
bearing
becoming
before
beggar
beginning
believe
believing
beneficial
benefited
berth
birth
biscuit
born
borne
boundaries
breath
breathe
bridle
brilliant

SPELLING LISTS — Sp 9c

Britain	commit	criticize
Britannica	committed	cruelty
Briton	committee	curiosity
bulletin	comparative	curious
buoyant	comparison	curriculum
bureau	compel	cylinder
business	compelled	dealt
busyness	competent	deceit
cafeteria	competition	deceive
calendar	complement	decent
candidate	completely	decide
cannot	compliment	decision
can't	comrade	deferred
canvas	concede	definite
canvass	conceivable	definition
capital	conceive	descend
capitol	conferred	descendant
captain	confident	describe
carburetor	connoisseur	description
career	conqueror	desert
carriage	conscience	desirable
carrying	conscientious	despair
cavalry	conscious	desperate
ceiling	considered	dessert
cemetery	consistent	device
certain	contemptible	devise
changeable	continuous	dictionary
changing	control	difference
characteristic	controlled	digging
chauffeur	convenient	dilapidated
choose	coolly	dining
chose	copies	dinning
chosen	corner	diphtheria
cite	corps	disappear
climbed	corpse	disappoint
close	council	disastrous
clothes	counsel	discipline
cloths	country	discussion
coarse	courageous	disease
colonel	course	dissatisfied
column	courteous	distribute
coming	courtesy	divide
commission	criticism	divine

173

doctor
doesn't
don't
dormitories
drudgery
dual
duel
dyeing
dying
ecstasy
effect
efficiency
efficient
eighth
eligible
eliminate
embarrass
eminent
emphasize
employed
employees
encouragement
encouraging
enemy
entirely
environment
equipment
equipped
equivalent
erroneous
especially
etc.
exaggerate
exceed
excel
excellent
except
exercise
exhaust
exhilaration
existence
exorbitant
expense

experience
explanation
extension
extraordinary
extremely
familiar
fascinate
February
fiery
Filipino
finally
financial
financier
forehead
foreigner
foremost
forfeit
forgo, forego
formally
formerly
forth
forty
fourth
frantically
fraternities
friend
fundamental
furniture
further
gage
gallant
gauge
generally
genius
ghost
government
governor
grammar
grandeur
grief
grievous
guarantee
guard

guidance
handkerchief
handsome
harass
having
height
hero
heroes
hesitancy
hindrance
hoping
hopping
huge
Hugh
hurriedly
hygiene
hypocrisy
imaginary
imitation
immediately
impromptu
incidental
incidentally
incredible
independence
indigestible
indispensable
inevitable
infinite
influential
ingenious
ingenuous
initiation
innocence
innocents
instance
instants
intellectual
intelligence
intelligent
intentionally
intercede
interested

invitation
irrelevant
irresistible
it's (it is)
its
itself
knowledge
laboratory
laid
later
latter
lead
led
legitimate
leisure
liable
library
lightning
likely
literature
livelihood
loneliness
loose
lose
lying
magazine
maintain
maintenance
maneuver
(manoeuver,
manoeuvre)
manual
manufacture
marriage
material
matériel
mathematics
meant
medicine
medium(*s*),
 media (*pl.*)
merely
messenger

metal
mettle
miniature
minute
miscellaneous
mischievous
misspell
momentous
moral
morale
mortgage
mosquitoes
murmur
muscle
mussel
mysterious
naïve
naphtha
naturally
necessarily
Negroes
neither
nevertheless
nickel
niece
nineteen
ninetieth
ninety
ninth
noticeable
notoriety
nowadays
nucleus
obedience
oblige
obstacle
occasion
occasionally
occur
occurred
occurrence
o'clock
of

off
officer
omission
omitted
oneself, one's self
operate
opinion
opportunity
optimism
optimistic
organization
origin
original
outrageous
overrun
pageant
paid
pamphlet
parliament
parliamentary
particularly
partner
passed
past
pastime
peace
perceive
perform
perhaps
permanent
permissible
perseverance
persistent
personal
personnel
perspiration
persuade
phenomenon(a)
physically
Philippines
physician
picnic
picnicking

Sp 9c

piece
plain
plane
planed
planned
pleasant
politician
politics
possess
possession
possible
potato
potatoes
practicable
practically
practice
prairie
precede
precedence
precedents
preceding
prefer
preference
preferred
prejudice
preparation
presence
presents
presidents
prevalent
primitive
principal
principle
prisoner
privilege
probably
procedure
proceed
profession
professor
prominent
pronounce
pronunciation

propaganda
propeller
prophecy
prophesied
prophesy
prove
psychology
publicly
pulling
purchase
pursuit
quantity
quarter
quiet
quite
quiz
quizzes
rarefied
ready
realize
really
recede
receive
recognize
recommend
refer
reference
referred
regard
region
reign
rein
relieve
religion
religious
remembrance
renown
repetition
replies
representative
reservoir
resistance
respectably

respectfully
respectively
restaurant
rhetoric
rheumatism
rhythm
ridiculous
sacrifice
sacrilegious
safety
salary
sandwich
scarcely
scene
schedule
science
scientific
secretary
seize
sense
sentence
sentinel
separate
sergeant
several
severely
shepherd
shining
shinning
shone
shown
shriek
siege
significance
significant
similar
sincerely
site
smooth
soliloquy
sophomore
source
speak

specimen
speech
statement
stationary
stationery
statue
stature
statute
stopped
stopping
strength
strenuous
stretch
strictly
studying
succeed
successful
suffrage
superintendent
supersede
supplement
suppress
surely
surprise
syllable
symmetry
temperament
temperature
tendency
than
their

then
there
therefor
therefore
they're
thorough
thousandths
threw
through
tired
to
together
too
tournament
track
tract
tragedy
transferred
treacherous
tries
truly
Tuesday
twelfth
two
typical
tyrannically
tyranny
unanimous
undoubtedly
universally

unnecessary
unprecedented
until
unusually
usage
using
valuable
vegetable
vengeance
view
vigilance
village
villain
warring
weather
Wednesday
weird
welfare
whether
which
wholly
who's
whose
witch
women
won't
writer
writing
written
yacht

5

Manuscript Conventions

Ms   Manuscript

Leg   1. Legibility, 180
                2. The page, 181
                    a. Paper, 181
                    b. Margins, 181

c. Spacing, 181

] or ¶   d. Indention, 182
                3. Paging, 182
                4. Endorsement, 182
                5. Final revision, 182

^   a. Insertions, 183

ꝃ   b. Cross-outs, material to be deleted, 183

¶ or *No* ¶   c. Designating paragraphs, 183
                6. Titles, 184
                    a. Capitalization in titles, 184
                    b. Titles as antecedents, 184

Cap, Lc   7. Capitalization and lower case, 184
                    a. Capitals, 184
                        1) Proper nouns and adjectives, 184
                        2) The first word of a sentence, 185
                        3) The first word of a quotation, 185

MANUSCRIPT CONVENTIONS — **Ms**

      4) The major words of a title, 185
      5) Titles of honor, 185
      6) The first word of a line of poetry, 185
      7) Salutation and complimentary close, 185
      8) *I* and *O*, 186
   b. No capitals (lower case), 186
      1) Points of the compass, 186
      2) Seasons, 186
      3) Nouns of family relationship, 186
      4) Academic classes, 186
      5) Academic courses, 186
      6) Words like *high school* and *college,* 187

Ital   8. Italics, 187
   a. Emphasis, 187
   b. Titles of complete works, 187
   c. Names of ships, planes, etc., 187
   d. Foreign words and phrases, 188
   e. Words, letters, etc., as symbols, 188

= / **or Syl**   9. Hyphens and syllabication, 188
   a. Hyphens, 188
      1) Compound nouns, 188
      2) Compound modifiers, 188
      3) Guides to compounding: The dictionary, 189
      4) Guides to compounding: Accent, 189
      5) Some categories, 189
         a) A prefix plus a proper noun, 189
         b) Compound numerals and fractions, 189
         c) Compounds with *self-*, 190
         d) Hyphens to avoid confusion, 190
         e) Coined compound adjectives, 190
   b. Syllabication, 190
      1) Division by syllables, according to pronunciation, 190
      2) A single-vowel syllable, 191
      3) A one-letter prefix and a two-letter suffix, 191
      4) Doubled consonants, 191
      5) Hyphenated compounds, 191
      6) Single-word compounds, 191

Ms 1 _____ MANUSCRIPT CONVENTIONS

        c. Other uses of the dividing hyphen, 191
           1) In spelling out, 191
           2) In representing stuttering, 191
           3) In pairing compounds, 192

Abr   10. Abbreviations, 192
N   11. Representation of numbers, 192
        a. General principles, 192
           1) Numbers of one or two words, 192
           2) Numbers of more than two words, 192
           3) Consistency, 193
        b. Special conventions, 193
           1) Numbers beginning a sentence, 193
           2) Figures for statistics, 193
           3) Figures for dates, 193
           4) Figures for street numbers, 193
           5) Figures for decimals, 194
           6) Forms for percentage, 194
           7) Figures with A.M. and P.M., 194
           8) Forms for numbered streets, 194
           9) Numbers standing side by side, 194

There are a number of conventional practices in handling manuscript with which you should be familiar. Most of them apply not only to themes, but to writing of any kind. Consult this chapter for advice if you find that you do not know how to handle one of the conventional, mechanical problems in writing.

1. LEGIBILITY—Leg

Your instructor will be pleased if you can type your papers; but even if you type, there will be many papers, like impromptu themes and examinations, which must be written in longhand. Remember that every paper must be legible. No one will ever discover the virtues of a paper that cannot be read. It is a sign of careless disregard of the reader, not of superior eccentricity, to form your letters so individually that they cannot be deciphered. Distin-

THE PAGE ——————————————————— Ms 2a–c

guish clearly between capital letters and lower-case letters. Distinguish between *a*'s and *o*'s, *e*'s and *i*'s and *l*'s, *m*'s and *n*'s and *w*'s and *u*'s and *v*'s. Avoid flourishes that encroach on letters in the lines above and below. Write at least as plainly as a fifth-grader does, or type your papers. The symbol **Leg** always calls attention to an illegible or a messy manuscript, and the general symbol **Ms** often does.

2. THE PAGE

a. Paper

Many colleges specify particular kinds of theme paper or bluebooks for college work. If no such specification is made, handwritten papers—in blue or black ink—should be submitted on 8½" × 11" white bond paper, ruled for ⅜" lines. Do not use colored paper or flimsy paper, either unglazed paper or the thin, ripply paper that is designed for carbon copies. Do not use legal-size paper or small notebook paper. Do not use narrow-lined notebook paper, which crowds your writing and makes it very difficult for the instructor to read it.

If you type your papers, use white, 8½" × 11" paper, unruled.

Use one side of the sheet only, with either typing or longhand.

b. Margins

Never crowd your pages. Leave your instructor room for helpful comments. Standard margins are, top, 1½"; left side, 1½"; right side, 1"; bottom, 1". If papers are submitted in a folder, allow extra margin at the left.

All lines, including the last line on the page, should be carried over as nearly as possible to the right-hand margin, except for the line that ends a paragraph.

c. Spacing—#

Typed papers are always double-spaced, except for business letters and inserted quotations of over six lines, both of which are single-spaced with double spacing between paragraphs or between quotations and text.

181

Ms 2c–d _____ MANUSCRIPT CONVENTIONS

In longhand on lined paper, write on each line. Do not skip lines between paragraphs.

Leave a space between your title and the text.

If you are not familiar with standard spacing in typing, such as the single space after commas but double after periods, consult any typing manual.

d. Indention—] or ¶

Paragraphs should be indented ¾". If the paper is typed, five or six spaces is standard for paragraph indention.

3. PAGING

Number all pages, after the first, with Arabic numerals, at the top center or in the upper right-hand corner. The first page is left unnumbered, or numbered with an Arabic 1 at the bottom.

Roman numerals are often used for sections or chapters or volumes, and preface pages are usually numbered (at the bottom of the page) by lower-case Roman numerals. Roman numerals are never used for text pages. Arabic numerals are rapidly superseding Roman numerals for all uses. To translate Roman numerals into Arabic, or vice versa, consult your dictionary, under *numbers* or *Roman numerals*.

Having numbered your pages, keep them in order.

4. ENDORSEMENT

Your instructor will probably prescribe the form you are to use in endorsing your themes. If no form is prescribed, be sure at least to put your name on the outside of all papers.

It is usually not necessary to endorse any but the last page of the paper.

5. FINAL REVISION

The final copy submitted to your instructor should be as neat as possible, and revisions should be kept to the minimum. But no instructor will object to a few neat corrections on the paper he reads. In deciding whether to correct on the page or recopy, apply common-sense tests: Does the paper look as if you thought it worth taking pains? Can it be read easily?

FINAL REVISION ———————————— Ms 5a–c

a. Insertions—∧

Insertions should be written above the line and centered over the point at which they are to be read into the text. A caret (∧) is used *below* the point of insertion, thus:

not
Children should be impertinent to their elders.
∧

In typing, a virgule (/) is often used instead of a caret.

not
Children should/be impertinent to their elders.

b. Cross-outs, material to be deleted—δ, ϑ

If you wish the reader to omit words or phrases, strike through them (cross them out) with a heavy straight line. Do not enclose them in parentheses. Parentheses have a quite different function (see page 143), so that your reader, instead of omitting your unwanted phrases, will try to read them in and will usually be confused as he tries to make sense of what you have said.

Commonly, the grading symbol δ means, "You have included something here which should have been omitted."

c. Designating paragraphs—¶, No ¶

If you decide, belatedly, that a passage should have been paragraphed separately, mark it at the beginning of the passage with the symbol ¶. If you have inadvertently set up as a paragraph a passage that really belongs with the preceding paragraph, mark it at the beginning **No** ¶. But use these two symbols rarely. Your paragraphing should mark turns of your thought as it advances, and excessive use of ¶ and **No** ¶ suggests that you have been careless in your thinking. It is usually better to recopy the page.

The principal use of these instructions for last-minute revisions should come in impromptu themes. These, too, should be legible and as neat as possible, but probably your instructor will not expect you to waste the limited time of a single class period by making an impeccable final copy. Put your time, instead, on planning, writing, and revising.

183

Ms 6/7a   MANUSCRIPT CONVENTIONS

6. TITLES

Titles are centered at the top of the first page, with a space between the title and the text.

a. Capitalization in titles

Major words of a title (all but the articles, and prepositions and conjunctions of less than six letters) are capitalized. The first word and the last word are capitalized. If you type your themes, full capitals may be used, throughout the title.

Do not use quotation marks or italics (underlining) unless they are called for. (See Italics, page 187, and Quotation Marks, page 146, for their special uses.)

b. Titles as antecedents

Your title and your theme are separate items. The title foreshadows the theme, to be sure, but it should not be treated as if it were the opening sentence. In particular, avoid using a first-sentence pronoun referring to the title as antecedent. For example, do not begin a theme entitled SHOES with, "They are an utter abomination." If necessary, repeat the title.

A common exception is the book review which uses the title of the book as the title of the review, and then begins, "This book . . ." or "Miss Scriver's new romance. . . ."

7. CAPITALIZATION AND LOWER CASE—Cap, Lc

a. Capitals—Cap

1) PROPER NOUNS AND ADJECTIVES

Capitalize the names of particular persons, places, things, events, periods, and so on, and adjectives derived from such proper nouns.

John Doe	General Motors
Louisville	the Civil War
the Treaty Oak	the Colonial Period
Wednesday	English
June	Spanish

the Coronation of Elizabeth II

CAPITALIZATION AND LOWER CASE ———— **Ms 7a**

Except in journalistic practice, *street, county, river,* and so on, in geographical names are usually capitalized as part of the proper name.

First Street, Fairfax County, the Ohio River

2) THE FIRST WORD OF A SENTENCE

Capitalize the first word of a sentence.

3) THE FIRST WORD OF A QUOTATION

Capitalize the first word of a direct quotation except when the quotation is incorporated in your own sentence.

He asked, "Where are you going, my pretty maid?"
The chairman's speech was "full of sound and fury."

4) THE MAJOR WORDS OF A TITLE

Capitalize the first word, the last word, and other major words of a title (all but articles, and prepositions and conjunctions of less than six letters).

A Guide to the Nation's Capital
All Is Lost
Thoughts Concerning Glory

5) TITLES OF HONOR

Capitalize titles of honor preceding proper names.

Dr. Cole, Professor Tupper, Mr. Green
BUT: He asked the professor to go over the paper with him.

6) THE FIRST WORD OF A LINE OF POETRY

Capitalize the first word of a line of poetry.

7) SALUTATION AND COMPLIMENTARY CLOSE

Capitalize the first and last words of the salutation of a letter, and the first word of the complimentary close.

Ms 7b — MANUSCRIPT CONVENTIONS

8) *I* AND *O*

Capitalize the pronoun *I* and the vocative interjection *O*.

b. No capitals—Lc

Lc means "lower case," no capital.
Do not capitalize unnecessarily.

1) POINTS OF THE COMPASS

Do not capitalize words naming points of the compass when you are indicating a direction. Such words, however, are capitalized when they refer to specific areas of the country.

> Indianapolis is east of Denver.
> He was born in the East.

2) SEASONS

Do not capitalize seasons.

> I like spring best of all the year.

3) NOUNS OF FAMILY RELATIONSHIP

Do not capitalize nouns of family relationship unless they are used as substitutes for names or as titles preceding the name.

> She is the mother of three children.
> Tell me, Mother, where you put it.
> He is my uncle.
> Give it to Uncle George.

4) ACADEMIC CLASSES

Do not capitalize academic classes.

> Most sophomores are more arrogant than most freshmen.

5) ACADEMIC COURSES

Do not capitalize academic subjects unless they name particular courses or are proper adjectives.

> I like history better than German.
> My best course is History 171.

ITALICS — Ms 7b/8a–c

6) WORDS LIKE *high school* AND *college*

Do not capitalize words like *high school* and *college* unless they are parts of proper names.

I never studied in high school, but I have to study in college.
He is a member of the Columbian College of The George Washington University.

8. ITALICS—Ital

In longhand or typing, indicate italics by a single straight underline.

a. Emphasis

Italics are used for emphasizing words or phrases. The device should be used sparingly; it is better to secure emphasis by means of the sentence structure.

Italics for emphasis should *not* be overused.

b. Titles of complete works

Italics are used for titles of books, magazines, newspapers, and other complete works, including works of art.

Lee's Lieutenants *Paradise Lost*
The Eroica Symphony The *Saturday Review*

The in newspaper or magazine titles is not italicized, and is not capitalized unless it begins the sentence. If an identifying city name is an integral part of the name of a newspaper, it is italicized as part of the title, otherwise it is not.

He always reads the *New York Times*.
The picture appeared in the Louisville *Courier-Journal*.

Titles of short poems, even though they are complete works, are usually put in quotation marks instead of italics.

Carl Sandburg's "Fog" is well known.

c. Names of ships, planes, and so on

Italics are used for names of ships, planes, trains, Pullman cars, and so on.

187

Ms 8d/9a MANUSCRIPT CONVENTIONS

> The U.S.S. *Missouri* the *Denver Zephyr*
> the *Spirit of St. Louis* the *Altamont*

d. Foreign words and phrases

Italics are used for foreign words and phrases and their abbreviations. If a foreign word has been established in English, it is not italicized. When in doubt, consult your dictionary.

> Private Jones addressed the general with complete *sang-froid*.
> He astonished the general, and vice versa.

e. Words, letters, and the like, as symbols

Italics are used for words, letters, figures, and the like, used as symbols without reference to their meaning. The older practice of enclosing such words in double quotation marks is less common, but is still sometimes seen.

> There are too many *and*'s in that sentence.
> Is that letter an *a* or an *o*?
> Avoid the symbol & in general writing.

9. HYPHENS AND SYLLABICATION— = / or Syl

Hyphens function in two ways: They join words or word-parts to form compounds, and they divide words at the end of a line to preserve margins. The hyphen should not be confused with the dash; the two serve quite different functions. (See P12.)

a. Hyphens— = /

1) COMPOUND NOUNS

English often runs words together to form new noun, adjective, or adverb concepts. Usage varies widely, but in general it may be said of compound nouns that first there are two words, then a hyphenated compound, and finally, as the compound becomes familiar, a single word, written solid. Thus, *base ball* became *base-ball* and finally *baseball*.

2) COMPOUND MODIFIERS

Compound adjectives and compound adverbs sometimes reach the stage of single words when both elements are monosyllables or when the compound is very common, as in *upstate, inshore, overnight, nearby;* but usually with adjectives and adverbs the choice is between two words or a hyphenated compound. Adverbs ending in *-ly* are never hyphenated. With adjectives, hyphens are often used when the adjective precedes the noun; but predicate adjective compounds are usually written as two words.

> A clear-cut example. The example is clear cut.

3) GUIDES TO COMPOUNDING: THE DICTIONARY

Whenever you are in doubt about whether to hyphenate a compound, consult your dictionary. If you do not find the compound you are seeking in the general vocabulary, study the discussion of the use of compounding hyphens in the special article in the dictionary. There are numerous subtleties in the use of compounding hyphens. The dictionary is the best guide.

4) GUIDES TO COMPOUNDING: ACCENT

One indication that a compound noun may have become a single word lies in the stress, pitch, and juncture patterns of the spoken sentence. If you strongly accent the first element of the compound and slight the rest—as in *baseball, basketball, playwright, scorekeeper*—the compound is probably one word. If you read two or more words together in a breath with a rising pitch, but divide the accent fairly evenly—as in *mother-in-law, hanger-on, light-year, city-state, soul-stirring, sky-high*—the compound is probably hyphenated. If the signals fall somewhere in between, the dictionary is the only guide.

5) SOME CATEGORIES

   a) A PREFIX PLUS A PROPER NOUN

Compounds composed of a prefix plus a proper noun are commonly hyphenated: *pro-British, un-Christian.*

   b) COMPOUND NUMERALS AND FRACTIONS

Compound numerals (numbers consisting of two words, from twenty-one to ninety-nine) and fractions are commonly hyphenated; but fractions containing a compound numeral as one member are not hyphenated between members: *twenty-three, two-thirds;* but, *three twenty-sevenths.*

c) COMPOUNDS WITH *self*

Compounds with *self-* are usually hyphenated: *self-styled, self-appointed.*

d) HYPHENS TO AVOID CONFUSION

Compounds resulting in confusing vowel combinations or possible confusion with other words are regularly hyphenated: *anti-imperialist, co-owner, re-creation* (distinguished from *recreation*).

e) COINED COMPOUND ADJECTIVES

Any coined compound adjective read together in a breath with evenly divided accent and preceding the noun is hyphenated: *a not-to-be-sneezed-at opportunity.*

b. Syllabication—Syl

Hyphens are used to separate syllables of a word that must be divided at the end of a line to maintain a margin. The hyphen always comes at the end of the line on which the word begins; it never precedes the succeeding line. The hyphen comes always between syllables, that is, between elements of the word that are pronounced as distinct units of sound. Never divide a one-syllable word, no matter how long: *stretched* is one unit of sound and cannot be divided. Never divide in the middle of a syllable.

The dictionary is the best guide to the proper syllabication of a word, but certain conventional practices may be indicated.

1) DIVISION BY SYLLABLES, ACCORDING TO PRONUNCIATION

Words are divided by syllables, according to pronunciation, and they should preferably be divided so that the part of the word left at the end of the line will suggest the pronunciation of the whole word. Avoid such breaks as *serv-iceman, prefer-ence.* Never separate a word which is pronounced as a single syllable, even though its written form contains a suffix which in some other word is pronounced as a separate syllable. *Stretched,* as noted above, has only one syllable, though *wretched* has two. (Even when the *-ed* forms an extra syllable, separating it saves only one space.)

2) A SINGLE-VOWEL SYLLABLE

With words containing a single vowel as a separate syllable, divide after the vowel: *sepa-rate*.

3) A ONE-LETTER PREFIX AND A TWO-LETTER SUFFIX

Avoid leaving a one-letter prefix on the first line and avoid carrying over a two-letter suffix to the second line. Avoid such breaks as *a-bove, wretch-ed*.

4) DOUBLED CONSONANTS

When the addition of a suffix has caused the doubling of a final consonant, or when a word normally contains a doubled consonant, break between the consonants, as *sit-ting, neces-sary*.

But a word normally ending in a doubled consonant retains the two consonants in the one syllable when a suffix is added, as *fill-ing*.

5) HYPHENATED COMPOUNDS

Hyphenated compounds are preferably divided only at the hyphen, as *soul-stirring*.

6) SINGLE-WORD COMPOUNDS

Single-word compounds are preferably divided between the elements of the compound, as *scorekeeper* becomes *score-keeper*.

c. Other uses of the dividing hyphen

1) IN SPELLING OUT

Hyphens are also used to divide the letters of a word to indicate that the word is being spelled out.

The answer is *n-o,* no.

2) IN REPRESENTING STUTTERING

Hyphens are also used to divide repeated letters representing stuttering.

I'm n-n-not f-frightened.

Ms 9c/10/11a   MANUSCRIPT CONVENTIONS

3) IN PAIRING COMPOUNDS

Hyphens are sometimes used to indicate that the last part of a compound has been suppressed but will be supplied by the last part of a paired compound to follow.

We live in a three- or perhaps a four-dimensional world.

10. ABBREVIATIONS—Abr

In general writing, *avoid abbreviations,* including the ampersand (&).

The following abbreviations, however, are established and may be used in any but the most formal writing. (And since *Mrs.* has no other form, it may be used whenever you need it.)

    TITLES PRECEDING NAMES: Mr., Messrs., Mrs., Dr., St. (saint)
    TITLES FOLLOWING NAMES: Esq., Jr., Sr., M.D., Ph.D., etc.
    COMMON LATIN PHRASES: i.e., e.g., etc., ad lib., viz., A.D. and B.C., A.M., P.M., vs.

In informal writing, government agencies, and the like, are now often abbreviated to their initials. Be sure, however, that the abbreviation will be clear to your reader.

For specialized writing, common abbreviations are listed in your dictionary.

11. REPRESENTATION OF NUMBERS—N

a. General principles

Usage in the representation of numbers is divided, but some general principles may be suggested.

1) NUMBERS OF ONE OR TWO WORDS

In general writing, write out numbers that can be expressed in one or two words, as *one, twenty-three, two hundred, seven million.*

2) NUMBERS OF MORE THAN TWO WORDS

Use figures for numbers requiring more than two words, as *276, 1337, 9,277,438.*

REPRESENTATION OF NUMBERS ———————— Ms 11a–b

3) CONSISTENCY

Be consistent in the representation of numbers within a single paper. If most of them can be expressed in one or two words, write out all of them. If most (or even many) would require more than two words, use figures for all.

b. Special conventions

A few special conventions are generally observed. (See also Paging, page 182.)

1) NUMBER BEGINNING A SENTENCE

Never begin a sentence with figures. Write out the number or rephrase the sentence.

> AVOID: $2,300 was the price of that car.
> BETTER: That car cost $2,300.

2) FIGURES FOR STATISTICS

In all but very formal writing, use figures for statistics. If some numbers in a paper are statistical and some are not, consistency may be ignored to indicate the difference.

> ACCEPTABLE: Each of the two investigators reported that 43,000 bushels had been wrongfully sold, that 37,000 bushels had been allowed to spoil, and that 750,000 bushels remained in storage.

3) FIGURES FOR DATES

Use figures for dates, except in very formal social correspondence.

Kenny was born June 14, 1914.

But ordinal numbers representing days of the month, when the year is not given, are more commonly written out.

> PREFERRED: He was born June fourteenth.
> POSSIBLE: He was born June 14th (or June 14).

4) FIGURES FOR STREET NUMBERS

Use figures for street numbers.

2802 Massachusetts Avenue

193

Ms 11b — MANUSCRIPT CONVENTIONS

5) FIGURES FOR DECIMALS

Use figures for decimals.

The tolerance allowed was .001 of an inch.

6) FORMS FOR PERCENTAGES

Figures are usually used for percentages.

He gets a 10 percent (or 10%, or ten percent) commission.

7) FIGURES WITH A.M. AND P.M.

Use figures for the time of the day when given with A.M. and P.M.

It is now 4:19 P.M.

8) FORMS FOR NUMBERED STREETS

Numbered streets are written out unless local usage prefers figures. Thus, in New York, numbered avenues are written out; numbered streets are given in figures: *Fifth Avenue, 42nd Street.*

9) NUMBERS STANDING SIDE BY SIDE

When two numbers must stand side by side, the first number is often written out and the second given in figures, to prevent confusion.

He owned six 10-ton trucks.

6 — Outlining

* The informal outline, 195
* The formal outline, 196
    The sentence outline, 199
    The topic outline, 202

  * There are exercises for items marked with an asterisk.

THE INFORMAL OUTLINE

    The informal outline is a stimulant to thought, a guide to purposeful writing, and a useful check during revision. Being informal, it need not be polished. But being an outline, it allows you to think your problem through in advance. Consequently, you can give all your attention during the actual writing to the phrasing of your sentences and the shaping of your paragraphs. It is only a rough preliminary sketch of your paper, but for a simple paper it will provide all the blueprint you need. Phrase your thesis or statement of purpose as precisely as you can, jotting down in brief topics all the details that might help to develop it, and then thinking about those details. Any that seem irrelevant as you reconsider them can be eliminated. Any that occurred to you out of the most logical order can be rearranged. Those that are related to a single phase of the development can be grouped together. Gaps can be filled in and connections can be briefly indicated. All the thinking necessary to plan a simple paper can be done by jotting down rough notes, drawing arrows, crossing out irrelevancies, and numbering items or groups of items to mark their ultimate order. A final quick check will let you sharpen the phrasing of the thesis itself as your own thinking is clarified.

    For example, an informal outline for a theme by an Engineering student on the topic "Advice to the Dean" might finally look like the following, which is neither neat nor conventional in form, yet would provide him with a quick sketch of what he meant to do.

> THESIS: The Engineering curriculum is too theoretical and too narrow, denying its students both the practical training they will need as engineers and the broad background they will need as human beings.

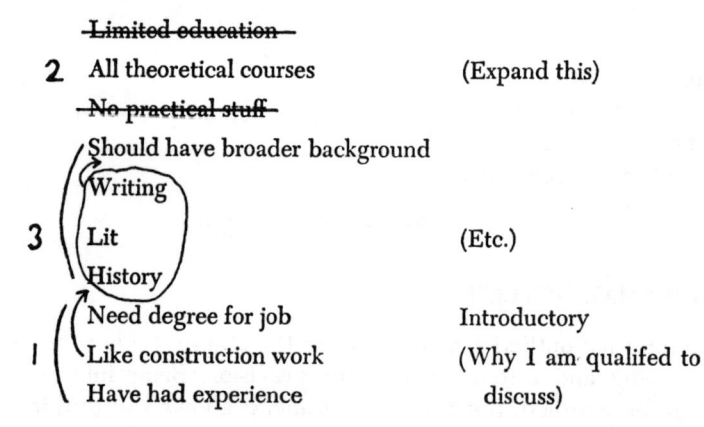

~~Limited education~~
2 All theoretical courses   (Expand this)
~~No practical stuff~~
{ Should have broader background
3 { Writing
   { Lit   (Etc.)
   { History
1 { Need degree for job   Introductory
  { Like construction work   (Why I am qualifed to
  { Have had experience   discuss)

THE FORMAL OUTLINE

For a long and complicated paper, an informal outline does not provide enough control to be very useful, though it does represent and help to capture the kind of preliminary thinking which must be done. We quickly forget what our rough notes meant to us; too many predicates could be fitted to the loosely phrased topics. For best control, we need careful phrasing of thesis and subpoints and lesser details, and we need a dependable device for indicating the relations between them. The conventions of the formal analytical outline provide just such control. Its thesis is carefully and precisely phrased and then is broken down into the subordinate parts which must be developed in order to develop the central idea. Like the informal outline, in other words, the formal outline subdivides the central thesis, breaking it down into its major parts and then similarly breaking down each part in turn, as far as the analysis needs to go for complete clarity to the writer and the reader. It is made by an analytical process of dividing and subdividing, treating at each stage smaller and smaller parts of the overall thesis.

This process of subdividing merely follows natural human habits of thought. We cannot think efficiently or even comfortably in units which are too large or too small. The continental United States, for example, is too big and too diverse for us to realize it as a whole. It is easier for us to visualize regions—New England, the Middle Atlantic states, the Middle West, the South, the Southwest, the West, the Northwest. Within each region we think of states—Maine, New Hampshire, Vermont, Massachusetts, Rhode Island, Connecticut. (They are unequal in size, but equal in legal status, equally important.) Within each state, we think of counties or parishes. Within each county we think of townships or hundreds or sections. Finally, we get down to quarter sections, town lots, or the fifty-foot frontage owned by an individual taxpayer. Analyzing by subdivision so that we can clearly see relations is a very familiar process, the basic one in making a formal outline.

The only thing really new about the formal outline is that it has conventional symbols for labeling the items at each stage of the subdividing.

We begin, as we always must, with the thesis, the central idea, the thing we want to say, and we label that **"Thesis."** The main points by which that thesis is to be presented (or the main points by which it was presented, if we are outlining something someone else has written) are given Roman numerals: **I, II, III.** Each Roman numeral point is in turn broken down into its parts, and the resulting secondary subdivisions are given capital letters: **A, B, C.** Tertiary subdivisions are given Arabic numbers: **1, 2, 3;** quaternary subdivisions are given lower-case letters: **a, b, c.** (You rarely need to go farther than that in your subdividing; if you do, use Arabic numerals in single parentheses first, then use lower-case letters in single parentheses.) The symbols which indicate each rank of subdivision stand out so as to be readily visible, and the outline looks like this:

THESIS: ─────────────────────────────
        ──────────────────.

  I. ─────────────────────────────
     ──────────────────.

OUTLINING

    A. _____.
    B. _____
       _____.
    C. _____.
       1. _____.
       2. _____
          _____.
          a. _____.
          b. _____.
II. _____.

(And so on, as far as your outline needs to go.)

    Because we are subdividing, chopping major ideas into smaller and smaller pieces, we cannot logically have a I without at least a II, nor an A without a B, a 1 without a 2, and so on. But we may have a III, or a V, or even a VII. You should be wary, however, of a IX, or a K, or a 12, because so many items of equal importance at any stage are hard to manage. Both the writer and the reader will get lost if they must keep too many points of similar rank in mind at one time. It is a good, if somewhat rough, rule to reconsider any section containing more than half a dozen items of similar importance; probably some of them could be grouped further.

    If a paper demands an extensive introduction, as distinct from a mere opening, the introductory idea should be included in the outline even though it does not directly contribute to the development of the thesis. It is labeled *Introduction,* and if necessary subdivided as if it were a primary point. Most outlines, however, do not include minor introductory material.

    There are three additional conventions to be learned. First, no item of whatever rank should deal with more than a single concept; consequently, no item should consist of more than a single sentence or a single topic. Second, each item expresses and summarizes the idea to be developed at that point in the paper; consequently, each item must be phrased as a declarative sentence or topic, not as a question whose answer would be the real idea concerned. And within each section, and wherever else the items are comparable, the sentences should be as nearly parallel as possible, to clarify the similarity of the ideas. Third, one purpose of the outline is to provide a readily clear visual breakdown of the thesis

THE FORMAL OUTLINE

idea; consequently, each item is indented so its identifying symbol will stand out clearly, and items which consist of more than one line are set up in block form, as in the schematic outline on pages 197–198.

Do not assume, finally, that each item, or even each primary subdivision, demands a paragraph in the final paper. Paragraphing, grouping ideas by convenience, is both a logical and a psychological problem to be solved with the thesis, the audience, and the length of the paper all in mind. If you were developing the thesis in answer to an examination question, for example, the whole paper might be only one paragraph in length. If you were writing a book, each primary subdivision might call for several chapters. Use your outline to ensure that you understand your ideas; write your paper to present your ideas to your intended audience.

There are only two really useful kinds of formal outlines: the sentence outline and the topic outline.[1]

THE SENTENCE OUTLINE

The sentence outline uses a full declarative sentence for every item of whatever logical value—thesis, primary subdivision, secondary subdivision, and so on down as far as the breakdown goes. It uses only declarative sentences because only declarative sentences directly state ideas, and the outline dispassionately states the ideas in the order of their relative importance. And it uses no more than one sentence for any one item. If you find yourself writing two or more sentences after any one outline symbol, see if those sentences can be combined into a single unified sentence. If they cannot, you must reconsider the item; there must be no more than one idea involved. But remember that a unified sentence need not be a simple sentence; you may use sentences of any necessary degree of complexity.

Sentence outlines have many advantages. Most important, they force you to decide at each step not only what topic you want to talk about, but exactly what you want to say about that topic, stating a complete idea at each point. Second, they fix your ideas in a form

[1] A third type of outline, the paragraph outline, is also common. It consists of the thesis, the topic sentences of each paragraph, and the subordinate details of each paragraph as subpoints. But because there is no necessary connection between the items of an analytical outline and paragraphs of the final paper, it is not very useful to the writer until his plans have been completely formed, and so will not be examined here in detail.

which will be just as clear six days or six weeks or six months later as it was at the moment of writing, so that if your outline is to be used long after you make it out, you will still be able to follow your original plan without stopping to wonder what on earth you had meant to do with some item whose relevance has completely escaped you. Third, a well-made sentence outline is very nearly as clear to someone else as it is to you. As you finish the preliminary work on your English 2 research paper, for example, your instructor can go over a sentence outline with you, see exactly what you are planning to do, and help you strengthen weak spots before the paper is written. The graduate student can submit the plan of his thesis to his adviser; the writer can show the publisher what he means to do with a projected book; the junior executive can get approval on his plans before the typist's time is wasted on an ill-advised manual. Because every idea of whatever rank is fully expressed, the sentence outline provides a clear and easily read blueprint that is understandable at any time, to any reader.

The following outline of an English 2 research paper illustrates not only the methods of formal outlining but also the value of the sentence outline as a blueprint for the final paper. The details still need to be filled in, but the plan to be followed and the approach to be taken is perfectly clear.

The Disappearance of the Greenland Colony

Thesis: After five centuries of varying prosperity, the medieval Norse disappeared from the Greenland colony, probably for a combination of several reasons.

Introduction: Greenland was for several hundred years a successful settlement.
  A. Discovered in A.D. 982, it was settled by Icelanders.
  B. As a republic, the settlement prospered.
    1. It was good-sized.
    2. The church was active.
    3. The Greenlanders could make a living by farming and hunting.
    4. They developed a brisk trade.
I. After Greenland joined Norway in 1261, trade decreased, and Europe gradually forgot Greenland.
  A. After Greenland joined Norway, trade fell off under Norwegian restrictions.

THE FORMAL OUTLINE

      1. Norway promised to foster Greenland trade, but broke trust by declaring a crippling monopoly.
      2. Under the monopoly legal trade ceased almost completely.
      3. Even illegal trade became unprofitable.
  B. Europe heard little good news from Greenland.
      1. Ivan Bardarsson reported that the West Settlement had been destroyed.
      2. Some of the Greenlanders returned to Europe because of unfavorable conditions in the colony.
  C. Europe gradually forgot the colonists.
      1. Recorded visits to Greenland stopped.
      2. Only isolated mention was made of the colony.
      3. Von Greenlander, about 1540, was the last outsider to see one of the colonists.
      4. Unsuccessful attempts were made to find the settlements again.
II. Greenland was rediscovered, and the extermination theory was proposed to account for the disappearance of the Norse colonists.
  A. Frobisher and others rediscovered Greenland, finding no Norsemen.
  B. The Norsemen were searched for unsuccessfully for many years.
  C. Egede resettled Greenland, looking for Norsemen but finding only Eskimo tales about them.
      1. Egede came to re-Christianize the Norse.
      2. Some time later, the Eskimos told him the Norse had all been killed.
  D. The theory of extermination by the Eskimos was proposed to account for the disappearance.
      1. The Eskimos had migrated into southern Greenland while the colony was still there.
      2. It was assumed that the Eskimos had killed the Norsemen, this being suggested by Egede's news.
      3. Bardarsson's account of the destruction of the West Settlement supported the idea.
III. Later it was suggested that the Norse had been absorbed by the Eskimos, not killed by them.
  A. The Eskimo way of life was well suited to Greenland.
  B. There is much white blood in the Eskimos today.
  C. Early reports support the theory.

D. The evidence of Bardarsson and Egede for extermination is not conclusive.
      1. Bardarsson merely assumed a reason for the abandonment of one farm; there could well be other reasons for the abandonment.
      2. Egede may himself have given the Eskimos the ideas they reported to him.
IV. Skeletal evidence suggests possible extermination by disease.
   A. Skeletons disinterred at Herjolfsnes suggested degeneration under changing climatic conditions.
      1. Skeletons, coffins, and clothes were recovered from the Herjolfsnes churchyard.
      2. The clothes dated the skeletons and showed that some trade must have continued into the fifteenth century.
      3. All the skeletons were degenerate, diseased, and deformed.
      4. Several factors indicate a change in climate.
         a. This change may at once have cut off trade and made life more difficult.
         b. Lacking necessities, the Norsemen died.
      5. But Herjolfsnes was an isolated case, and more material was needed to prove the theory.
   B. Skeletons excavated in other parts of Greenland show different conditions.
      1. Twelfth-century skeletons from Gardar were strong and healthy.
      2. Twelfth- to fourteenth-century material from the West Settlement also contradicts the earlier findings.
         a. The material was extensive and well preserved.
         b. The skeletons were normal: neither degenerate nor diseased.
      3. The skeletons do not prove much, but they do suggest that disease and degeneration were not everywhere important.
V. Perhaps the real solution is that the Norse, already diminished in numbers, turned to the Eskimo life, except for those at Herjolfsnes, who degenerated and died.

THE TOPIC OUTLINE

The topic outline, like the sentence outline, begins with a full sentence which expresses the central thesis of the paper. After that, however, all items are phrased as topics only, not as full-sentence

THE FORMAL OUTLINE

predications expressing ideas about the topics. Consequently, the topic outline is far less clear than a sentence outline, even when the topics are carefully polished and made as meaningful as possible within the limits of brevity. Topic outlines are less useful than sentence outlines if any time is to elapse between making the outline and writing the paper, or if the outline is to be submitted to an adviser for scrutiny and suggestion.

The topic outline follows the same conventions of subdivision, subordination symbols, and indention that the sentence outline follows.

For illustration, we can reduce to a topic outline the sentence outline we have just examined.

> Thesis: After five centuries of varying prosperity, the medieval Norse disappeared from the Greenland colony, probably for a combination of several reasons.
> Introduction: Greenland as a republic.
>   A. Settlement.
>   B. Prosperity.
>   1. Size.
>   2. Church activity.
>   3. Farming and hunting.
>   4. Trade.
>   I. Decay as a Norwegian colony.
>   A. Trade under Norwegian restrictions.
>   1. Crippling monopoly.
>   2. Cessation of legal trade.
>   3. Unprofitability of illegal trade.
>   B. Discouraging reports.
>   1. West Settlement destroyed.
>   2. Return of some colonists.
>   C. Oblivion.
>   1. Cessation of visits.
>   2. Rare mention.
>   3. Last visitor.
>   4. Settlements lost.
>   II. Rediscovery: Extermination theory.
>   A. Rediscovery: absence of Norse.
>   B. Unsuccessful search.
>   C. Egede: Eskimos.
>   1. Missionary resettlement.
>   2. Norse reported killed.

    D. Extermination theory.
       1. Early Eskimo migration.
       2. Extermination by Eskimos suggested.
       3. Confirmation in destruction of West Settlement.
III. Absorption theory.
    A. Eskimo culture suitable.
    B. White blood in Eskimos.
    C. Confirmatory early reports.
    D. Extermination evidence inconclusive.
       1. Only one farm involved.
       2. Idea possibly induced.
IV. Degeneration theory.
    A. Skeletons from Herjolfsnes.
       1. Recovered from churchyard.
       2. Evidence of late trade.
       3. Evidence of disease.
       4. Evidence of climatic change.
          a. Worsened conditions.
          b. Resultant death.
       5. Isolated case.
    B. Other skeletal evidence.
       1. Gardar: Healthy skeletons.
       2. West Settlement: further contradiction.
          a. Extensive evidence.
          b. Healthy skeletons.
       3. Dubiety of theory.
V. Probable solution.

Such a topic outline is scarcely more useful than the informal outline, although it does have the advantage of more clearly identifying the relative importance of the subordinate ideas. But too many predicates could be fitted to most of the topics for the topic outline to be wholly clear to anyone other than the original writer, and even he will soon forget exactly what he planned to say about each point. A good paper could certainly be written from that sample topic outline, but perhaps a poor one could be written just as easily. All the topic outline really ensures is that an intelligent writer will treat the topics in a logical order.

For a complex subject, for a paper to be written some time after the outline has been made, for a plan to be submitted to an adviser, a sentence outline is far superior.

THE FORMAL OUTLINE

EXERCISES

A. The following very rough notes on the topic, "The freshman and his final choice of major subject," are already partially arranged in logical order. No thesis, however, is expressed and the notes are sometimes phrases, sometimes declarative sentences, and sometimes questions or imperatives. Examine them carefully, phrase a thesis, and prepare an analytical sentence outline using all pertinent items. You may rearrange, modify, eliminate, or add items at need.

> Some college freshmen genuinely know what they want to specialize in.
> An overriding interest in science, or literature, or history, or religion, or engineering, or business (yet which, among all the choices in each field?) may be already established.
> The born and confident doctor, lawyer, etc.
> Some think they know.
> Limited experience may steer them into the wrong fields.
> The scientifically minded may go into physics, when he would have gone into astronomy if he had ever met it.
> A born Classicist may mistakenly major in Spanish.
> Parental occupation may set them wrong.
> Good doctors, lawyers, etc., often insist that their children study medicine, etc., regardless of interest or aptitude.
> Some know they are in the wrong curriculum, but accede to pressure.
> Chiefly that of parents.
> "I want my child to have what I missed."
> "I suppose I'll have to be a businessman. Most people are."
> It's a rare freshman who is strong enough to rebel.
> An Engineering freshman who wanted to write musical comedies worked out his own curriculum, over both parental and college objections.
> The lawyer's son who wanted to be an engineer.
> Many don't know, and know it.
> "I'm not interested in anything, really."
> "What shall I take?"—sometimes means, "What is required?" Sometimes means, "Help. What will I find of permanent interest?"
> Aptitude tests are sometimes useful.
> General requirements in first two years are in part designed to force undecided students to sample various kinds of subjects.

(Also designed to introduce all students to the varied approaches to different kinds of truth.)

Indecision not necessarily bad.

Why should an eighteen-year-old completely know his own mind?

Better to sample and find himself than to be forced into the wrong work—which is not always easy to escape.

At least, transfer from one curriculum to another should not be made too difficult.

Let the student who finally does decide have as easy access to his real field as possible.

B. Under your instructor's guidance, select a well-organized expository essay and prepare a thesis and sentence outline showing its structure.

7

The Research Paper

* The use of the library, 208
    The card catalogue, 209
    Periodical indexes, 212
    Newspaper and pamphlet indexes, 213
    Specialized indexes, 213
    References, 214
        General encyclopedias, 214
        Dictionaries, 215
        Biographical dictionaries, 215
        Yearbooks, 215
        Atlases, 216
Research paper procedure, 217
    The preliminary bibliography, 217
        Books, 218
        Reference books, 221
        Magazine articles, 222
        Government publications, 224
        Newspaper articles or news stories, 225

* There are exercises for items marked with an asterisk.

Unpublished manuscripts, 225
Annotating your bibliography, 226
Taking notes, 227
Plagiarism through ignorance, 229
The final outline, 231
* The final paper, 231
Footnoting, 232
The final bibliography, 239
A final word, 239
Sample short research paper, 240

A vast amount of learning and wisdom is preserved in the libraries of the world, and one major purpose of education is to teach students how to find it, examine it, evaluate it, and make it their own possession. Many college courses consequently require library research and term papers, both to familiarize students with the resources of each discipline and to force them to get at least a little way below the surface of one or more concepts. Knowledge of libraries and of term paper procedure is therefore essential.

THE USE OF THE LIBRARY

For thousands of years, the human race has been storing up its collective wisdom in libraries. No two libraries are exactly alike. The region in which a library is located, the interests of its donors or its directors, the accumulated results of losses and acquisitions—all these factors make the collection of any one library different from that of any other. Your library's share of "the best that has been thought and said in the world," however, will give you quite enough raw material for your freshman research paper. It is obvious that you do not have the time or the energy to read through all the books, magazines, newspapers, pamphlets, and manuscripts it contains in the hope of stumbling on facts or opinions which have a bearing on a particular subject you are interested in; but, fortunately, you do not have to. Even though the collection of each library is unique, the machinery by which you can search that collection for material you can use is standardized. The same research tools and methods can be used in any library in the country. Standard reference books, catalogues, and indexes save you from having to guess where to look for material, or from having to wonder what your library owns and what it lacks.

The Card Catalogue

The card catalogue—rows of filing cabinets filled with three-by-five-inch cards listing every book in the library's collection, usually in three different ways—is an invaluable aid to research. From it can be found what *books* the library contains, alphabetically listed by the author's name, the first important word of the title, and the subjects treated. Whether the library contains twenty thousand books or eight or nine million, a knowledge of the nature of the card catalogue is essential to the student.

The basic card is the author card, printed by the Library of Congress and distributed to libraries all over the country.

```
    E
  175.9
  .S34  Schlesinger, Arthur Meier, 1888–
  1934         New viewpoints in American history, by Arthur Meier
            Schlesinger ...  New York, The Macmillan company, 1934.
            x p., 2 l., 299 p.  20½ cm.
            Originally published 1922.
            "Bibliographical note" at end of each chapter.
            CONTENTS.—The influence of immigration on American history.—
            Geographic factors in American development.—Economic influences in
            American history.—The decline of aristocracy in America.—Radical-
            ism and conservatism in American history.—The rôle of women in
            American history.—The American revolution.—Economic aspects of
            the movement for the Constitution.—The significance of Jacksonian de-
            mocracy.—The state rights fetish.—The foundations of the modern
            era.—The riddle of the parties.
                 1. U. S.—Hist.—Philosophy.  2. U. S.—Hist.  3. U. S. Pol. govt.
               I. Title.
                                                                34–25367
                    Library of Congress         E175.9.S34   1934
                                                    [3]                 973.04
```

The typed number in the upper left-hand corner is the "call number," the number by which the librarian knows where in the stacks of books the particular volume is shelved. It is not important that you understand how the librarian arrives at that number, but it is extremely important that you copy it down exactly and completely as you fill out a "call slip" for a book. If you do not, you will have to go back to the card catalogue and get it.[1]

The first line of the printed card gives you the author's name, surname first, and the dates of his birth and, unless he was living when the card was printed, his death.

Second is the title of the book (capitalizing only the first word and proper names), the author's name as it appears on the title page, the edition (if other than the first), and the facts of publication, that is, the place of publication, the publisher, and the date.

In your final paper, you will need that information; consequently you should note carefully everything offered in the first two elements of the catalogue card.

The rest of the information provided by the card does not appear in your final paper. But do not, on that account, ignore it. From the third item you can get an idea of the size of the book—how many pages and how large a volume. You can tell whether or not it contains illustrations, maps, charts, or a bibliography that might be useful to you, and even sometimes how many times it has been reprinted, which suggests something of its value.

Even more important is the fourth item (which, unfortunately, does not often appear), the analysis of the contents. If that analysis is given, it will tell you at once whether or not the book will touch your particular phase of the general subject the book deals with.

Next—and again very important to you—are the subject headings under which the book has been classified. This element of the card will often suggest related subjects that should be consulted, and will give you key terms to keep in mind as you consult not only the card catalogue but also the other kinds of indexes to library material.

Finally, there are a series of numerical entries that are useful chiefly to librarians—the Library of Congress call number (which will also be listed in the upper left-hand corner if your library uses the Library of Congress system), the Dewey Decimal classification number (which will be listed as the call number if your library

[1] If you wish to know more about the classification systems, study any one of several good handbooks on library practice which your librarian can recommend.

follows that system), the Library of Congress card number, the copyright number, and so on.

Most books are listed not only by author but also by title and subject. From whichever angle you approach the card catalogue, you will get clues that will lead you to book sources. You should, however, follow up the other avenues of approach besides the avenue you first took. Usually, for example, you will begin with subject cards. But you should remember to look also at the author cards of an authority who turns up frequently; there may be other books of his bearing on the subject which the library has neglected to list under that particular subject heading. The subject headings are rather specific—history, for example, touches and overlaps many other concepts. They must be used intelligently and imaginatively, because your material may be scattered widely. Check related subject headings; they may lead you to useful sources. And use the cross-reference cards suggesting other ways of cataloguing related material, or use the *Library of Congress Subject Headings*, a ready-made cross-reference volume. A "see" card or a "see also" card should never be ignored. The first indicates that you are consulting the catalogue through a key term the library does not use and tells you what term to look for; the second suggests a closely related subject heading that may provide important additional material.

One important source of material is often overlooked. Biography may not be filed under any other subject matter heading, so that such a major source, say, as Freeman's four-volume *R. E. Lee* may not appear at all under U.S.—History—Civil War. Yet Volumes II and III are at least as important as Freeman's *Lee's Lieutenants*. Be sure to check biographical material for people who are importantly involved with your topic.

A few remarks might be made about the ways in which librarians file the catalogue cards. A little browsing in the catalogue will do more to teach you than any amount of direct advice, but some helpful hints may be offered.

Books *by* a writer are filed before books *about* him.

Abbreviations are filed as if they were written out in full— *U.S.* comes where *United States* would come. *Mac, Mc,* and *M'* are all filed as if they were *Mac*. Numerals are filed as if they were spelled out. *Von* and *de* are ignored, and the last name is used instead, as in *Rochambeau, Comte de.*

Single key words in phrases come before compounds, or, as the librarian phrases it, "short comes before long."

    Slave labor   Slavery
    Slave songs   Slavery and abolition
    Slave-trade   Slavery and the church

Historical subdivisions are arranged chronologically; otherwise subdivisions of a topic are arranged alphabetically.

    U.S.–History–Colonial Period
    U.S.–History–King William's War, 1689–1697
    U.S.–History–King George's War, 1744–1748
    U.S.–History–French and Indian War, 1755–1763
    U.S.–History–Revolution

But

    Slave-trade
    Slave-trade, Africa, West
    Slave-trade, Brazil
    Slave-trade, History
    Slave-trade, U.S.
    Slave-trade, West Indies

Follow through the listings under all possible subject headings before you decide the library contains no books dealing with your topic (including general books overlapping the topic).

Periodical Indexes

Magazine articles provide much of our current reading, but magazine articles are not listed in the card catalogues, though the magazines themselves will be. To find articles which have appeared in magazines or in other publications issued periodically, there are many very useful periodical indexes. Every student should be aware of the major indexes: *Poole's Index to Periodical Literature* (indexing many periodicals published during the nineteenth century), the *Reader's Guide to Periodical Literature* (a more useful index covering popular magazines of the period from 1900 to the present), the *International Index to Periodical Literature* (which lists articles in many scholarly magazines in the humanities and some of the sciences), the *Industrial Arts Index* (engineering and business), and the specialized indexes, of which there are many, covering the student's particular interest. The last two, and the specialized indexes which can include more periodicals as they try to cover less ground, are especially important. *Never* stop with the *Reader's Guide*. It indexes the popular magazines on the newsstands, and the authors of the feature articles listed in it are very likely to have acquired what they know by the same process of library research that you are learning. They are professional writers, but amateurs in the subject matter. Like them, you need to consult the experts, whose contributions are in the professional journals and the scholarly books.

As you use any of the periodical indexes, be sure that you understand the system they follow. Consult the explanatory material at the front of the volumes for full discussion of their abbreviations, the order of details, and so on. We shall later see that you need to record all bibliographical material according to a specialized system conventionally followed in research papers. Before you can translate an index entry into the system you must use, it will be essential that you understand both systems thoroughly.

Newspaper and Pamphlet Indexes

Most newspapers are not indexed, but since most papers print the same news on the same day, two particular newspaper indexes can be used to locate news stories in nearly any paper. One is the *New York Times Index,* and the other is the (London) *Times Index.*

Pamphlets are less completely indexed, but two indexes are very useful, as far as they go. The *Vertical File Service Catalog* indexes much pamphlet material and should be consulted. The *Document Catalogue* and the subsequent *Monthly Catalogue* list many government publications.

Specialized Indexes

There are many specialized indexes of various kinds and of varying value; among them are the following:

Agricultural Index
Art Index
Book Review Digest
Chemical Abstracts
Dramatic Index

213

Education Index
Engineering Index
Index to Legal Periodicals
Index Medicus
*Modern Humanities Research
   Association Bibliographies*
Psychological Abstracts
Public Affairs Information Service

Make use of any specialized indexes available; you can locate them by consulting Winchell, *Guide to Reference Books,* Robert W. Murphy, *How and Where to Look It Up,* the *Bibliographic Index,* or—after you have really looked for yourself—the librarians.

Reference Books

Reference books, like the telephone directory, are designed to be consulted for specific and classified information about limited subjects. The periodical indexes we have just been considering are reference books, and there are many others, some of which, like the general dictionaries, are already familiar to you. Among the most important are the encyclopedias, the dictionaries, the biographical dictionaries, the yearbooks, and the atlases.

GENERAL ENCYCLOPEDIAS

General encyclopedias attempt to present objective and authoritative articles on as many topics of general interest as possible. Because they differ, of necessity, one from another and edition from edition, it is well to consult several rather than only one. Among the best edited and most dependable are the following:

Encyclopedia Americana and its annual supplement *The Americana Annual*

Encyclopædia Britannica and its annual supplement *The Britannica Book of the Year*

Collier's Encyclopedia (This is designed primarily for high school use and will often provide a good introductory article from which you can—and should—go on to the adult encyclopedias listed above.)

It is usually best to use the latest available editions, which will present the results of the most recent scholarship. Only if you wish to know what was thought about a given topic at an earlier period (or if your topic has been dropped from late editions) should you consult an edition other than the most recent one.

DICTIONARIES

In addition to the standard unabridged dictionaries,

The New Century Dictionary of the English Language
Funk & Wagnall's New Standard Dictionary of the English Language
Webster's Third New International Dictionary of the English Language,

every student should be aware of two or three comprehensive historical dictionaries.

Dictionary of American English on Historical Principles
Mitford M. Mathews, *Dictionary of Americanisms*
Oxford English Dictionary on Historical Principles (also called the *New English Dictionary* or the *Murray Dictionary*)

These multivolumed dictionaries are invaluable in tracing the development and change of meanings and in determining what a word may have meant to an author writing in an earlier time—the Anglican *Book of Common Prayer,* for example, in praying, "Prevent us, O Lord, in all our doings," is confusing until you understand the sixteenth century use of *prevent.*

BIOGRAPHICAL DICTIONARIES

At least four biographical dictionaries should be familiar to every student, and there are many others in specialized fields.

Dictionary of American Biography, and supplement
Dictionary of National Biography (British), and supplements
Who's Who in America
Who's Who (British)

The first two are concerned with prominent persons no longer living, the second two with prominent living persons.

YEARBOOKS

Yearbooks contain valuable factual information about events

215

of each year. There are many, but among the most important are the following:

The Americana Annual
The Britannica Book of the Year
American Year Book
Facts on File
New International Year Book
World Almanac and Book of Facts

ATLASES

The three best-known atlases are the following:

Encyclopædia Britannica World Atlas
Columbia Lippincott Gazetteer of the World
Rand McNally Commercial Atlas and Marketing Guide

Early in your work on the research paper you should familiarize yourself with the very important general reference works that have been listed. In addition, you should examine carefully the specialized periodical indexes, biographical dictionaries, technical dictionaries, and encyclopedias offering information about your special field of study. Consult Winchell, *Guide to Reference Books* or some similar guide (there are many), browse through the library Reference Room, and consult the reference librarian. Remember that she should not be expected to do your work for you, but part of her job is to know the best reference sources for specialized investigations. Make use of her expert knowledge.

EXERCISES

A. What would be the best source to consult if you wished to find the following information?

1. A list of the principal books by Sir Winston Churchill.
2. The tonnage of steel produced last year in the United States.
3. The career of Francis Scott Key.
4. A sketch of the early history of Jamaica.
5. The approximate date at which *prevent* appeared in print with its modern meaning.
6. The philosophical publications of Herbert Spencer, who lived in England from 1820 to 1903.
7. The location and height of Mount Everest.

8. Articles in historical periodicals, between 1950 and 1960, on King Richard III of England.
9. Newspaper accounts of the death of Ernest Hemingway in 1961.
10. Specialized encyclopedias in religion and ethics.

(If you go to the library to look up the information, handle the reference books carefully. When many students look up the same items, books wear out rapidly.)

B. Prepare and submit to your instructor a list of the specialized encyclopedias, specialized periodical indexes, and specialized biographical dictionaries necessary to anyone doing research in the field in which you expect to major.

C. After careful examination of the books, write out and submit to your instructor a brief statement of the content and scope of the following: *Oxford English Dictionary, Cambridge History of English Literature,* Bartlett's *Familiar Quotations, Book Review Digest,* Webster's *Biographical Dictionary,* Winchell, *Guide to Reference Books.*

D. Consult your library's card catalogue to discover how many books your library contains from which you could secure detailed information about Lady Jane Grey. Include in your list biographies, specialized histories of the period, and the pertinent volumes of general histories. Follow up all "see" and "see also" cross-references.

RESEARCH PAPER PROCEDURE

The Preliminary Bibliography

As you find titles of books or articles that may provide information about a subject chosen for a term paper, make a careful record of each one on a separate three-by-five inch card and arrange the cards in alphabetical order.

The purpose of the preliminary bibliography is to give you a convenient list of the sources that might be helpful. After your paper is finished, you will be expected to append a final bibliography which will give your readers a list of the sources you have actually used. It will save time and trouble and will help prevent mistakes if you take down the items for your preliminary bibliography in the

217

form and with the detail you will ultimately need. Your instructor, indeed, will probably examine your bibliography cards to be sure you understand the method, so that care from the beginning not only will save you trouble with the paper itself, but may even save your having to do much of the work over again to satisfy some of the course requirements.

The form of the bibliographical entry differs slightly for each type of source—for books, encyclopedia articles, magazine articles, pamphlets, and unpublished manuscripts, like theses.

But for all types of sources, three bits of information are expected: *author, title, facts of publication.* (The facts of publication are also called the "imprint.") As we shall see, the three-by-five-inch bibliography card recording each source may and often should contain additional information, but those three items are standard. For each source, *take these three items down in full* when you first come across the source and save yourself possible trouble later. And take them down in the recommended form, avoiding abbreviations or other shortcuts.[2]

BOOKS

Author: Last name first, to facilitate alphabetizing. If two or three authors are listed on the title page (not the cover or the spine), the book will be alphabetized in your bibliography under the surname of the first author listed. That author's name is given surname first. The names of the other authors, however, are recorded in normal order.

If more than three authors are given on the title page, the first alone is used, and the rest are indicated by *et al.,* meaning "and others."

If the work of many authors has been collected in one volume, as in an anthology, the book is listed under the name of the editor, with his function indicated by the abbreviation *ed.*

An edition of a classic work, or a translation of a foreign work, is listed under the name of the author (unless that name has become

---

[2] The bibliographical forms discussed and illustrated are those of the revised *Style Sheet* of the Modern Language Association with one major modification, the inclusion of the publisher, borrowed from Kate L. Turabian, *A Manual for Writers of Term Papers, Theses, and Dissertations* (Chicago: University of Chicago Press, 1955).

almost part of the identifying title, as in Homer's *Iliad*), and the name of the editor or translator follows, identified as *ed.*, or *trans.*

If no author is listed, the book should be listed alphabetically by title, disregarding initial *A* or *The*.

Title: The title of the book, as it appears on the title page, is entered on the second line of the card. If the title is extremely long, it may be shortened, but be sure to include all significant, identifying terms.

The titles of complete works, like books, are put in italic type by the printer; in longhand or in typing, they are underlined.

Facts of publication: For books, the standard entries are place of publication, publisher, and date. (The date may be given on the title page, or as a copyright date on the back of the title page, or merely as a date appended to a preface or introduction. Use the title page date if one is given.)

All three of the standard entries need to be entered in your bibliography so that a reader who wishes to follow up your references may easily find the same edition (with the same pagination, misprints, revisions, and other details) that you used.

If for any reason one of the three entries cannot be found, indicate that fact by the abbreviations *n.p.* (no place given), *n. pub.* (no publisher), or *n.d.* (no date).

The normal bibliography card for a book by one author looks like this:

> Yarwood, Doreen
>
> The Architecture of England
>
> London: B. T. Batsford, 1963

Examples of the various complexities you are likely to run across follow *in the form the entries should take in your final bibliography*. (On the preliminary cards, author, title, and facts of publication should each be listed on a separate line, as in the sample card above.)

One author:

    Yarwood, Doreen. *The Architecture of England.* London: B. T. Batsford, 1963.

A second work by the same author:

    ———. *English Costume.* London: B. T. Batsford, 1953. [The use of a long dash instead of repeating the author's name emphasizes the repetition. In this book, the title page uses the abbreviation *Co.* You may either follow the title page usage, or put all entries in one consistent form, or omit the word altogether.]

Two authors:

    Batho, Edith, and Bonamy Dobrée. *The Victorians and After.* New York: Robert M. McBride Company, 1938.

More than three authors:

    Dock, Lavinia, *et al. History of American Nursing.* New York: The Macmillan Company, 1922. [Omitted: Sara Elizabeth Pickett, Clara D. Noyes, Fannie F. Clement, Elizabeth G. Fox, Anna R. van Meter.]

A collection of the work of many authors:

    Kreymbourg, Alfred, ed. *An Anthology and a History of American Poetry,* 2 vols. New York: Tudor Publishing Co., 1930.

An edition other than the first:

    Benns, F. Lee. *Europe, 1914–1939.* New York: Appleton-Century-Crofts, 1965.

An edition of a classic:

    Carlyle, Thomas. *Sartor Resartus,* ed. by Charles Frederick Harrold. New York: The Odyssey Press, 1937.

A translation of a foreign work:

    Zweig, Stefan. *Mary Queen of Scotland and the Isles,* trans. by Eden and Cedar Paul. New York: The Viking Press, 1935.

Lang, Andrew, Walter Leaf, and Ernest Myers, trans. *The Iliad of Homer.* New York: The Modern Library, n.d. [The author's name has become so merged with the title that the translators are more important in identifying the edition used.]

A book of more than one volume:

Trevelyan, G. M. *History of England,* 3 vols. Garden City, N.Y.: Doubleday & Company, 1953.

One volume of a set of volumes:

Trevelyan, G. M. *History of England,* Vol. I. Garden City, N.Y.: Doubleday & Company, 1953.

A book in a series:

Faulkner, Harold Underwood. *American Political and Social History,* 4th ed. Crofts American History Series, Dixon Ryan Fox, general ed. New York: F. S. Crofts & Co., 1946. [Notice that this entry also identifies a late edition and an editor distinct from the author.]

A book with a "corporate author":

Workers of the Writers' Program of the Works Project Administration. *Washington, D.C.: A Guide to the Nation's Capital,* revised ed. American Guide Series. New York: Hastings House, 1942.

REFERENCE BOOKS

The following form is suitable for articles from many kinds of reference books, like the *Dictionary of National Biography,* as well as from the general encyclopedias.

Author: As with book entries, last name first on the first line of the bibliography card.

Many, though not all, encyclopedia articles are signed by the authors' initials at the end of the article. The authors' full names are listed at the front or back of the volume, or sometimes of the first or last volume of a set. If you are certain that the article is not signed, the first entry on your card cannot be an author entry and is the title entry instead. But find the author if possible.

Title: The title of the *article,* not of the encyclopedia, is the title of your source. Titles of works which appear as parts of larger wholes, as one article is part of the larger encyclopedia, are put in quotation marks.

Facts of publication: The facts your reader needs before he can understand where your article appeared are the title of the encyclopedia (underlined), the date or edition of the encyclopedia (normally the most recent, unless an earlier edition is somehow superior), the volume number, and the inclusive pages of the article in that volume.

The normal bibliography card for an encyclopedia article looks like this:

> Fraser, Alexander Campbell, and Richard Ithamar Aaron
> "John Locke"
> <u>Encyclopaedia Britannica</u> (1964),
> XIV, 273-274

The entry would appear in the final bibliography as

> Fraser, Alexander Campbell, and Richard Ithamar Aaron. "John Locke," *Encyclopaedia Britannica* (1964), XIV, 273–274. [An alternative form, equally acceptable, would enter the date, volume, and pages as: (1964), 14:273–274. Whichever form you adopt, use it consistently.]

MAGAZINE ARTICLES

Author: Last name first, if the article is signed. If the article is anonymous, alphabetize it under the first key word of the title.

Title: The title of the article, in quotation marks.

Facts of publication: The underlined title of the magazine (in full, not abbreviated as it is to save space in the periodical indexes), the volume, the date, and the pages. Two forms are common, as with encyclopedia entries. Whichever form you use, be consistent throughout your bibliography.

RESEARCH PAPER PROCEDURE

If, in addition to numerals representing volume and pages, you need to use numerals representing series, numbers, or sections, identify the numerals by the abbreviations **ser., no., sec., vol.** (or **vols.**), and **p.** (or **pp.**).

The normal bibliography card for a magazine article looks like this:

> Viertel, John
> "Generative Grammars"
> <u>College Composition and Communication</u>
> XV (May, 1964), 65-81.

The entry would appear in the final bibliography as

Viertel, John. "Generative Grammars," *College Composition and Communication*, XV (May, 1964), 65–81.

Or

15:65–81 (May, 1964).

Many magazine articles, as well as chapters or excerpts from books, are reprinted in anthologies or in casebooks for composition courses. When such reprints are used in research papers, the author and title are, of course, those of the original article or excerpt. If the original facts of publication are indicated, they should also be given in the bibliography. In addition, however, full credit must be given to the immediate source. The result is in effect a double entry.

An excerpt in an anthology:

Becker, Carl L. "The Ideal Democracy," from *Modern Democracy*. New Haven, Conn.: Yale University Press, 1941. Reprinted in Kenneth L. Knickerbocker, ed. *Ideas for Writing*, 3rd ed. New York: Holt, Rinehart and Winston, Inc., 1962, pp. 318–332.

An article in a casebook:

Reed, Glenn A. "Another Turn on James's *The Turn of the Screw*," *American Literature*, 20:413–423 (January, 1949). Reprinted in Gerald Willen, ed. *A Casebook on Henry James's "The Turn of the Screw."* New York: T. Y. Crowell Company, 1960, pp. 189–199.

GOVERNMENT PUBLICATIONS

Author: Often, no author is named in government, industrial, and similar publications. If the author is named, of course his name should be entered, but if the work is anonymous and the government agency or the corporation assumes responsibility for it, enter the name of the agency or corporation as a "corporate author." Use the smallest division of government that will be recognizable to your reader; the author card in the card catalogue may or may not help you reach your decision. Arrange the name to alphabetize the work under the key term; that is, use Agriculture, United States Department of, rather than United States Department of Agriculture or list the work under the title.

Title: As the title of a complete work, underline it.

Facts of publication: This is often the hardest part of the entry to determine. Remember that the purpose of the entry is to enable a reader to secure a copy of the work, and to provide whatever information will be most useful to him. For example, most federal government publications are printed by the Government Printing Office, and publications designed for general distribution are usually available through a branch of the same agency. For such publications, the Government Printing Office should be listed as publisher. But if the work is for use within a government agency, the agency using it should be listed as publisher. If the publication is one of a series, the titles and numbers of the series should be given if they will be useful. Dates, when available, should always be given.

The following examples illustrate a few typical entries:

Commerce, United States Department of. *Employee Handbook.* Washington, D.C.: United States Department of Commerce, 1949. [No author is listed; the work is designed to be used within the department.]

Goheen, Howard W., and Samuel Kavruck. *Selected References on Test Construction, Mental Test Theory, and Statistics, 1929–1949.* Washington, D.C.: United States Government Printing Office,

1950. [The work is designed for general circulation and may be obtained through the Government Printing Office.]

Hall, Milton. *Getting Your Ideas Across through Writing.* Training Manual No. 7. Washington, D.C.: Federal Security Agency, 1950.

Electronic Determination of Tolerances. Washington, D.C.: Industrial Researches Company, 1964.

NEWSPAPER ARTICLES OR NEWS STORIES

Author: If the article or news story is signed, the author's name should of course be recorded. Usually, however, no author is identified, and the title of the article or story must serve as the first entry.

Title: The title (often no more than a headline or a single topic, like a name heading an obituary) should be enclosed in quotation marks, as part of a larger whole.

Facts of publication: The underlined title of the newspaper (the name of the city is underlined only if it is part of the title of the paper), the date, the page and section number if the paper has section numbers, and sometimes the column—all these help the reader find the article you are citing. It is often difficult to determine which of several editions is involved. That information would be useful, because the makeup of newspapers changes from hour to hour; but the clues to the edition are usually hidden, and in general the same edition will be distributed to libraries beyond the immediate place of publication. As a result, editions are rarely identified in bibliographical citations.

A typical signed newspaper entry would appear in the final bibliography like this:

Raskin, A. H. "Steel Talks Wait as Owners Want Light on Prices," *New York Times,* April 1, 1952, sec. 1, p. 1.

UNPUBLISHED MANUSCRIPTS

University students often have access to specialized treatments of their topics in the form of typed and bound manuscripts prepared as theses for the master's or doctor's degree. These should be consulted if they are available, and of course should be included in the bibliography if they prove useful.

Author and title are always given and should be listed. The title, somewhat oddly, is enclosed in quotation marks even though the work is complete in itself. Since the work is unpublished, there are no "facts of publication," but to let the reader know where the source may be found, it is identified as an unpublished thesis (or dissertation), and the university and the date are indicated.

A typical thesis entry would appear in the final bibliography like this:

> Rorabacher, Louise E. "Victorian Women in Life and in Fiction." Unpublished thesis, Ph.D. (Illinois, 1942).

Make out a bibliography card for each promising source as you come across it. Take down all the information you will later need in the form you will later need to use. Keep your cards in alphabetical order as you go. The method may seem like a good deal of extra trouble at first, but in the long run it will save time and effort.

ANNOTATING YOUR BIBLIOGRAPHY

At least two additional entries should be made on each card, not for the final bibliography, but for your own working convenience. The first is the library call number by which you may get the book or bound volume of the periodical from the library stacks. When you first locate the item in the card catalogue, enter the call number in a corner of your bibliography card; thus you will save later unnecessary trips back to the card catalogue when you want to withdraw the volume. The second additional entry on the bibliography card is a brief note indicating the value of the source to your paper. When you examine a book or article, make a note of its value on the bibliography card. If you discover, for example, that a source with a promising title is really of no use to you, a note to that effect will save your having to look at it again after you have forgotten what you thought of it. Similarly, a source may give you valuable information without actually providing a single specific detail for your paper; yet a reader following up the subject should know about it. A note on the bibliography card will remind you to include that item in your final bibliography even though you make no direct reference to it in your paper.

The preliminary bibliography, carefully kept, is an invaluable tool. Use it in any way that you can.

EXERCISE

Submit to your instructor the cards on which you have listed your preliminary bibliography. Be sure that you have consulted both general and specialized periodical indexes as well as the card catalogue. Do not overlook pertinent chapters or sections in books covering wider topics.

Taking Notes

As you read, you will find yourself constantly coming across new facts, and, particularly, new ways of looking at the old facts. Take careful notes on everything new to you and important to the subject, so that when you write your final paper you will know whom to credit for the ideas you are borrowing.

Notes, like the preliminary bibliography entries, should be taken on cards so that they can be rearranged, added to, and otherwise shuffled at will. Facts and important opinions and pertinent questions will come to you in the accidental order determined by the purpose of whatever authority you happen to be consulting. They would soon be hopelessly jumbled if you tried to keep them on the pages of a notebook. Instead, use four-by-six-inch cards (large enough to give you room but not too large to handle easily) and *take one note to a card.* If an item happens to be related to two or three of the topics in your tentative outline, fill out a card to be filed under each topic. Though this may seem tedious at the time, it will save some desperate hunting for notes as you write.

As you take each note, record its source carefully, so that you may know later exactly where you got it. It is not necessary, however, to write down author, title, and the facts of publication on every card. If you are using only one book, for example, by Joseph Wood Krutch, all you need to identify the note is "Krutch," and the page or pages on which you found the item. Later, your bibliography card will provide you with all the additional information you need. If you have two sources by the same author, use a short title to identify each one. If you have two authors with the same last name, use initials. And so on.

At the top of the card, write the topic from your tentative outline under which the item belongs. That way, no matter in what accidental order you pick up useful details, you can always keep related details together, and from the beginning will have your material at least loosely arranged in manageable form.

Most of your notes should be summaries of what your authorities are saying. Be sure your summaries are *your own words,* not thinly veiled quotations of the source. Take down in direct quotation only phrasings that are particularly striking, or statements for which you may later want the prestige of the exact words of a recognized authority. Such quotations as you do take must be copied exactly as they are in the text (spelled and punctuated, for example, as the original writer left them). They must fairly represent the author's intended meaning, not distort it when they are taken out of context. You may omit parts of the original, indicating the omission by the three dots of the ellipsis mark; you may insert explanatory material in square brackets; and you may use capitals and lower-case letters according to the final sentence pattern of your own paper. But you must be sure no distortion of the writer's original meaning results. Mark all quotations in your notes with quotation marks, to be sure you will later know exactly where paraphrase stops and quotation begins.

A typical note card looks like this:

Daniel, p. 62　　　　　　Chamber Tombs:
　　　　　　　　　　　　　　Distribution

"Single chambers occur in two areas" of south-west Iberia: Almeria (circular, dry wall or orthostat wall); central and northern Portugal ("polygonal megalithic chambers"). Rectangular tombs rare in south-west, and when covered are round barrows. "...the long barrow... is non-existent in Iberia."

Except as aids to your own memory, you will not need source notes on details that are presented by virtually all the authorities, such as the birth dates of prominent people (on which all your sources will agree). But in your final paper, you will be expected to acknowledge your indebtedness for any details that have come, or that look as if they probably came, from particular sources, for individual interpretations of facts, for statistics or charts or tables you have borrowed from one of your authorities, and for passages you are quoting verbatim. For your own protection and convenience, record carefully the sources of all such material. You will need the information as you write the final paper.

Plagiarism through Ignorance

It is important here to consider briefly the nature of summary and paraphrase and the problem of plagiarism. When a teacher, or a textbook, says, "Most of your notes should be summaries," or, "Mark all quotations in your notes with quotation marks to be sure you will know exactly where paraphrase stops and quotation begins," the matter seems so elementary and the injunction so clear that often no more is said about it. But when the final paper comes in, the instructor recognizes phrases and sentence patterns that are completely unlike the student's usual writing; no quotation marks indicate that the student is borrowing directly, although a footnote may acknowledge indebtedness for the ideas. When the instructor checks the source, he finds that the striking phrases and the uncharacteristic sentences come from the source, though perhaps with slight modifications. He calls the student in to examine the honesty of the paper, and often the student is genuinely bewildered. He has been taught to write précis in high school; he has not copied his source word for word; he has given credit for the information in a footnote. What has gone wrong? Sometimes he is expelled from college without ever finding out. (Sometimes, unhappily, he knows perfectly well.)

Just what does it mean to "use your own words"? We can best explain by using examples. William Gaunt, in a book entitled *London* (New York: Viking Press, 1961), p. 25, wrote:

> Would you know how a merchant prince of the fifteenth century lived? In what stately surroundings, Crosby Hall, moved stone by stone and timber by timber from Bishopsgate to Cheyne Walk in 1908, can tell. . . . It is just as it was, . . . with its oriel window and oak roof, as when it belonged to a prosperous wool-stapler of the late Middle Ages; when after his death in 1475 it was occupied by Richard, Duke of Gloucester; and after 30 years again by Sir Thomas More.

Those are his exact words, and if they are used, they will of course

229

be given a footnote to acknowledge the source. As a long quotation —say, over six lines—they will be indented and single-spaced, as in the sample page on page 240. The format means "this is quoted," so no quotation marks are needed. (A shorter quotation, with quotation marks, would be double-spaced and folded into the text, with the sentence patterns of the text adapted to the grammar of the quotation so that they fit smoothly together.)

There are several ways the passage may be used, *all calling for a footnote reference;* there is one way it may *not* be used.

1. It may be paraphrased. Using the names and the date and such key terms as *wool-stapler,* and in this case using the unavoidable chronological organization, you may say essentially the same thing in your own words and in your own way. It would not be indented in the paper:

> Crosby Hall, although it has been moved from Bishopsgate to Cheyne Walk, is unchanged from the days of its occupancy by a London wool-stapler who died in 1475, its occupancy after that by Richard, Duke of Gloucester, and thirty years later by Sir Thomas More. With its oriel window and its oaken roof it is a fine example of the home of a wealthy merchant at the end of the Middle Ages.

Because the idea and the information came from Gaunt, the paraphrase calls for the same kind of footnote as the direct quotation.

2. It may be summarized:

> Crosby Hall, successively occupied by a wool-stapler who died in 1475, by Richard, Duke of Gloucester, and by Sir Thomas More, exemplifies the houses of wealthy fifteenth century merchants.

A footnote is still necessary.

3. Part of the information may be borrowed as fact:

> Sir Thomas More lived in Crosby Hall, in Bishopsgate, about 1505.

A footnote is still necessary, unless your topic is such that the same information can be found in most of your sources.

4. Part of the phrasing may be borrowed directly:

> Crosby Hall shows the "stately surroundings" in which "a merchant prince of the fifteenth century" lived.

A footnote is still necessary.

The only way in which it may *not* be used, the way which

raises strong suspicion of an intention to gain for oneself the credit for organization and phrasing that rightfully belongs to William Gaunt, is to adopt his wording with only slight modifications:

> Would you like to know how a merchant prince of the fifteenth century lived? In what stately surroundings, Crosby Hall can tell. It is just as it was, including its oriel window and oak roof, as when it belonged to a prosperous wool-stapler; when it was occupied after 1475 by Richard, Duke of Gloucester; and after thirty years more by Sir Thomas More.

No footnote can prevent the reader from thinking that you must have known that the sparkle in that passage, as well as the facts, belonged to Gaunt.

Unless you are careful as you take notes to mark all direct quotations clearly, you may not know, later, what phrasing is your own and what belongs to your sources. The college Disciplinary Committee may well regard the matter as very serious.

The Final Outline

When the reading is finished, think about what you have learned and what you want to say about it in your paper. Phrase your central idea in a carefully worded thesis sentence and plot the development of that thesis in a formal, analytical sentence outline (see Chapter 6) by which your instructor, if he wishes, can evaluate your plans and with which you yourself can control the writing of the paper. For a term paper, a detailed sentence outline is invaluable.

EXERCISE

Submit to your instructor your final outline, the cards on which you have listed your final bibliography, and the cards on which you have taken your notes.

The Final Paper

The final paper will consist of four sections: the title page, the outline, the text complete with footnotes indicating the sources of your detailed evidence, and the final bibliography. The third of these, the text, is obviously the most important of the four.

The title page should contain at least the title of your paper, your name, and the course and section number.

The outline that accompanies the final paper may well be the sentence outline that served as a guide to the writing of the paper, or your instructor may require that that sentence outline be reduced to a carefully phrased topic outline. In either case, it is often useful to treat the final outline as a combined table of contents and index, indicating the pages in the text at which each idea is presented.

The text, the paper itself, is the heart of the project. The material in it has come to you from reading rather than from experience, but the unity, the organization, the development, and the phrasing are your own. It is you who give meaning to the information you have accumulated. Except for indicating where you learned what you know, writing the paper is no different from writing any other paper. You need not try to work in all the evidence you have collected if honest and judicious selection can make your point just as well. You must not distort what seems to be the truth by ignoring inconvenient evidence, of course, but you may and should select the clearest and most pertinent. Since it is the most important single piece of writing done in the course, the paper on which you have spent the most time and the one dealing with the most complex material, bring to bear in writing it all you have learned about writing during the year. You should find, as a matter of fact, that it is also the easiest paper of the year to write. You know more about the subject matter than usual, you have given more thought to the development of the idea, and you have, besides, steeped yourself in the writing others have done on the same subject. Perhaps for the first time during the course, you can put your full attention on the actual writing job and can concentrate on phrasing your ideas in the most effective way, on making the clearest and most graceful transitions, on saying well the things you want to say. If you have done the work you should have done in preparation, you may well be surprised and proud over the results.

FOOTNOTING

There is only one thing new about the text of the research paper: the necessity for using clear and conventional footnotes to acknowledge your indebtedness to the writers from whom you are borrowing details. It is not necessary or expected, remember, that you use footnotes to document details that might be found in most treatments of the subject. But it *is* necessary to use a footnote at any point at which you know that a particular source provided the fact, the opinion, the pattern, or the exact phrasing you are presenting. As you read, especially in the scholarly journals, notice how your authorities footnote their articles.[3]

Footnotes are conventionalized shorthand devices for saying to the reader, "I got the information I have just given you from so-and-so. He said it in his book or article with such-and-such a title. If you care to look into the matter further, you will find it on such-and-such a page."[4]

That thirty-nine word remark to the reader can immediately be shortened to the name of the author, the work cited, and the page, as in

    Arthur Guilfoyle, *The Ebb of the Confederate Tide at Gettysburg,* p. 327.

And there are a number of conventional abbreviations that make subsequent notes even briefer. See pages 237–239 for a full list. Here, we may consider the most common. If the next note should refer again to the same work and the same page, the useful abbreviation *ibid.* (for the Latin word *ibidem,* "the same") will shorten your remark to the reader to those four letters alone. Or if another author's name and work intervenes, you may after the first reference to Guilfoyle's book use his last name only and the page, as in

    Guilfoyle, p. 390.

A numeral after and slightly above the end of the detail you are documenting will announce to the reader that a note is ap-

---

[3] There are in fact, many different systems, but the differences are matters of minor detail, such as punctuation. Most of them are based on the University of Chicago *Manual of Style,* and the pertinent forms may be examined in Turabian, *A Manual for Writers of Term Papers* (see note, page 287). The form here recommended is that of the revised Modern Language Association *Style Sheet,* which is somewhat simpler and is now widely followed.

[4] That description applies to the most common type of footnote, the source note. There are also explanatory notes, like this one, which add useful information that could not gracefully be blended with the text. A third type of note combines the other two by citing a source and then adding explanatory comment.

pended; the same numeral at the foot of the page (before and slightly above the note) tells him which note to consult.

A sample passage would look like this:

```
some illegal trade, most of which probably
came from Lynn and Bristol in England.¹⁶ Dur-
ing the last years of the fourteenth century,
however, Greenland trade became unprofitable
to Europeans. African ivory, Russian fur, and
Dutch and English cloth had replaced Greenland
commodities in the European market, and the
voyage to Greenland had become increasingly
risky.¹⁷ The trade dwindled and ceased.
```

About 1345, Ivar Bardarsson, steward of the bishop's farms in the East Settlement, accompanied an expedition sent to find out why there had been no news from the West Settlement for several years. He found no human beings at the one farm he stopped to investigate, but there were cattle there, and sheep roamed about

---

[16] Stefansson, _Greenland_, p. 160.

[17] Norlund, p. 143.

untended. From this limited evidence he concluded that the Skraelings (Eskimos) had recently slaughtered the entire settlement.[18] In 1355, another expedition was sent to find the missing Greenlanders, but it was unsuccessful.[19]

After 1367, we hear little about the colonies. In such isolation, life must have become more unattractive and difficult. Some of the settlers took passage on visiting vessels and returned to Europe.[20] The last recorded visit of Ice-

---

[18] The story is told in Vilhjalmur Stefansson, Unsolved Mysteries of the Arctic (London, 1939), pp. 28-29; Nansen, p. 127; Norlund, p. 134.

[19] Nansen, p. 128.

[20] Stefansson, Greenland, p. 86; Nansen, pp. 96, 100.

Typical footnote problems are illustrated in the following sample notes.

A first reference to a book:

[1] William Carter, *Charles Dickens* (New York, 1964), p. 28.

An immediately succeeding second reference to the same book and page:

[2] *Ibid.*

An immediately succeeding reference to the same book but a different page:

[3] *Ibid.*, p. 328.

A first reference to a magazine article:

[4] Edward Wagenknecht, "Dickens and the Scandalmongers," *College English*, 11:374 (April, 1950).

Or (an alternative form):

[4] Edward Wagenknecht, "Dickens and the Scandalmongers," *College English*, XI (April, 1950), 374.

An immediately succeeding reference to the same article and page:

[5] *Ibid.*

A reference to Carter's book, last cited in footnote 3:

[6] Carter, pp. 42–44.

A reference to Wagenknecht's article, last cited in footnote 3:

[7] Wagenknecht, p. 376.

A reference, at secondhand, to something available to you only as a quotation by another source:

[8] Pieter de Haugen, *Hoera de Koningin*, as quoted by Edgar Gilbert, *Modern Holland*, II, 269. [If it is possible to examine the original source, of course you should do so; if one useful detail is there, others might be also. Footnote 8 also illustrates, incidentally, a reference to a work of more than one volume.]

An immediately succeeding reference to Gilbert's book cited in footnote 8:

[9] Gilbert, II, 297. [*Ibid.* could not be used here, since that would refer not to Gilbert, but to de Haugen.]

A reference to editorial material in an anthology:

[10] Stephen F. Fogle, "What Poetry Does," in *A Brief Anthology of Poetry*, ed. by Stephen F. Fogle, p. xi.

A reference to an unsigned newspaper editorial:

[11] "Interstate Tax Chaos," *Washington Post*, June 18, 1964, p. A22.

A reference to an encyclopedia article:

[12] Morris William Travers and H. Grayson Smith, "Liquefaction of Gases," *Encyclopædia Britannica* (1951), 14:176. [The only difference between this first footnote reference and the bibliography entry is that the note cites the specific page to which reference is made, but the bibliography entry cites the inclusive pages covered by the article.]

A later reference, not immediately succeeding, to the same article:

[14] Travers and Smith, p. 180.

A reference to an authority personally consulted:

[15] Wood Gray, Professor of American History, The George Washington University, in a personal interview, February 27, 1964. [Such a note is rare, because a reader would find it difficult to consult the same source to check your accuracy or to obtain additional information. But an important point should not be omitted from your paper merely because it is not based on a published source, and if you consult an authority in person, you must credit him with the material he provides.]

A second reference to an author with more than one entry in the bibliography:

[16] Harrison, *Over the Hill*, p. 77. [The title must be repeated, since a reader referring to the bibliography could not easily tell which work had already been cited. If the note immediately preceding had referred to the same work, however, *Ibid.* would be perfectly clear.]

Other footnote problems will occur as you work, but if you remember that the purpose of the footnote is to inform your reader of the source of borrowed material, and if you understand the details of the method illustrated, you should be able to adapt your notes to the system.[5]

Abbreviations and symbols: The following abbreviations and symbols are conventional in footnoting. You will often see them in your sources, and you may have occasional need for them yourself. For any others that you find, consult your dictionary. (Those in italics are from Latin and are put in italics because they are foreign words. They are underlined in longhand or typing.)

above: appearing earlier in the same article. See *supra*.
art(s).: article(s).
below: later in the same article. See *infra*.
bk(s).: book(s).
c. or ca.: about, approximately; used with dates.

[5] The system presented is that commonly used by scholars in the humanities. The sciences frequently follow a different pattern, numbering their alphabetized bibliography items and making source references to those items by inserting in the text, in parentheses, the bibliography number and the page to which reference is made, as (17:39). Even science majors, however, will have occasion to write papers for advanced courses in the humanities, and the system illustrated in detail in the text should consequently be learned. Unless your instructor otherwise directs, follow the models in the text in your composition course research paper.

cf.: compare.
chap(s).: chapter(s).
col(s).: column(s).
ed(s).: editor(s), edition(s).
et al.: and others.
etc.: and so on. Not italicized, because it is now common English. But use it sparingly.
et seq.: and following; used of the pages following a cited page.
ff.: and following; used of the pages following a cited page. Now more common than *et seq.*
fig(s).: figure(s); used to refer to charts, diagrams, and so on.
ibid.: the same, used as a ditto sign to refer to an immediately preceding reference. May be used with a page change. When it is the first word in the footnote, as it usually is, it is capitalized.
infra: later in the same article. Not an abbreviation, it is not followed by a period. "Below" is now more common.
loc. cit.: in the place cited; used instead of *op. cit.* for magazine and encyclopedia articles, or for any source which is part of a larger, integral whole. Usage of *loc. cit.* varies, but this is its essential function. The author's name (or the title of an unsigned work) must accompany it. Often used with a page change.
MS(S).: manuscript(s).
n.d.: no date given.
n.p.: no place given.
n. pub.: no publisher given.
no(s).: number(s).
op. cit.: the work (opus) cited; used to refer to a previously cited book. The author's name and the page reference must always accompany it.
p(pp.): page(s).
passim: here and there throughout. Used, rarely, to indicate that pertinent material is scattered all through an indicated work. Use specific pages wherever possible. No period because it is not an abbreviation, but a complete word.
sec.: section.
ser.: series.
[*sic*]: thus in the original; used to indicate that an obvious error occurs in the source and that the quotation is exact. Used in square brackets, because it is a remark inserted in the quoted text. No period, because it is not an abbreviation.

supra: earlier in the same article. Not an abbreviation, it is not followed by a period. "Above" is now more common.
trans.: translator(s), translation.
vol(s).: volume(s).

Make use of these common abbreviations to save yourself the trouble of writing unnecessarily long footnotes. Since you will be expected to recognize and use these abbreviations in papers written for advanced courses, your instructor will not look with favor on long footnotes which appear to be attempting to evade the task of learning the use of the shorter forms.

THE FINAL BIBLIOGRAPHY

The final bibliography, the last section of your research paper, presents an alphabetized list of the sources you have found helpful in preparing the paper. All sources to which you have made footnote reference must be included, and it is often helpful to your reader to include any particularly good sources that you have not referred to directly. The bibliography thereby gives your reader a selected reading list on the topic you have studied. Practice differs here. Consult your instructor.

The forms of the final bibliography entries have already been illustrated in the discussion of the preliminary bibliography (pages 220–226). Consult those examples, and study the models offered in the attached student research paper. Follow the models exactly, in the order of details, in the information given, and in punctuation.

A FINAL WORD

You have a long, hard job ahead of you; there is no way in which digging information out of the library can be made painless. But if you follow the advice and the methods we have been discussing, and if you work intelligently and steadily throughout the time allotted to the project, you will find that it is not as hard as it may seem at first, and you will even discover, about the time you get into the intensive reading, that it really can be fun.

Examine the following typical student research paper for its methods of unifying material gathered from varied sources, its development of its topic, and its use of documentation.

The Problems of Slums and Urban Blight

JAMES A. INCE

The problems arising from slums and urban blight are not new; they have probably been with civilization for as long as there have been cities. At least, references to slums and related problems have been found in the earliest written histories.[1] The major factors responsible for slums are varied and intermingled, a combination of social and economic problems.

> The slum is a residential area (comprising one or more lots, city blocks, or rural plots) in which the housing is so deteriorated (through poor upkeep ordinarily combined with obsolescence, age, depreciation, or change in consumer demand), so substandard (owing to builders' or owners' ignorance of principles of construction, planning, equipment, and hygiene, or to the deliberate ignoring of such principles), or so unwholesome (owing to narrowness of streets, crowding of buildings upon the land, or proximity of nuisances such as noxious factories, elevated railways, overshadowing warehouses, railroads, dumps, swamps, foul rivers, or canals) as to be a menace to the health, safety, morality, or welfare of the occupants.[2]

This definition by no means encompasses all the factors that produce slums, but it is comprehensive enough to indicate the scope of the problem.

Although slums have been with us since the beginning of history, only in comparatively recent times has the general public become fully aware of the deplorable conditions existing in these areas.[3] This condition is due in part to the concept of democracy as it has developed over the past two centuries. We know now that to say that a child raised in a slum area has equality of opportunity with a child raised in more favorable surroundings is absurd.[4] The foul atmosphere in which a slum child is raised saps his vitality, corrupts his morals, and usually leaves him with a hostile attitude toward society. It thus materially reduces his chances of becoming

---

[1] Harold M. Lewis, *Planning the Modern City* (New York, 1949), II, 17.
[2] James Ford, *Slums and Housing* (Cambridge, Mass., 1936), I, 13.
[3] *Lewis*, p. 19.
[4] *Ibid.*

a well-adjusted and useful member of society. Another reason for public awareness is our rising standard of living, which has widened the gap between slum dwellings and the average home. This consciousness of the wide difference between the living conditions of different segments of our population is being manifested in legislation by federal and local governments for the redevelopment of blighted areas. Examples of such legislation are the Housing Act of 1949 and the subsequent amendment in 1954, with major emphasis on the prevention of slums and blighted areas.[5] In order to eliminate slums completely, we must first eliminate the factors responsible for our blighted areas. It will be necessary to make detailed studies of the causes and effects of slums. The redevelopment problems will have to be studied and solutions recommended. Most of all, there will have to be cooperation between the federal government, local governments, and the general public.

The factors responsible for slum conditions can be divided into the broad categories of primary and secondary causes. Obsolescent housing is an important primary cause of slum conditions. With the advance of design and technology in building houses, the old structures are no longer attractive to most tenants. As it becomes increasingly difficult to keep tenants in these obsolete buildings, the rents are usually lowered and the buildings allowed to deteriorate because it is no longer profitable to keep them in good repair.[6] Other important factors are overcrowding, development of heavy traffic, noxious industrial odors, and uneconomic use of land.[7]

> Finally the important factor of land speculation is a cause of blight, in that properties are held for prices at which there is no possibility of appropriate and economic development in the location. The speculator anticipates sale for a higher-value use than exists, and so reduces his expenditures for maintenance to a minimum. He is not interested in the property as presently used in the existing community, hoping only to make a profit on his invested capital by sale. The tragedy of this practice is that there is little or no possibility of such sales except in isolated and fortuitous cases; yet each such high-priced sale is used by scores of owners in the neighborhood as an indication that they also may expect a windfall.[8]

[5] *Ibid.*
[6] *Ibid.*, p. 36.
[7] Ford, I, 446.
[8] Lewis, p. 36.

The secondary factors responsible for slum conditions are not very important individually, but collectively they constitute a major problem. Some of these factors are physical, such as unsuitable building sites, inadequate street systems, or the shift of a city's business district to a new location.[9] Other secondary factors are mainly economic. Incomes that are too low to provide money for adequate housing chain many people to slum areas.[10] On the other hand, high costs, including taxes and mortgages, which are not in keeping with the earning ability of an area may cause its abandonment and subsequent deterioration.[11] The two causes interact disastrously. The effects of these various factors which tend to bring about slum conditions are felt not only by the individuals directly concerned but also by the entire community as the blight spreads.

There are, of course, other bad effects within the slum itself. Slums in general have a higher juvenile delinquency rate than surrounding areas. The lack of playgrounds and supervision of children's activities in these areas aggravates this condition.[12] Adult crime seems to flourish more in blighted areas than in other sections of the city. High disease and mortality rates are commonplace in slum areas. Communicable diseases are easily spread by the overcrowded conditions, filth, and lack of adequate sanitation.[13] One of the many studies made of the social effects of slums should illustrate the magnitude of the problems.

> The San Francisco Planning and Housing Association made a study of two contrasting residential areas with results that students of the subject know to be common in all cities. The "clean bright" Marina area of 53 blocks and 12,188 people was checked against the blighted area known as Geary-Fillmore with 41 blocks and 13,750 people. Marina had, in the period studied, 133 fires, Geary-Fillmore had 251; Marina had 17 juvenile court cases, Geary-Fillmore had 100; Marina had 39 "police" cases, Geary-Fillmore had 4,771; Geary-Fillmore had 36 times as many tuberculosis cases, 66 times as many hospital cases, and three times as many infant deaths as Marina.[14]

[9] *Ibid.*, p. 35.
[10] Robert E. Alexander and Drayton S. Bryant, *Rebuilding a City* (Los Angeles, 1951), p. 6.
[11] Ford, I, 447.
[12] *Ibid.*, p. 448.
[13] *Ibid.*, p. 376.
[14] James Dahir, *Communities for Better Living* (New York, 1950), p. 78.

RESEARCH PAPER PROCEDURE

This is not an isolated example. Similar studies in other large cities have found the same results—crime, juvenile delinquency, and disease are widespread in slum areas. The social effects of slums on a community are only part of the problem. The cost of fire and police protection for blighted areas is exceedingly high, and these areas drain heavily on the city treasury for such services as relief and medical attention.[15] Without a doubt, if the cost of social services for the entire city were as high as the services for slum areas, the city would go bankrupt.[16] Since the people living in these deteriorated sections of a city have low incomes, the revenue to pay for the social services must come from taxpayers residing in other sections.[17] This inequality causes many people to move to the suburbs, thereby lowering the city's already faltering tax base.[18] If concrete proposals are not made for the redevelopment of blighted areas, this flight to the suburbs will continue to grow in the years to come.[19]

The redevelopment of a blighted area is a complex undertaking and requires a well-organized and aggressive city plan. Often redevelopment plans pay too much attention to slum clearance and too little to slum prevention.[20] Sufficient consideration is not given such problems as size of city lots, architecture, and recreation areas. Little is accomplished by erecting developments that will be tomorrow's slums. Effective zoning is essential to any redevelopment project. Industries should be near, but not in residential areas.[21] Considerable attention must be given to housing standards. Each room of a house should have adequate light and ventilation. Minimum standards should be established for sanitation and general cleanliness of buildings. These housing standards should be applied to suburban communities as well as redeveloped urban areas, for suburban developments that lack adequate design and planning can easily become the slums of the future.[22] ——— Park, Virginia, located about thirty miles from Washington, D.C., is a good example of a poorly designed community that is very likely to become a

[15] Ford, I, 431.
[16] Ibid.
[17] Alexander and Bryant, p. 1.
[18] Lewis, p. 35.
[19] Ibid.
[20] Ford, I, 495.
[21] Ibid., p. 615.
[22] Ford, I, 477.

blighted area within the next twenty years. The entire community consists of houses having the same architectural layout. The houses are small and poorly constructed, and have the general appearance of summer cottages. Many of the residents work in Washington, D.C., thereby creating a transportation problem. Elimination of housing developments similar to —— Park is one of the major problems in preventing future slums.

One of the most difficult problems in redeveloping blighted sections of a city is relocating the displaced population. In almost every location where slums are torn down and replaced by new housing developments, there are more families in the slum than can be adequately housed in the rebuilt area.[23] Care must be taken that these displaced families do not move to areas already overcrowded. Because of the low incomes of these families, the only practical solution seems to be an expanded program of low-cost government housing.

Another major obstacle in the way of urban redevelopment is financing. Slum rehabilitation through private effort is usually economically unfeasible. If private capital were used to finance redevelopment projects, the rents of the new buildings would have to be quite high.[24] Using private capital would therefore defeat the purpose of slum rehabilitation: to replace slum areas with housing developments for low-income groups.[25] As mentioned earlier, land speculation is one of the main causes of high costs. Some method must be found to obtain at a fair price the land that needs redeveloping.[26] Other high costs stem directly from our postwar inflation, and little can be done about them. The only way these financial problems can be overcome and an adequate slum clearance program can be carried out for the country as a whole is through government assistance.

In fact, the federal government already gives considerable assistance to local slum clearance projects.

> In the Housing Act of 1949, the Congress declared, in part, that the general welfare and security of the nation and the health and

[23] Coleman Woodbury, ed., *The Future of Cities and Urban Redevelopment* (Chicago, 1953), p. 517.
[24] Ford, II, 572.
[25] *Ibid.*
[26] Lewis, p. 38.

living standards of its people require the elimination of substandard and other inadequate housing through the clearance of slums and blighted areas, and the realization as soon as feasible of the goal of a decent home and a suitable living environment for every American family, thus contributing to the development and redevelopment of communities and to the advancement of the growth, wealth and security of the nation.[27]

Federal financial assistance is available to local governments to assist them in the clearance of slum areas and for future redevelopment of these areas. These programs are carried out by private enterprise in accordance with local plans. The federal government does make decisions on the acceptability of the plans, but local governments can proceed on most general matters without further approval.[28] The federal government provides up to two-thirds of the net project cost, and the local government must furnish the rest in the form of cash, land, public utilities, or site improvements.[29]

Another way in which the federal government aids local communities in the fight against urban blight is through low-rent public housing. Since the main economic factor compelling most families to live in substandard housing is low incomes, these housing projects are essential to the elimination of slums. The housing projects are constructed, owned, and maintained by local housing authorities operating under state enabling acts.[30] If the United States Public Housing Administration determines that a community has a need for low-cost public housing, it usually grants a loan, which must be approved by local authorities, for preliminary work. After the housing is complete, the federal government pledges a subsidy which will cover the difference between operating expenses of the project and the amount obtained in rent.[31]

It appears that federal assistance will have to be continued for an indefinite period. Local governments are unable to raise sums of money large enough to finance adequate slum clearance programs because the federal and state governments have tapped available

[27] Meyer Kestnbaum, "Twenty-five Federal Grant-in-Aid Programs," *Final Report of the Commission on Intergovernmental Relations* (Washington, D.C., 1955), p. 147.
[28] *Ibid.*, p. 148.
[29] *Ibid.*
[30] Kestnbaum, *Final Report of the Commission on Intergovernmental Relations* (1955), p. 223. Hereafter cited as *Final Report.*
[31] *Ibid.*

sources of revenue to such an extent that little more can be added to the tax burden.[32] While cities are unable financially to undertake a large-scale renewal program, however, most cities could accept more responsibility for the prevention of slums than they are presently willing to do.

> The shocking neglect of many municipal governments in failing to enforce and modernize existing housing and building codes has done much to bring about widespread conditions of urban blight and has resulted in governmental subsidies on an increasing scale. Local governments should accept responsibility for the broad goals of raising housing standards, eliminating and preventing slums and blight, establishing and preserving sound neighborhoods, and laying a foundation for healthy community development. Local governments should recognize the interrelationship of these activities and should work continuously to improve administrative and fiscal coordination among all local agencies and programs involved in planning, development and enforcement of codes and ordinances, slum clearance, public housing, and other related elements.[33]

State governments have also shirked their responsibilities in the field of slum clearance.[34] This is one of the primary reasons why the federal government has been forced to enter the field of public housing on such a large scale, despite the fact that slum clearance is an exercise of police power and ideally belongs at the municipal and state levels.[35]

Together with government assistance, furthermore, slum clearance needs the support of the general public. In order that our governmental units may plan expansion and renewal of our cities effectively, it is necessary for the private citizen to give his support.[36] The people of a community must let their elected officials know how they feel about having a well-planned community.[37] Groups of public-spirited citizens can do much to prevent the occurrence of slum conditions. They can encourage the improvement and

[32] Guy Greer, *Your City Tomorrow* (New York, 1950), p. 113.
[33] Kestnbaum, *Final Report*, p. 224.
[34] *Ibid.*
[35] *Ibid.*
[36] John Popham, "National Citizens Planning Conference," *New York Times*, June 11, 1957, sec. 1, p. 26.
[37] Luther Gulick, "Five Challenges in Today's New Urban World," *American City*, 71:149 (December, 1956).

upkeep of tenements and call on homeowners with suggestions on how their property can be improved. If they cannot secure voluntary cooperation, they should report all violations of the housing code and make sure that city officials require property owners to clear up all discrepancies. If enough private citizens actively support slum clearance projects, the job of ridding our cities of slums will progress at a faster pace.

The success or failure of slum clearance and urban renewal will ultimately depend on the success of modern city planning techniques.[38] City planning, like any large undertaking, requires a great deal of teamwork. This is why it is important that government and private persons cooperate to rid our cities of slums and blighted areas. It should be the goal of everyone concerned to see that adequate housing is brought to the level of our public school system—available to the entire population.[39]

[38] Henry S. Churchill, "City Planning in the United States," *Encyclopedia Americana* (1957), 6:718.
[39] Lewis, p. 21.

BIBLIOGRAPHY

Alexander, Robert E., and Drayton S. Bryant. *Rebuilding a City.* Los Angeles: The Haynes Foundation, 1951.

Churchill, Henry S. "City Planning in the United States," *Encyclopedia Americana* (1957), 6:718–726.

Dahir, James. *Communities for Better Living.* New York: Harper and Brothers, 1950.

Ford, James. *Slums and Housing.* 2 vols. Cambridge, Mass.: Harvard University Press, 1936.

Greer, Guy. *Your City Tomorrow.* New York: The Macmillan Company, 1950.

Gulick, Luther. "Five Challenges in Today's New Urban World," *American City,* 71:149–150 (December, 1956).

Kestnbaum, Meyer, chairman. *Final Report of the Commission on Intergovernmental Relations.* Washington, D.C.: United States Government Printing Office, 1955.

———. "Twenty-five Federal Grant-in-Aid Programs," in *Final Report of the Commission on Intergovernmental Relations.* Washington, D.C.: United States Government Printing Office, 1955.

Lewis, Harold M. *Planning the Modern City,* Vol. II. New York: John Wiley & Sons, Inc., 1949.

Popham, John. "National Citizens Planning Conference," *New York Times,* June 11, 1957, sec. 1, p. 26.

Woodbury, Coleman, ed. *The Future of Cities and Urban Redevelopment.* Chicago: University of Chicago Press, 1953.

8

Glossary of Troublesome Phrases

This section is designed to provide brief advice on the use of words and phrases that often trouble college students. The trouble stems from a variety of sources. Sometimes it arises because a locution that is common in the student's dialect is not used in the dialect of educated writing. Sometimes it arises because of changing linguistic custom, so that older readers (and all college teachers are at least slightly older) are conscious of shibboleths that may no longer be observed by contemporary writers of the first rank. (Some shibboleths have never been observed, even by those who are most disturbed when someone else violates them. The disturbance, however, is itself an important fact to be remembered.) Sometimes, perhaps most often, the trouble arises because a locution which is perfectly appropriate in writing of one level of formality (stylistic level) or of one tone is not appropriate to the level or tone of the paper in which you have used it. (This may occur, notice,

249

if the phrasing is either overformal or too informal: On occasion *eschatology* can be as badly out of place as *catterwampus*.)

It is scarcely possible to say of a given phrase or word, "This may only be used in writing of such-and-such a level." Yet it can and must be said that the locutions in a given piece of writing should be appropriate to the topic, tone, and level of the piece as a whole. And it can be said of many of the phrases in this glossary that they tend characteristically to appear in writing of one sort rather than of another. Here and there, consequently, phrases are labeled to call your attention to the responses they may evoke, even though the intention is not flatly to prohibit their usage, but rather to warn you that they must be used judiciously.

The labels employed must be understood. *Nonstandard:* "not used by the educated writer except to secure special effects, as in dialogue"; *dialectal:* "used regionally, but not standard, not in general use"; *conversational:* "used in general educated speech, but rarely in writing, except of a highly informal, colloquial sort"; *informal:* "used in educated writing, but probably not on the most serious subjects or occasions"; *formal:* "used in educated writing on serious subjects or occasions."

Occasionally, you will find a word or phrase characterized as "acceptable," or "established," but with the added recommendation that it be avoided in college writing. This means that even though the dictionaries record the locution without any special label, many college instructors will disapprove of its use in papers prepared for college classes because they know that many readers object to the phrase and would be distracted by it. The wise writer will generally be conservative when faced with a choice. His purpose is to present his idea as clearly and as effectively as possible, not to disturb and distract his readers unnecessarily by his phrasing. If he knows that many readers will object to a locution, he will avoid it even though he himself is aware that the linguistic authorities have demonstrated its complete propriety.

Accept—except. *Accept* means "to take" or "receive." *Except* means "to exclude," "with the exception of."

> I accept your invitation.
> If I were inviting your guests, I would except Jim.
> All may come, except Jim.

Ad, exam, phone, photo. Such "clipped forms" are informal; many readers object to them unless the tone of the paper is clearly casual. Avoid in college writing.

A.D. *Anno Domini,* "in the year of Our Lord." Usually precedes a specific year date. Avoid with centuries. B.C., "before Christ," follows year or century.

Adapt—adopt. *Adapt* means "to make suitable." *Adopt* means "to take as one's own."

> He adapted the suggestion to suit his own plans.
> I will adopt your suggestion as it is.

Note: In the nouns of action made from these verbs, *adaptation* contains four syllables, *adoption* contains three.

Affect—effect. In student writing, *affect* is usually a verb meaning "to influence"; *effect* is usually a noun meaning "the result."

> Your words do not affect her.
> The effect of your words is negligible.

Note: Affect, verb, may mean "to adopt as an affectation." *Effect,* verb, means "to bring to pass."

> He affects a Harvard accent.
> The law was inadequate to effect the desired change.

Aggravate—irritate. Formally, *aggravate* means "to intensify."

> His carelessness aggravated the seriousness of the disease.

Informally and conversationally, *aggravate* means "to irritate." Avoid this use in college writing.

Ain't. This once useful contraction for "am not" has been successfully banished by repeated strictures against it. It is not used by educated American writers.

Alibi. Formally, *alibi* (Latin for "elsewhere") means that one was elsewhere at the time some act was committed. Informally, *alibi* means simply "excuse."

All—all of. Either is acceptable, although *all* is somewhat more formal. *All of* is usual before a pronoun. "All of it."

All ready—already. Not interchangeable. Distinguish between "They are all (All of them are) ready" and "We have already (before this time) decided."

All right. *All right* is strongly preferred to *alright*.

All the farther. Dialectal for "as far as," as in "This is all the farther (as far as) I mean to go."

All together—altogether. Distinguish between "They are all (All of them are) together" and "You are altogether (entirely) too insistent."

Allude—refer. *Allude* means "to refer indirectly."

> In your speech you referred to Lee, but didn't you also allude to Jackson?

Almost—most. *Almost* is an adverb and is used before adjectives, verbs, or other adverbs. *Most* is an adjective and is used before nouns.

> Almost every person present agreed.
> Most people agreed.

Note: The *every* of *everyone, everybody,* and the *any* of *anyone,* etc., still retain enough adjective force to require the adverb *almost.*

> Almost everyone agreed.

A lot. See **Lot.**

Alright. See **All right.**

Altho. One of the simplified spellings never used in the carefully edited publications. It should be avoided because it distracts and often annoys the reader.

Although—though. Virtually interchangeable. The choice is largely a matter of sentence rhythm. *Although,* however, can be used only to introduce its clause. It is never inserted parenthetically.

Among—between. *Among,* strictly, is used of more than two, *between* of two. The distinction is weakening and *between* is becoming common in both situations. In college writing, the strict usage is usually preferred.

Amount—number. *Amount* refers to quantity, *number* to countable units in a group.

> Any amount of time.
> Any number of people.

TROUBLESOME PHRASES — At

And etc. *Et cetera* means "and other things." *And etc.,* is redundant. See also **Etc.**

Anybody else's. The standard form. Do not use the stilted *anybody's else.*

Anyway—anyways. *Anyway* is normally preferred, though *anyways* is possible in the sense of *anywise,* "in any manner."

Apt—liable—likely. *Apt* means "habitually tending," but chiefly means "suited," "to the point." *Liable* means "obligated to" or "exposed to the danger of." *Likely* means "of a nature to render possible."

> She is apt to get excited in a crisis.
> That was an apt remark.
> You are liable to fall if you climb too high.
> It is likely that he will come.

As—for—because—since. All of these conjunctions are used in rough synonymy with *because,* but avoid using them in a sentence which might be confusing, as in "As you were speaking (Because? While?), I slept briefly." Restrictive adverbial clauses use *because.* In formal writing, nonrestrictive, explanatory clauses use *for,* as in "Critical revision is important, for even Homer nods."

As . . . as—so . . . as. *As . . . as* is used in both affirmative and negative statements, but many still prefer *so . . . as* after a negative.

As if—as though. Virtually interchangeable.

As—like. In meticulous usage, *as* is usually a conjunction introducing a clause (containing a subject and a verb); *like* is a preposition taking a substantive object.

> Do not do as I do, do as I say.
> Do not act like me.

As, "in the role of," is a preposition: "He was employed as a reporter."

As—that. Use *that,* not *as,* to introduce noun clauses.

> UNACCEPTABLE: I don't know as I do.

As to. Redundant in such sentences as "I inquired as to whether he was ready."

At. Nonstandard and redundant in such sentences as "Where is he at?"

253

At about. Avoid this noncommittal phrase in such sentences as "He came at about five o'clock." (Which was it, at five or about five?)

Auto. A "clipped form" perhaps best avoided in college writing.

Awful. A counter word, meaning roughly "very bad." Do not overuse it. Strictly, it means "awe-inspiring."

Back of—in back of—behind. *In back of* is conversational. *Back of* or *behind* may be used without apology, although *behind* is somewhat more formal.

Bad—badly. *Bad* is an adjective; *badly* is an adverb. After such verbs as *look, feel, seem,* use the predicate adjective *bad,* as in "I feel bad."

Balance. Avoid this commercial term in the sense of "remainder," "rest of."

Because. See **As**.

Because. See **Reason is because**.

Being as—being that. Dialectal for *because*.

AVOID: Being as (that) I'm already here, I'll stay.

Beside—besides. *Beside* is usually a preposition, meaning "by the side of."

He sat beside the Prom Queen.

Besides is now chiefly an adverb, meaning "in addition."

I'm too tired to go. Besides, I can't afford it.

Between—among. See **Among—between**.

Boy friend—girl friend. Informal. Many people object violently to these terms. They should be avoided even though there is no other easy way to express the concept.

Bring—take. *Bring* means "to carry with oneself to this point." *Take* means "to carry with oneself away from this point." Avoid the dialectal use of *bring* in both senses.

Broke. Slang for "bankrupt," "without money."

But—hardly—scarcely. These words, implying negation, are not used with an additional negative.

NONSTANDARD: I haven't but a dime.
NONSTANDARD: I didn't hardly hear you.
NONSTANDARD: I haven't scarcely started.

But what. Dialectal.

Can—may. Strictly, *can* means "to be able"; *may* means "to have permission." Informally, *can* is used in both senses, but in college writing the distinction between the two might well be observed.

Can't hardly. See **But.**

Can't seem. Informal for "seem to be unable."

Character. Avoid in the sense of "person," as in, "This character spoke up and said . . ."

Claim. Often objectionable as a synonym for "say" or "assert," because it suggests a pugnacious contradiction of a prior assertion. Avoid for the sake of tactful phrasing.

Climactic—climatic. *Climactic* means "pertaining to climax." *Climatic* means "pertaining to climate."

Common—mutual. *Common* means "shared by others." *Mutual* means "sharing equally, jointly, and reciprocally."

> Common experiences
> Mutual obligations

Complected—complexioned. *Complexioned* is the standard adjective.

Considerable. Avoid *considerable* as a noun: "He did considerable." As an adjective, use it with *amount, degree, extent,* as in "It cost a considerable amount of money," not "It cost considerable money."

Contact. Informal in the sense of "to get into communication with." But even in informal writing many readers object to it violently.

Continual—continuous. *Continual* means "with prolonged and frequent recurrence." *Continuous* means "in an uninterrupted stream."

> My morning was ruined by continual interruptions.
> The distracting noise of the power mower was continuous throughout the class hour.

Could of. See **Have—of.**

Couple. Colloquial in the sense of "any two," as in "Give me a couple of days to decide." Standard at all levels in the sense of "an associated, especially a married, male and female pair."

Cute. A much overworked counter word. Find a more exact synonym, such as *attractive, charming, dainty, pretty.*

Date. Informal in the sense of "an appointment for a particular time" and "a social engagement with a person of the opposite sex."

Deal. A commercialism in the sense of "agreement," "arrangement": avoid. *A great deal* means "a great amount," not "a great number."

Definitely. An overworked counter word. Find a more exact synonym, or simply omit the word, unless you are using it necessarily and precisely in the sense of "clearly defined."

Different from—different than. *Different from* is preferred in American usage, but *different than* is common before a clause as object.

Dove—dived. *Dived* is the preferred past tense in American usage, but *dove* is an established alternative form.

Due to. Clearly established in the sense of "because" or "because of." Many readers, however, still strongly object to the use of *due* except as an adjective. *Due to* and especially *due to the fact that* often result in wordiness.

> AVOID: Due to illness, I missed the examination.
> AVOID: Due to the fact that I was ill, I missed the examination.
> PREFER: Because of illness, I missed the examination. Because I was ill, I missed the examination.
> RIGHT: My absence was due to illness.

Dumb. Informal for *stupid*.

Each other—one another. Virtually interchangeable.

Effect. See **Affect**.

Either—neither. *Either* and *neither* are singular and normally require singular verbs and pronouns. Used of two things. When more than two are involved, use *any—none*.

> Either (of two) was willing, but neither was chosen.
> Any of the class could have explained the problem, but none of them was called on.

Enthuse. Informal for "to make or become enthusiastic." Avoid *enthuse,* because many readers strongly object to it.

Equally as. Do not confuse *equally* with *as good* (etc.) *as*. In such a sentence as, "He was equally as prepared as she," the two constructions overlap.

TROUBLESOME PHRASES — Fix

He was as prepared as she.
They were equally prepared.

Etc. *Etc.* is an abbreviation of the Latin *et cetera*, "and other things." Never write *and etc.* Never write *ect.* Avoid *etc.* in general writing. It weakens a series which by its nature is evidently not intended to be exhaustive.

> AVOID: He is very energetic, always swimming, riding, playing tennis, dancing, etc.

If you need to indicate that the series is not an exhaustive list, prefer "and so on," "and so forth," or "and the like."

Every so often. Conversational for "every now and then."

Exam. See **Ad**.

Except. See **Accept**.

Expect—suppose. *Expect* is informal in the sense of "suppose."

Famous—notorious. *Famous* means "widely and favorably known." *Notorious* means "widely but unfavorably known."

Farther—further. More or less interchangeable, but many writers use *farther* for "greater distance" and *further* for "additionally," and many readers are disturbed if these distinctions are ignored.

Feature. Established as a verb in the sense of "to display conspicuously," but it has a flavor of theatrical or journalistic cant and probably should be avoided in college writing. Slang in the sense of "imagine," as in "Feature him in an apron!" Avoid.

Fellow. Low informal in "Tom's her fellow." Informal (but not entirely complimentary) in the sense of "person": "He's a dependable fellow." Established for all levels, as an adjective or a noun, in the sense of "associate(d)": "fellow worker," "the Fellows of the Graduate Council."

Fewer—less. *Fewer* refers to number; *less* refers to amount.

> Fewer students, less noise.

Fine. An overworked counter word in the sense of "superior," as in "a fine man." Select a more exact synonym.

Fix. Informal in the sense of "repair," "arrange," as in "to fix a leaky faucet." Many regard it as slang, in the sense of "to settle or dispose of," as in "That fixed him," and in the sense of " a predicament," as in "He's really in a fix."

257

Folks. Conversational in the sense of "relatives," as in "Meet my folks." Avoid in the sense of "you people," as in "Watch closely, folks, while I demonstrate this indispensable carrot juicer."

For. See **As.**

Former—latter. Used of two: "the first mentioned," "the second mentioned."

Funny. Informal in the sense of "strange." Standard in the sense of "humorous," "amusing."

Gentleman—lady. Avoid *gentleman* and *lady* as genteelisms for *man* and *woman*. Never use the vulgar *gents*.

Get. *Get* has many slang and informal uses in addition to its formal use in the sense of "to obtain," "to receive." It might be well to consult the dictionary on the status of *get* in any dubious construction.

Girl friend. See **Boy friend.**

Good. *Good* is an adjective, not an adverb.

>NONSTANDARD: He writes real good.
>STANDARD: He writes very well.

But after such verbs as *look, feel, seem* the syntax often calls for a predicate adjective.

>INFORMAL: I feel good.
>FORMAL: I feel exuberant (or unconquerable, etc.)

Good and. Informal as an intensive.

>INFORMAL: I was good and tired.
>FORMAL: I was very tired.

Got—gotten. Both are established past participles of *to get*. *Have got to* is a common and emphatic informal synonym for *must*, as in, "I have got to do it." At more formal levels, "I must do it" would be preferred. To secure the same degree of emphasis at the formal level, a stronger synonym may be necessary, as "It is imperative that I do it." *Gotten* is obsolete in British usage, hence the occasional objection to it for formal writing.

Grand. An overworked counter word for *magnificent*, etc. Save it for use with nouns of superlative impressiveness.

Guess. Long established in the sense of "think," "suppose," "believe," but many readers object to it. Prefer a more exact word in college writing.

TROUBLESOME PHRASES

Guy. Low informal for "male person."

Hanged—hung. *Hung* is the normal past tense and past participle of *hang*. *Hanged*, however, is regularly used in reference to the execution or suicide of human beings.

Hardly. See **But.**

Have—of. Do not confuse the verb *have* (or its contracted form *'ve*) with the preposition *of*.

> WRONG: I should of known.
> INFORMAL: I should've known.
> FORMAL: I should have known.

Have got to. See **Got.**

Heap. Informal or jocular in the sense of "a considerable amount," as in, "It takes a heap of living to make a house a home."

Height—heighth. Do not add an extra and nonstandard *h* to *height*. The misspelling *heightH* presumably occurs in mistaken analogy with *length, breadth,* etc.

Human. Avoid *human* as a noun. Many readers object to it and prefer *human being*.

If—though—whether. *If* in the sense of "though" is acceptable at the informal level, as in "I approve, even if you don't." In clauses of doubt or uncertainty, *if* may be used in the sense of "whether," as in "I wonder if she meant what she said." If the alternatives are clear, *whether* is preferred, as in "I do not know whether to believe her or not."

Imply—infer. *Imply* means "to express or suggest indirectly." *Infer* means "to draw conclusions from the evidence."

> Your tone implies that you doubt my statement.
> I infer your doubt from the tone you use.

In—into. *In* means "being within an enclosure, etc." *Into* means "moving from outside to inside."

> He is in his seat.
> He walked into the room.

In back of. See **Back of.**

Individual. Avoid *individual* in the sense of "person," as in "He's an odd individual." It is properly used in the sense of "a distinct entity," "particular as opposed to general," as in "The state in

259

peacetime should respect the rights of the individual," or as an adjective, as in "He has a highly individual style."

In regards to. Avoid. Say *in regard to,* or *about,* or *regarding.*

Inside of. In the sense of "in," the *of* is redundant.

> He was inside the room.

In the sense of "within," "by the expiration of," *inside of* is informal.

> INFORMAL: He'll be here inside of an hour.
> FORMAL: He will be here within an hour (or, in less than an hour).

Intrigue. Many readers strongly object to *intrigue* in the sense of "to arouse interest." You might well avoid it in college writing.

Irregardless. A redundant vulgarism for *regardless.*

Is where—is when. Avoid the "something is where" definition.

> AVOID: Security is where you don't have to worry about anything.
> PREFER: Security is freedom from anxiety.

Its—it's. Do not confuse *its,* the possessive pronoun, with *it's,* the contraction of *it is* or *it has.*

Kind of—sort of. Redundant or conversational as synonyms for *rather,* as in, "kind of tired." In the sense of "group," "class," as in "That kind of carelessness irritates me," the phrases are singular and require singular verbs. Plurals are formed normally, both the pronoun and the noun taking plural forms: "These kinds are . . ."

Lady. See **Gentleman.**

Later—latter. *Later* means "at a subsequent or a more advanced time," as in "John came at five; Jack came later." "Jack comes to class later every day." *Latter* means "the second of two things mentioned," as in "Of work and sleep, I prefer the latter." See also **Former—latter.**

Lay—lie. *Lay (laid, laid)* always takes an object.

> Lay that pistol down.

Lie (lay, lain) takes no object.

> I lie down.
> The pistol lies where it fell.

Lead—led. *Lead* is a metal, a noun. *Lead, led, led* are principal parts of the verb, *to lead.* Do not allow the similar pronunciation of *lead* the metal and *led* the verb to mislead you in spelling the latter.

Learn—teach. *Learn* means "to acquire knowledge." *Teach* means "to impart knowledge."

Leave—let. *Let,* proposing a course of action, is not interchangeable with *leave* in such a construction as "Let us arise and go now." In the sense of "to allow to be undisturbed," however, use either *let* or *leave,* depending on precisely what you mean. "Let me alone" suggests "Do not disturb me." "Leave me alone" suggests "Go away."

Let's. *Let's* is a contraction of *let us. Let's us,* consequently, is redundant. When *let's* is followed by an appositive, the appositive is in the objective case, as *us ('s)* is.

> Let us (you and me) go.
> Let's you and me go.

Less. See **Fewer.**
Liable. See **Apt.**
Lie. See **Lay.**
Like—as. See **As.**
Likely. See **Apt.**
Line. *Line* in the sense of "a department or kind of activity or business" is recorded by the dictionaries without comment, but many readers regard it is commercial slang, and it probably should be avoided in college writing. *Line,* as in "the Communist party line," is acceptable in all but very formal use. *Line* in the sense of "social technique" is slang. *Along the line of* is verbose.

> AVOID: His activities are along the line of banking.
> PREFER: He is a banker.

Loan—lend. *Loan* is a noun or a verb. *Lend* is a verb. The verb *lend* is more formal and is preferred by many readers.

Locate. Informal in the sense of "to recall" and in the sense of "to establish a residence."

Loose—lose. *Loose* means "to be unfastened" or "to unfasten."

> The dog is loose.
> Loose the dogs.

Lose means "to misplace."

> Don't lose my place in that book.

Lot—lots

The pronunciations differ: *Loose* = lōōs; *lose* = lōōz.

Lot—lots. Colloquial in the sense of "a large amount." *A lot* is two words. Do not confuse with *allot*.

Lovely. An overworked counter word. Select a more exact adjective.

Mad. Colloquial in the sense of "angry."

Math. A slang, "clipped form" of *mathematics*.

Mean. Colloquial for *bad tempered, malicious, vicious*, etc.

Medium-media. *Medium* is singular, *mediums* and *media* are plural. Of the latter two, *media* is the more formal.

Mighty. A colloquial intensive, as in "a mighty big job."

Most. See **Almost**.

Must. The recent dictionaries disagree over the status of *must* as an adjective and a noun ("A must book." "This book is a must.") and many readers object to it; consequently it should probably be avoided in college writing.

Mutual. See **Common**.

Myself—me. Avoid the use of the reflective or intensive pronoun *myself* where the syntax calls for the personal pronoun *I* or *me*.

>   AVOID: John and myself are responsible.
>   AVOID: It was done by John and myself.

Nice. An overworked counter word signifying little more than vague approval. Select a more exact modifier. Even in its strict sense of "discriminating," it should be used with caution, unless you are certain no confusion could result.

None. Used as singular or as plural.

>   None of them is present.
>   None of them are present.

Not as—not so. See **As . . . as**.
Nowhere near. Informal for *not nearly*.
Nowheres. Dialectal for *nowhere*.
Number—amount. See **Amount**.
Of—have. See **Have—of**.
Off of. The *of* is redundant.
O.K. Conversational or informal.
Only. Place *only* as near to the word it modifies as possible, even

TROUBLESOME PHRASES ——————————— **Provided**

though in conversational and informal use its position is highly fluid and confusion rarely results.

> CONVERSATIONAL AND INFORMAL: I only have a dime.
> FORMAL: I have only a dime.

Out loud. Informal. Formal: *aloud.*
Outside of. The *of* is usually redundant in the sense of "beyond."

> PREFER: His actions put him outside (or beyond) the pale.

Conversational in the sense of "except."

> CONVERSATIONAL: I've done nothing outside of a little reading.
> INFORMAL AND FORMAL: I've done nothing (but) except read a little.

Party. Dubious (and suggesting commercial cant) for *person.*
Passed—past. *Passed* is the normal past tense and past participle in verb forms. *Past* is normally an adjective or a noun.

> He passed the course.
> We have passed the middle of the twentieth century.
> Judge him by his past performance.
> The time for action is past.
> History is our interpretation of the past.

Per. Commercial cant.
Percent—per cent—percentage. *Percent* may be written as one word or as two. Use *percent* (or *per cent*) after a number; otherwise use *percentage.*

> He gets a 10 percent (or per cent) commission.
> He gets a fixed percentage of the net income.

Phone. See **Ad.**
Photo. See **Ad.**
Plan on. Conversational. Informal and formal: *plan to.*
Plenty. Avoid *plenty* as an adverb, as in "He was plenty tired."
Prof. College slang. Avoid it as an abbreviated title in addressing a letter, endorsing a paper, etc. Many professors object to it.
Proposition. Slang as a verb. A commercialism as a noun in the sense of "proposal."
Proved—proven. Both are past participles of *prove.*
Provided—provided that—providing. *Provided,* with *that* expressed in formal writing and implied when it is informally

Put across ──────────────────────── GLOSSARY OF

omitted, is a conjunction meaning "on condition," "if." *Providing* may similarly be used as a conjunction, but many object to it in formal writing.

Put across—put in—put over. Conversational.

Raise—rise. *Raise* (*raised, raised*) always takes an object.

> Raise your hands.

Rise (*rose, risen*) takes no object.

> She rises reluctantly in the morning.

Raise—rear (children). Informally, *raise* is now more common in American usage. For strictly formal writing, *rear* is preferable.

Real—really. *Real* is a conversational intensifying adverb, as in "I was real pleased," but *really* (or in such constructions, *very*) is preferred in written English.

Reason is because. Frequently used, but violently disturbing to many readers. Prefer *reason is that*. Avoid particularly the wordy "The reason I did it is because. . . ." Say, "I did it because. . . ."

Reckon. Dialectal in the sense of "think," "suppose."

Regular. Informal in the sense of "complete," "genuine," as in "He's a regular fellow."

Right. Dialectal in the sense of "rather," "very," as in "We had a right nice time."

Rise. See **Raise**.

Run. Informal in the sense of "to manage," as in "He runs a restaurant."

Said—same—such. Avoid as pronouns. *Same* and *such*, however, are well established as pronominal adjective modifiers in such phrases as "the same thing," "until such time as."

Scarcely. See **But**.

Seldom ever. Illogical and confusing.

> AVOID: She is seldom ever on time.
> PREFER: She is seldom on time. She is never on time.

Self. Avoid in the sense of "the present writer or speaker," as in "I wish to reserve a table for self and party."

Set—sit. *Set* (*set, set*) always takes an object.

> Set the trunk over by the window.

264

Sit (sat, sat) takes no object.

> Sit there until the dean can speak to you.

Shape. Conversational for *condition,* as in "After the exam, he was in bad shape."
Should of. See **Have—of.**
Show. Informal for *theatrical performance,* etc.
Show up. Colloquial in the sense of "to expose" or "to appear."
Sick. Slang in the sense of "disgusted." In the sense of "unwell," *sick* is well established in American usage.
Since. See **As.**
Sit. See **Set—sit.**
Situation. An overused counter word in the sense of "the circumstances of the moment."
Size up. Conversational in the sense of "to evaluate a person or a situation."
Slow—slowly. Both forms are well established as adverbs. They are not, of course, interchangeable in all constructions.
So. *So,* as a conjunctive adverb meaning "consequently" and as a subordinating conjunction meaning "so that," is grossly overused. Other connectives (*consequently, accordingly, therefore, as a result,* etc.) or further subordination of the *so* clause would often be more exact. *So* as an intensive ("I was so tired") is colloquial. In written English, where vocal emphasis cannot be given the word, it suggests an incomplete comparison ("I was so tired that . . . .")
So . . . as. See **As . . . as.**
Some. Informal or slang in the sense of "noteworthy," as in "That was some party last night."
Somebody else's. See **Anybody else's.**
Sort. See **Kind.**
Sure. Conversational as an adverb. Use *surely* in college writing.
Suspect—suspicion. *Suspect* and *suspicion* are both nouns.

> The suspect was arrested as soon as the suspicion of the police was supported by enough evidence.

Suspect alone may be used as a verb.

> AVOID: I didn't suspicion him at all.
> PREFER: I did not suspect him at all.

Swell. Slang in the sense of "splendid."
Take. See **Bring.**
Take in. Conversational in the sense of "view," "attend," as in "Let's take in a show." Slang in the sense of "fool," "hoodwink," as in "You can fool some of the people, but you can't take me in."
Taxi. A "clipped form" of *taxicab*. Well established for all but strictly formal usage, it is nevertheless objected to by readers who prefer *taxicab* without realizing that it itself is in origin a double clipping of *taximeter cabriolet*.
Terrible—terribly. Overworked counter words meaning *difficult* or *very*, as in "a terrible job," "terribly tired." Best used in the sense of "dreadful," "dreadfully," "invoking terror," as in "a terrible storm," "terribly frightened."
Terrific. Often used, as slang, to avoid the weakened counter word *terrible*, or merely as an intensive, as in "He's a terrific dancer." *Terrific* retains more of its root idea of "invoking terror" than *terrible* does.
Than—then. *Than* is used in comparisons.

He is taller than his father.

Then implies time, or means *consequently*, etc.

We saw the flash and then heard the report.
If you understand me, then, you will do as I say.

The two words do not sound alike, are not spelled alike, do not function in the same way. Do not confuse them.
That. See **Which.**
That there—this here. *There* and *here* are redundant. *That* means "the one over there." *This* means "the one over here." *That one there*, or *this one here*, however, are well established as emphatic locutions.
Tho. One of the simplified spellings never used in the carefully edited publications. It should be avoided because it distracts and often annoys the reader.
Though. See **If.**
Through. *Through* is rather informal in the sense of "finished," as in "Are you through yet?" In college writing, *finished* will normally be preferred.
Thru. One of the simplified spellings never used in the carefully

edited publications. It should be avoided because it distracts and often annoys the reader.

Till—until. Virtually interchangeable. Never use the spelling *'til*. *Till* is not a contraction of *until*.

To—too—two. *To* is a preposition: "Give it to John." *Too* is an adverb: "John went, too." "He works too hard." *Two* is an adjective or a noun: "Two sides to an argument," "the number two." Avoid *too* as an intensive, as in "He is not too careful in his speech."

Toward—towards. Interchangeable, although *toward* tends to be preferred in American, *towards* in British usage.

Try and. *Try and* plus an infinitive is colloquial and low informal. *Try to* is preferred.

Unique. *Unique*, strictly, means "the only one of its kind." In the sense of "rare," "very unusual" it is informal. But because many readers find that usage objectionable, it should be avoided in college writing.

Used to. Do not omit the *d*. In origin, the phrase means "was accustomed to"; now often "formerly did." It is used only in the past tense.

Used to could. Vulgar for *used to be able to*.

Very. A standard intensive, sometimes unnecessarily used.

Wait for—wait on. *Wait for* means "to await."

I will gladly wait for you.

Wait on means "to serve."

I can't find a clerk to wait on me.

Wait on in both senses is informal.

Want in—want out. Dialectal. Use "want to get (or go or come) in or out."

Ways. Dialectal in such phrases as "come a long ways." As a combining form, as in *endways, sideways*, it is almost interchangeable with *-wise*. *-Ways* suggests extension in space; *-wise* suggests manner. (See also *-Wise*.)

Well. See **Good.**

Where. *Where* in place of *that*, as in "I read in the paper where you had won a prize," is unacceptable in college writing.

Where—when. See **Is where—is when.**

Where at. The *at* is redundant.

Whether. See **If.**

Which. *Which* is used of nonpersons; *who* is used of persons; *that* is used of either: "The dog which, the place which, the man who, the man or dog or place that." *That,* however, is used only with restrictive modifiers.

While. See **As.**

While. Avoid *while* in place of *and* or *but* in such sentences as "I came as quickly as I could, while he dawdled." *While* suggests the duration of time.

> I came as quickly as I could while (during the time that) he dawdled.

Who. See **Which.**

Who's—whose. Do not confuse *who's,* the contraction of *who is* or *who has,* with *whose,* the possessive case of *who.*

> Who's going to the game?
> The man whose pocket you picked has complained.

Whose, informally, is often used as a possessive with nonpersons, in place of the formal *of which.*

-Wise. As an adverbial suffix, *-wise* has been used since Anglo-Saxon days to form adverbs of manner from substantives, as in *lengthwise, otherwise, clockwise,* but has long been obsolete for new formations. Its recent disinterment to form such adverbs as *time-wise* ("When do you expect to finish, time-wise?") seems deplorable to many readers. Avoid its use in college writing.

Wonder. In form, sentences with *wonder* as the verb are usually declarative. In purpose they are often interrogative. They are normally (and formally) closed with a period, but question marks are used in all but strictly formal writing if the interrogative note is strong.

> RIGHT: I wonder whether I should go.
> RIGHT: I wonder whether I should go?

Would have. Avoid the use of *would* phrases when the syntax requires the simple past tense.

> WRONG: If you would have asked, I could have told you.
> RIGHT: If you had asked, I could have told you.
> RIGHT: Had you asked, I could have told you.

TROUBLESOME PHRASES — You

Would of. See **Have—of.**

Yes. Avoid "the announcer's Yes." *Yes* is an affirmative adverb used to agree with what someone else has said. Its use in television commercials ("Yes, we all need Brand X Mange Cure now and then") does not need to be imitated.

You. Beware of the indefinite and impersonal *you* because of its strongly personal flavor. It is often used in informal writing, however, when all readers could accept it personally.

To write well, you must be prepared to rewrite.

In formal usage, *one* (often followed by *he*) is preferred.

If one is to write well, he must be prepared to rewrite.

INDEX

A, B, and C series: punctuation of, 123–125
Abbreviations: conventional use of, 192; in footnotes, 237–239
Absolute construction: defined, 49–50; interjections, 86; nominative absolutes, 89–90, 112–113; nouns of address, 115; parenthetical remarks, 114–123; participial phrases as, 89–90, 115; punctuation of, 115
Abstract noun, 55
Abstract words, 55
Accusative case (*see* Objective case)
Active voice, 74
Address: nouns of, 115
Addresses: punctuation in, 130
Adjectives, 80–81; *a* and *an*, 81; clause, 94–95, 115–120; compound, 188–189; confusion of adjective and adverb, 83–84; coordinate punctuation of, 124–125; function of, 80–81; infinitives as, 77–78; as interrupter, punctuation of, 114–123; after linking verb, 45–46; modifying noun, 80–81; noun or pronoun as, 54–55, 57, 62; participle as, 76–77; phrase, 87, 88, 89, 90; predicate, 45–46, 52, 80–81, 95; prepositional phrases as, 88; punctuation of coordinate adjectives, 124–125
Adjective clause, 94–95; punctuation of, 115–116
Adjective phrase, 87, 88, 89, 90
Adverb, 81–84; classification of, 81–82; clause, 96–97, 115–120; compound, 188–189; confusion of adjective and adverb, 83–84; conjunctive, 82, 109; function of, 81; infinitive as, 77–78; as interrupter, punctuation of, 114–123; *-ly* ending, 81, 166; modifying verb, adjective, adverb, 81; prepositional adverbs, 40, 69, 83; prepositional phrase as, 87–88; squinting modifier, 15; verb-adverb phrases, 40, 69, 83
Adverbial clause, 96–97; punctuation of, 112–113, 114–123
Adverbial conjunction (*see* Conjunctive adverb)
Adverbial phrase, 87–88, 89, 90

Agreement: pronouns, 19–22; verbs, 22–25
Almanacs, 215–216
Almost: position of, 14–15
And: in faulty parallelism, 30; overuse of, 8; plural pronoun with antecedents joined by, 20; plural verb with subjects joined by, 22
Antecedent, 19–22; reference to, 16–18
Apologetic quotation marks, 145–146
Apostrophe, 148–149
Appositive, 119; faulty, 28; punctuation of, 115–120
Article, 81
Articles, titles of: quotation marks with, 146, 221–222, 226
As: case of pronoun after, 60
As well as: number of verb not affected by, 22
Atlases, 216
Auxiliary verb, 64–68, 70, 87; *of* as, 70
Awkwardness, 31–33

Be: case after, 59, 60; case after infinitive *to be*, 60; complement after, 45–46, 58, 59, 65–70; illogical use of, 28; as linking verb, 65–70
Bibliography (*see* Research paper)
Bibliographies: guides to, 213–216
Biography: dictionaries of, 215
Books, titles of: italics with, 187, 219, 222, 224, 225
Brackets, 144, 228

Call numbers, 209–210
Capitalization: rules for, 184–187
Card catalog, 209–212
Caret, 183
Case, 58–62
Choppy sentences, 8–9
Clause, 91–97; adjective, 94–95, 115–120; adverbial, 86, 96–97, 115–120; conditional, contrary to fact, subjunctive in, 73–74; coordinate punctuation of, 107–112, 138–139, 140, 142; dangling elliptical, 13; dependent, 91–97; elliptical, 13; independent, 91–92; introductory, punctuation of, 112–113; modifier,

271

48, 94–97; nonrestrictive, 115–120; noun, 92–93; as object, 92–93; position of, 93, 95, 97; restrictive, 115–120; as subject, 92
Clipped words, 251
Coherence: within paragraph, 8–9
Collective nouns: number of, 21–22
Colloquialism, 250
Colon, 139–140
Comma: with absolutes, 115; in compound sentences, 107–111; with contrasted elements, 129; with dates, 129–130; with elements out of order, 120; with geographical items, 130; after introductory elements, 106, 112–113; with nonrestrictive appositives and modifiers, 115–120; with nouns of address, 115; overuse of, 132–134; with parenthetical interrupters, 106, 114–123; to prevent misreading, 129; with quotation marks, 146; with series, 123–125; to set off direct quotations, 130
Comma splice, 5–6, 109–110, 130
Common noun, 55
Comparison: incomplete, 28–29, 265
Complement, 44–47; adjective as, 45–46, 76–81; case of, 58–62; position of, 45, 52–53, 62, 92–93
Compound adjective, 188–189
Compound adverb, 188–189
Compound noun, 188
Compound sentence: punctuation of, 5–6, 6–7, 107–111, 138–139, 140, 142
Compound words: hyphenation of, 188–189
Compounding hyphens, 188–190
Conclusion: in outline (*see* Introduction)
Concrete words, 55
Conditional clause: contrary to fact, subjunctive in, 73–74
Conjugation, 68–70
Conjunction, 84–86; adverbial (*see* Conjunctive adverb); coordinating, 85, 107–109, 110–111, 133–134; correlative, 85–86; function, 85–86; subordinating, 86, 92–93, 96
Conjunctive adverb, 82; punctuation of, 5–6, 109–110, 138–139
Connectives, 8–9, 48–49, 84, 86; *see also* Conjunction, Preposition
Consonant: final, before suffix, 165, 168–169; plus *y* before vowel, 169; suffix beginning with, 169
Construction: shifts in, 26–29

Contractions: apostrophe in, 148–149
Conversation (*see* Dialogue)
Conversational level of language, 250
Coordinate elements: punctuation of, 107–110, 123–125
Coordinating conjunction, 85–86
Copulative verb (*see* Linking verb)
Correlative conjunction: parallelism with, 30, 85–86

Dangling modifiers, 12–13
Dash: use of, 141–143
Dates: punctuation of, 129–130
Declarative sentence: in outlines, 199
Deletions from manuscript, 143, 183
Demonstrative pronoun, 56; with implied antecedent, 18
Dependent clause, 92–97
Derivation of words: as aid to spelling, 161–162
Dewey Decimal System, 210
Dialect, 250
Dialogue: comma splices and fragments in, 5–6; punctuation of, 5–6, 130, 144–147, 150
Diction: abstract words, 55; clipped words, 251; colloquialisms, 250; concrete words, 55; glossary of troublesome phrases, 249–269; syllabication, 190–191; vulgar, 250
Dictionaries, 215
Digression: punctuation of, 114–123, 141–142, 143
Direct address: nouns in, 115
Direct discourse: punctuation of, 5–6, 130, 144–147
Direct object, 46; case of, 59, 62; position of, 52–53, 54
Direct quotation: punctuation of, 5–6; 130, 144–147
Division of words at end of line, 190–191
Documentation of research paper, 217–226, 232–239

E: silent, 165, 169
Editorial interpolation: brackets with, 228, 518
Editorial omission: suspension points with, 149–150, 228
Ei-ie: in spelling, 167–168
Either . . . or: parallelism with, 85–86
Ellipsis marks (*see* Suspension points)
Ellipitical clauses: dangling, 13
Emphasis: italics for, 187; positional, 8–9, 97
Emphatic present in verbs, 69
Encyclopedias, 214–215

INDEX

End: as emphatic position, 8–9, 97
Endorsement of themes, 182
English: history of, as aid to spelling, 154–156
Equation: false, 28
Etymology: as an aid to spelling, 161–162
Everybody, etc.: modified by adverb, 252
Excessive coordination, 8–9
Exclamation point, 137
Exclamatory sentence, 137
Expletive: agreement with, 23

False series, 30
Faulty parallelism, 8, 29–31
Faulty predication, 27–29
Faulty subordination, 11
Feminine *so* (*see So*: overuse of)
Figures (numbers): representation of, 192–194
Final consonant: before suffix, 165, 168–169
Finite verb, 5, 64, 65–66
Flexible sentence, 9
Footnotes (*see* Research paper)
For: as coordinating conjunction, 85, 107
Formal English, 250
Fractions: hyphens in, 189–190
Fragmentary sentence: faulty, 4–5, 108, 135, 142
Function words, 38
Fused sentence, 6–7, 110–111
Future perfect tense, 68–69
Future tense, 68–70, 71; *shall* and *will*, 71
Future time: verb forms expressing, 68–69, 71

Gaps in thought, 27
Gazeteers, 216
Gender, 19–20, 62
General words: distinguished from specific, 55
Genitive case (*see* Possessive case)
Gerund, 75–76; phrase, 89; possessive with, 60
Glossary of troublesome phrases, 249–269
Government publications: indexes to, 213
Grammar: clauses, 91–96; as description of language, 38–40; function words, 38; functions of sentence elements, 41–50; importance of, 38–40; morphology, 38; parts of speech,

discussion, 53–76; patterns of sentences, 51–53; phrases, 87–90; pitch, stress, juncture (*see* Pitch); varieties of, 39–40, 42; word order, 38, 43–97 *passim*

Harmony of tone, 40
Historical present, 72
Hyphen: uses of, 188–192

Ie-ei: in spelling, 167–168
Illiterate English, 250
Imperative mood, 73
Impersonal *you*, 23, 269
Incomplete comparison, 28–29, 265
Incomplete predication: verb of (*see* Linking verb, Transitive verb)
Indefinite pronoun, 57; agreement with, 21, 23; *everybody*, etc.; modified by adverb, 252; shift in person or number, 26–27; *you* as, 23, 269
Indention: in outlines, 197, 203; in the paragraph, 182
Independent clause: defined, 92
Indexes to reference material, 213–216
Indicative mood, 67–68, 73
Indirect discourse, 144–145
Indirect object, 46, 52–53
Indirect question: punctuation with, 136
Indirect quotation: punctuation with, 144–145
Infinitive, 77–78; dangling, 13; phrase, 90; split; 78; subject of, 60; tense sequence, 79
Informal English, 250
Insertions in manuscript, 183
Intensive pronoun, 57
Interjection, 86; punctuation of, 115
Interpolation: editorial, brackets with, 144, 228
Interpolated elements: punctuation of, 114–123
Interrogative pronoun, 56
Interrogative sentence: parenthetically, punctuation of, 136
Interrupting elements: punctuation of, 114–123
Intransitive verb, 65
Introduction: in outline, 198, 200
Introductory modifier: punctuation of, 112–113
Inversion: punctuation with, 120
Irregular verb, 68
It: as expletive, 17, 23, 43
Italics: use of, 187–188, 219, 222, 224, 225

Juncture (*see* Pitch)

L.c. (*see* Lower case letters)
Legibility, 180–181
Length: of vowels as indication of spelling, 165, 169
Library: card catalog, 209–212; indexes to reference material, 212–216; use of, 208–216
Library of Congress classification, 210
Linking verb, 65–66
Lower case letters, 186–187
-*ly*: spelling with, 166

Magazines: indexes to, 212–214
Main clause (*see* Independent clause)
Manuscript conventions, 180–194
Margins, 181
Misplaced modifiers, 13–15
Mode (*see* Mood)
Modifiers, 48, 80–82; adjectives, 80–81, 83–84; adverbs, 81–82, 83–84; clauses, 94–95, 96–97; dangling, 12–13; introductory, punctuation of, 112–113; misplaced, 13–15; nonrestrictive, 114–123; nouns as, 54, 60; phrases, 87–90; position of, 48, 80, 81, 88, 94–95, 97; restrictive and nonrestrictive, punctuation of, 115–120; squinting, 15; verbals, 76–78
Mood, 26–27, 73–74; shift in, 26–27
Morphology, 38

Newspapers: indexes to, 212
Nominative absolute, 89–90, 115
Nominative case (*see* Subjective case)
Nominative predicate (*see* Subjective complement)
Nonrestrictive appositives, 115–120
Nonrestrictive modifiers, 115–120
Nonstandard English, 250
Normal order: inversions in, punctuation of, 114–123
Notetaking (*see* Research paper)
Noun: abstract, 55; as adjective, 54; as appositive, 54; classification, 55; clause, 92–93; collective, agreement with, 21–22; common, 55; as complement, 54, 55; compound, 188; concrete, 55; defined, 54; in direct address, 115; functions of, 54, 55; gerund as, 75–76; infinitive as, 77–78; as modifier, 54; number, 62; as object, 54, 55; objective complement, 54, 55; person, 22, 68; possessive used as adjective, 58; predicate nominative, 54–55; proper, 55, 184–185; as subject, 54, 55, of gerund, 75–88, of preposition, 54, 55, 84, 87–88, of verb, 54, 55; subjective complement, 54, 55
Noun clause, 92–93
Number: nouns, 62; pronouns, 20–23, 62; shifts in, 26–29; verbs, 67–68
Numbers: hyphen with compounds, 189–190; representation of, 192–194
Numerals: Arabic, 182; Roman, 182

O: plural of nouns ending in, 166–167
Object: direct, of verb, 46; indirect, of verb, 46; position of, 46, 52–53; of preposition, 46 47, 87–88; of verbal, 46–47, 75, 87
Objective case, 58, 59, 60, 62
Objective complement, 46, 52–53
Omission, editorial: suspension points with, 149–150, 228
Omissions: confusing, 27; *see also* Deletions from manuscript
Only: position of, 14–15
Or: agreement with antecedents joined by, 20; with subjects joined by, 22
Outline: analytical subdivision, 196–198; conventions of, 197–199; formal, 196–204; informal, 195–196; sentence, 199–202; thesis in, 195, 196, 202; topic, 202–204; value of, 195, 196, 200

Paging, 182
Pamphlets: indexes to, 213
Paper and ink for themes, 181
Paragraph: coherence, within paragraph, 8–9; indention, 182; symbol, use of, 183
Parallelism: faulty, 8, 29–31
Paraphrasing, 228, 229–231
Parentheses: uses of, 143–144
Parenthetical elements: errors, in case with, 61, in number with, 22; punctuation of, 114–123, 142, 143–144
Parenthetically interrogative sentence: punctuation of, 136
Participle: dangling, 12; defined, 76–77; tense sequence, 79
Participial phrase, 89; absolute, 89–90; dangling, 12
Parts of speech: adjective, 80–81; adverb, 80–81, 86; changes in, 53; conjunction, 84–86; in dictionaries, 83; discussed, 53–86; interjection, 86; noun, 54–55; preposition, 54; pronoun, 19–22, 56–62; verb, 22–24, 63–74

INDEX

Passive voice, 74–75
Past perfect tense, 68–69
Past tense, 68–69
Patterns of sentences, 52–53
Perfect tenses, 68–69
Period: uses of, 135–136
Period fault (*see* Fragmentary sentence)
Periodicals: indexes to, 212–214
Person, 19; shifts in, 26–27
Personal pronoun, 56–57
Phrase: absolute, 89–90; adverbial, 87–88, 89–90; as complement, 89, 90; defined, 87; gerund, 89; infinitive, 90; as modifier, 87–88, 89, 90; participial, 89–90; prepositional, 87–88, 113; as subject, 89, 90; verb, 87; verbal, 88–90, 112–113
Pitch, stress, juncture: 4, 15, 38, 40–41, 104–144 *passim*
Plagiarism, 229–231
Plurals: of figures and other symbols. 149; formation of, 67–68, 167; of nouns, ending in *o*, 167, ending in *y*, 166–167; possessives of, 148–149
Point of view: shifts in, 26–27
Positional emphasis, 8–9, 97
Possessive case: with gerunds, 60; spelling of, 58, 148–149; substantives in, as modifiers, 57, 58–59, 60; use of apostrophe in, 58, 148–149
Predicate adjective, 45–46, 52, 80–81, 94–95
Predicate noun or pronoun, 43–44, 44–47, 48, 52, 54, 57
Predication: faulty, 27–29; reducing, 111
Prefixes: spelling with, 165–166
Preposition, 84; as adverb, 40, 69, 83; at end of sentence, 40, 83
Prepositional phrase, 87–88, 113
Present perfect tense, 68–69
Present tense, 68–69; special uses of, 71–72
Principal parts of verb, 68
Progressive present in verbs, 69
Pronoun: agreement, 19–22; antecedent, ambiguous, 17–18, implied, 16–17, 18, too remote, 16, in subordinate construction, 18; case of, 58–62; classification, 56–57; as complement, 44–47, 57; declension of personal, 57; defined, 56; demonstrative with implied antecedent, 18; functions, 57; impersonal *you*, 23, 269; as modifier, 57, 60; number, 19–22; reference of, 16–18; with different antecedents, 17–18;

shifts in person, 26–27; spelling of possessives, 58, 148–149; as subject, 57; title as antecedent, 184; *who*, *which*, and *that*, 57, 268; *who* and *whom*, 61–62
Pronunciation: as guide, to hyphenation, 189, to spelling, 160–161, 165, 169–170
Proper adjectives: capitalization of, 184–185
Proper nouns, 55; capitalization of, 184–185
Punctuation: absolutes, 115; addresses, 130; apostrophe, 148–149; brackets, 144; colon, 139–140; comma, 107–134; comma splice, 5–6, 109–110; compound sentences, 107–111; contrasted elements, 129; coordinate elements, 107–111, 123–125, 132–134, 138–139, 139–140, 142, 143–144; dash, 141–142; dates, 129–130; direct address, 115; elements in series, 123–125; exclamation point, 137; four troublesome sentence patterns, 107–127, graphically illustrated, 126–127; fragmentary sentence, 4–5, 130–131, 132, 136, 142; fundamental principles, 105–107; geographical items, 130; hyphen, 190–192; importance of, 104–105; indirect questions, 136; of interrupting elements, 106, 114–123; of introductory elements, 106, 112–113; of inversions, 120; of nonrestrictive modifiers and appositives, 115–120; overuse of comma, 132–134; parentheses, 143–144; period, 135–136; to prevent misreading, 129; question mark, 136–137; quotation marks, 144–147, 221–222. 226; quotations, 5–6, 130, 144–147; run-on sentence, 6–7, 110–111; semicolon, 138–139; of series (A, B, and C, coordinate adjectives), 123–125; suspension points, 149–150, 228

Question: parenthetical, punctuation of sentence with, 136
Question mark, 136–137
Quotation marks, 144–147, 221–222, 226
Quotations: acknowledgment of (*see* Research Paper: footnotes); capitalization, 185; long, indention of, 230; punctuation of, 5–6, 130, 144–147; single spacing of, 181–182, 230

Reciprocal pronoun, 57
Reference aids in libraries (*see* Library)
Reference books, 214–216; almanacs, 215–216; atlases and gazetteers, 216; biographical dictionaries, 215; dictionaries, 215; encyclopedias, 214–215; form of entry in bibliography, 220–222; guides to, 213, 216; indexes, to government publications, 213, to newspapers, 213, to pamphlets, 213, to periodicals, 212–214; year books, 214–216
Reference of pronouns, 16–18
Reflexive pronoun, 57
Relative pronoun, 24, 57, 61–62, 94–95; agreement, 24
Research paper: bibliography, final, 217–226, 232, 239, form of, 220–227, preliminary, 217–227; final outline, 232; footnotes, abbreviations used in, 237–239, form of, 227–229, 232–239, position of, 234–235, when required, 227, 228–231, 232–233; model pages, 234–235; notetaking, 227–231; procedure, 217–239; quotations in, 228, 229–231; sample paper, 240–248; title page, 232
Restrictive appositives, 115–120
Restrictive modifiers, 115–120
Revision: of first draft, 182–183
Roots: unchanged in spelling with prefixes, 165–166
Run-on sentence, 6–7, 110–111

SEED words: spelling of, 169–170
Semicolon, 108, 109–110, 138–139
Sentence: choppy, 8–9; compound, punctuation of, 107–111; defined, 41–42; elements of, 42–43; emphasis, inversion for, 120; excessive coordination in, 8–11; flexible, 9; fragmentary, faulty, 4–5, 108, 135, 142; fused, 6–7, 110; interrogative, 136–137; inversion in, for emphasis, 120; normal order, 51–53; patterns, 51–53; positional emphasis in, 9; reducing predication in, 8; run-on, 6–7, 110; shifts in, 26–29; stringy, 8; subordination, effective, 9, faulty, 11–12; thesis, in outline, 196, 197, 199, 202; unity, 111; variety, 9
Sentence elements: function of, 43–47
Sentence outline, 199–202
Sentence patterns: basic, 51–53

Sequence of tenses: verbs, 73; verbals, 79
Series: A, B, and C, punctuation of, 123–125; coordinate adjectives in, punctuation of, 124–125; faulty, 30
Shall and *will*, 71
Shifts in construction, 26–29
Short-circuited thought, 27
Silent *e:* as indication of spelling, 165, 169
Slang: apologetic quotation marks with, 145–146
So: overuse of, 109–110, 265; punctuation with, 109–110
Sources: documentation of, 217–226, 232–239
Spacing: in manuscript, 181–182
Specific contrasted with general, 54–55
Spelling: diagnosing difficulty, 158–160; dictionary, as guide to, 160–162; etymology, as aid to, 161–162; finger, 163; history of English as aid to, 154–156; lists, 170–177; *ly*, 166; memory aids, 163–164; personal spelling list, 158, 162; plurals, 166–167; possessive nouns, 58, 148–149; pronunciation as key to, 160–161, 165, 169–170; using regular patterns, 165–167; visual images, 157, 162–163
Spelling rules: consonant plus *y*, 169; doubling final consonants, 165, 168–169; *ie-ei*, 167–168; SEED words, 169–170; silent *e*, 165, 169
Split infinitive, 78
Squinting modifier, 15
Stress: positional, 9, 97; *see also* Pitch
Subject of verb, 43–44, 52–53, 54, 55; agreement of verb with, 22–25; case of, 58; position of, 52–53, 93; pronoun as, 57; substantive as, 55
Subjective case, 58–60, 61
Subjective complement, 44–47, 48, 52, 54, 57, 80–81
Subjunctive mood, 73–75
Subordination: faulty, 11
Subordinate clause (*see* Dependent clause)
Subordinating conjunction, 86, 92–93, 96–97
Substantive: defined, 55
Suffixes: spelling with, 165–166
Summarizing, 229–231
Suspension points, 149–150, 228
Syllabication, 190–192
Symbols: outline, 197; plural of, 149

INDEX

Tense: in verbs, 68–73, needless shift of, 26; sequence in verbs, 73; sequence in verbals, 79
Than: case of pronoun after, 60
That: with restrictive clauses, 57, 133, 268
That, who, which, 57, 268
There: as expletive, 23, 43
Thought gap, 27
Time: indicated by tenses, 68–70
Titles: as antecedents of pronouns, 184; of articles, *et cetera,* quotation marks with, 146, 221, 226; of books, italics with, 187, 219, 222, 223, 224; capitalization of, 185
To be: case of complement, 59, 60; case after the infinitive, 60; illogical use of, 28; as linking verb, 65–66
Tone: harmony of, 40
Transition: within paragraphs, 8–9; within sentence (*see* Connectives)
Transitive verb, 65
Troublesome words and phrases, 249–269

Unity: in the sentence, 111
Usage: as determinant of correctness, 106–107, 156, 249–250

Variety: sentence, 9
Verb: agreement, 22–25; auxiliary, 69–70, 87; classification, 65–66; complements with, 44–47, 58–62; conjugation, 68–70; copulative, 65–66; defined, 63–64; finite, 5, 64, 65–66; function, 44, 64; intransitive, 65; irregular, 68; linking, 65–66; mood, 73–74; number, 67–68; person, 68; phrases, 87; position of, 52–53; principal parts, 68; tense, 68–74; special problems of, 70–73, sequence, 73; transitive, 65; voice, 74
Verb-adverb phrase, 40, 69, 83
Verbals: dangling, 12–13; defined, 75; gerund, 75–76; infinitive, 77–78; participle, 76–77; phrase, 88–90; tense sequence, 79
Voice, 74–75; shifts in, 26–27; weak passive, 74–75
Vowels: length as indication of spelling, 165, 169
Vulgar English, 250

Weak passive, 74–75
When, where, why clauses as nouns, 92–93
Who, which, that, 57, 268
Who and *whom,* 61–62
Whose, who's, 62, 268
Wonder sentences: punctuation of, 268
Words: (*see* Diction); compound, hyphenation of, 188–190; function, 38
Words as symbols: italicized, 188
Word order, 13–15, 38, 43–97 *passim,* 51–53, 61

Y: final, before suffix, 169; plural of nouns ending in, 166–167, 169
Year books, 215–216
You: impersonal, 23, 269

CORRECTION SYMBOLS

Abr	Abbreviations, 192	
Cap	Capitalization, 184	
Case	Faulty case form, 58	
Colloq	Used chiefly in conversational English, 250	
Co-ord	Excessive coordination, 8	
Cs	Comma splice, 5	
Cst	Faulty construction, shift in construction, 26	
Dng	Dangling modifier, 12	
Frag	Faulty fragmentary sentence, 4	
Glos	Consult the glossary, 249	
Gr	Faulty grammar (see outline of grammar chapter, 35)	
Ital	Use italics (underline), 187	
K	Awkward passage, 31	
Leg	Legibility, 180	
Log	Illogical as phrased, 27; faulty predication, 401	
Mm	Misplaced modifier, 13	
Ms	Messy manuscript, 180; manuscript conventions, 178	
N	Representation of numbers, 192	
P	Punctuation (see outline, 100)	
	The Comma, 107	
	1. Independent clauses, 107	
	2. Introductory elements, 112	
	3. Parenthetical elements, 114	
	4. Elements in series, 123	
	5. Miscellaneous uses of comma, 129	
	a. Prevent misreading, 129	
	b. Contrasted elements, 129	
	c. Dates, 129	
	d. Geographical items, 130	
	e. Quotations (including **Cs, Frag** in dialogue), 130	
	6. Overuse of the comma, 132	
	Other Punctuation	
	7. Period, 135	
	8. Question mark, 136	
	9. Exclamation point, 137	
	10. Semicolon, 138	
	11. Colon, 139	
	12. Dash, 141	
	13. Parentheses, 143	
	14. Brackets, 144	
	15. Quotation marks, 144	
	16. Apostrophe, 148	
	17. Suspension points, 149	
PAgr	Faulty pronoun agreement, 19	
Pas	Weak passive, 74	
Pred	Faulty predication, 27	
Ref	Faulty pronoun reference, 16	
Run-on	Run-on sentence, 110	
Sp	Misspelling (see outline of spelling chapter, 153)	
Sub	Faulty subordination, 11	
Syl	Faulty syllabication, 190	
Tense	Shift in tense, faulty sequence, 26, 73, 79	
VAgr	Faulty verb agreement, 22	
δ or $\wp$	Delete, omit, 183	
¶, No ¶	Paragraph or no paragraph, 183	
//Cst	Parallelism needed, or misleading, 29	
=/	Hyphen, 188	
$\wedge$	Insert, omission, 183	